Human Resources Support

April 2014

United States Government
US Army

Contents

		Page
	PREFACE	v
	INTRODUCTION	vi
Chapter 1	HUMAN RESOURCES (HR) SUPPORT	1-1
	Objective	1-1
	Enduring Principles	1-1
	Focus of HR Support	1-2
	Strategic HR Support	1-2
	Operational and Tactical HR Support	1-3
	Functions of HR Support	1-3
	Core Competencies Overview	1-4
	The Role of the Adjutant	1-6
	HR and Sustainment Relationships	1-7
	HR Sustainment Roles	1-8
Chapter 2	HR ORGANIZATIONS AND STAFF ELEMENTS	2-1
	Army Human Resources Command (HRC)	2-1
	Army Service Component Command (ASCC) G-1/AG	2-1
	Corps and Division G-1/AG	2-4
	Brigade S-1 Section	2-8
	Battalion S-1 Section	2-10
	Human Resources Sustainment Center (HRSC)	2-12
	Human Resources Operations Branch (HROB)	2-14
	Military Mail Terminal (MMT) Team	2-16
	Theater Gateway Personnel Accountability Team (TG PAT)	2-17
	HR Company Headquarters	2-18
	HR Platoon	2-19
	Postal Platoon	2-20
	Personnel Accountability Team (PAT)	2-21
	Casualty Liaison Team (CLT)	2-21

Distribution Restriction: Approved for public release; distribution is unlimited.

*This publication supersedes FM 1-0, dated 6 April 2010.

Standard Requirements Code (SRC)-12 Units at Home Station
Recommendations 2-21
Army Bands... 2-23
HR Rear Detachment Responsibilities... 2-25

Chapter 3   MAN THE FORCE 3-1
General 3-1
Section I – Personnel Readiness Management (PRM) 3-1
Responsibilities 3-3
Distribution Process 3-6
Unit Reset 3-7
Pre-Deployment Readiness 3-9
SECTION II – PERSONNEL ACCOUNTABILITY (PA) 3-12
General 3-12
Responsibilities 3-14
Section III – Strength Reporting (SR)..3-17
Key Terminology 3-19
Responsibilities 3-20
Battlefield Flow.. 3-21
Section IV – Retention Operations 3-22
Career Counselor's Role in Preparation for Deployment.................................... 3-22
Responsibilities 3-23
Section V – Personnel Information Management (PIM) 3-25
Responsibilities 3-26
HR Automation Support 3-28

Chapter 4   PROVIDE HR SERVICES 4-1
Section I – Essential Personnel Services (EPS) 4-1
HR Customer Service 4-3
Awards and Decorations.. 4-4
Evaluation Reports.. 4-5
Promotions and Reductions... 4-5
Transfer and Discharge Program... 4-6
Leave and Pass Program 4-6
Military Pay.. 4-7
Other S-1 Support... 4-7
HR Division of Labor 4-10
Section II – Postal Operations 4-10
Proponency.. 4-11
Responsibilitles.. 4-11
Other Postal Information 4-15
Use of Contractors for Postal Support 4-18
Battlefield Flow.. 4-18
Section III – Casualty Operations 4-20
Responsibilites 4-23
Pre-Deployment Actions 4-29
Casualty Estimation 4-30
Battlefield Flow.. 4-33

Chapter 5	**COORDINATE PERSONNEL SUPPORT**	**5-1**
	Section I – Morale, Welfare, and Recreation (MWR) Support	**5-1**
	Responsibilities	5-2
	American Red Cross (ARC)	5-7
	Army and Air Force Exchange Service (AAFES)	5-7
	Battlefield Flow	5-8
	Section II – Command Interest Programs	**5-9**
	Section III – Army Band Operations	**5-10**
	Responsibilities	5-11
Chapter 6	**CONDUCT HR PLANNING AND OPERATIONS**	**6-1**
	HR Planning and Operations	6-1
	Running Estimate/HR Planning Considerations	6-2
	HR Planning Using the Military DecisionMaking Process (MDMP)	6-2
	HR Input to Operation Orders	6-7
	Postal Input to Operation Orders	6-8
	Rules of Allocation (ROA) for HR Units	6-9
	Operate HR Mission Command Nodes	6-9
Chapter 7	**THEATER OPENING AND REDEPLOYMENT OPERATIONS**	**7-1**
	General	7-1
	Section I – Theater Opening	**7-1**
	Personnel Accountability	7-2
	Casualty Operations	7-2
	Postal Operations	7-3
	Section II – Theater Redeployment	**7-4**
	Personnel Accountability	7-5
	Casualty Operations	7-6
	Postal Operations	7-6
	Brigade and Battalion S-1	7-8
Chapter 8	**CIVILIAN SUPPORT**	**8-1**
	General	8-1
	Responsibilities	8-2
	Personnel Accountability	8-4
	Casualty Operations	8-4
	Postal Support	8-4
	MWR Support	8-5
	Other HR Support	8-5
	Deployment and Redeployment of Civilians	8-5
	Contracting HR Support Functions	8-6
	GLOSSARY	**Glossary-1**
	REFERENCES	**References-1**
	INDEX	**Index-1**

Figures

Figure 1-1. HR support... 1-4

Figure 1-2. HR/sustainment structure relationship 1-8

Figure 1-3. Theater sustainment command with an HRSC 1-9

Figure 2-1. Organizational design – ASCC G-1/AG 2-4

Figure 2-2. Organizational design - Corps G-1/AG... 2-8

Figure 2-3. Organizational design – Division G-1/AG 2-8

Figure 2-4. Organizational design – Brigade S-1 section 2-10

Figure 2-5. Organizational design – Battalion S-1 section... 2-12

Figure 2-6. Organizational design – Human Resources Sustainment Center (HRSC) 2-14

Figure 2-7. Organizational design – HR Operations Branch (HROB) 2-15

Figure 2-8. Organizational design – Military Mail Terminal (MMT) team.......................... 2-17

Figure 2-9. Organizational design – TG PAT... 2-18

Figure 2-10. Organizational design – HR Company headquarters................................... 2-19

Figure 2-11. Organizational design – HR platoon.. 2-20

Figure 2-12. Organizational design – Postal platoon.. 2-21

Figure 2-13. Organizational design – Army band small... 2-24

Figure 2-14. Organizational design – Army band medium 2-24

Figure 2-15. Organizational design – Army band large 2-25

Figure 3-1. Replacement flow 3-3

Figure 3-2. Distribution process... 3-6

Figure 3-3. Personnel accountability reporting process... 3-13

Figure 3-4. Strength reporting process 3-18

Figure 3-5. Sample joint personnel status (JPERSTAT) 3-18

Figure 4-1. Mail flow... 4-19

Figure 4-2. DA Form 1156, Casualty feeder card... 4-22

Figure 4-3. Benchmark rate structure (BRS) with key parameters 4-32

Figure 4-4. The casualty reporting flow... 4-34

Figure 4-5. The casualty reporting and tracking flow (reporting process) 4-35

Figure 6-1. The operations process 6-2

Figure 6-2. Military decisionmaking process (MDMP) 6-4

Tables

Table 3-1. Unit reset model... 3-8

Table 4-1. Essential personnel services (EPS) responsibilities...................................... 4-1

Table 4-2. Casualty operations 4-23

Table 5-1. Morale, Welfare, and Recreation (MWR) support 5-3

Table 5-2. American Red Cross (ARC) Support.. 5-7

Preface

Field manual (FM) 1-0 provides the fundamentals, principles, and concepts of Army human resources (HR) support doctrine. It provides the doctrinal bases for developing operational plans (OPLANS) and standard operating procedures (SOPs) that support national objectives that reinforce the Army's vision that Soldiers and readiness are the principle focus of HR support. This publication applies to the range of military operations and supports Army doctrine publication (ADP) 3-0, *Unified Land Operations* and ADP 4-0, *Sustainment*.

The principle audience for FM 1-0 is all members of the profession of arms. Commanders and staffs of Army headquarters serving as joint task force or multinational headquarters should also refer to applicable joint or multinational doctrine concerning the range of military operations and joint or multinational forces. Trainers and educators throughout the Army will also use this manual.

Commanders, staffs, and subordinates ensure that their decisions and actions comply with applicable United States, international, and, in some cases, host-nation laws and regulations. Commanders at all levels ensure their Soldiers operate in accordance with the law of war and the rules of engagement. (See FM 27-10.)

FM 1-0 applies to the Active Army, Army National Guard/Army National Guard of the United States, and the United States Army Reserve unless otherwise stated.

The proponent of FM 1-0 is the United States Army Training and Doctrine Command. The preparing agency is the United States Army Adjutant General School, Soldier Support Institute. Send comments and recommendations on the Department of the Army (DA) Form 2028 (Recommended Changes to Publications and Blank Forms) directly to Commander, Solider Support Institute, ATTN: ATSG-CDI, 10000 Hampton Road, Fort Jackson, SC 29207.

Introduction

Field manual (FM) 1-0, Human Resources Support, is the second revision of this publication. FM 1-0 provides human resources professionals and commanders an understanding of how human resources support contributes to current and future operations and how human resources professionals, organizations, and systems play an increasingly critical role in support of the total force. This manual provides basic doctrinal discussion on the organization and operations of human resources entities within the Army, as well as standard requirements code (SRC)- 12, Adjutant General Corps, organizations.

FM 1-0 makes numerous changes from the first version. The most significant is the elimination of all the appendices included in the previous version. This information has been modified and embedded throughout the publication which has increased by two chapters from the first version.

FM 1-0 contains eight chapters.

Chapter 1 discusses human resources support at the tactical, operational, and strategic levels, in the context of HR objectives, enduring principles, and focus of HR support. The chapter also more clearly articulates the role of the Adjutant than previously published.

Chapter 2 provides an overview of HR organizations and staff elements, including SRC-12 organizations. This chapter provides recommendations for home station employment of the aforementioned organizations, while also discussing HR rear detachment responsibilities previously addressed in appendix A.

Chapter 3 through 6 discuss the four HR core competencies of man the force, provide HR services, coordinate personnel support, and conduct HR planning and operations. A section covering HR automations support is now included in chapter 3, detailing the many HR enabling systems. Additionally, chapter 5 further defines command interest programs and program oversight responsibilities.

Chapter 7 was formerly appendix B. This chapter discusses theater opening operations and redeployment operations.

Chapter 8 was formerly appendix D. This chapter covers civilian support to include contractor support.

FM 1-0 was developed in close coordination with the United States Army Combined Arms Support Command and input taken throughout the Army human resources community.

FM 1-0 does not introduce, modify, or rescind any Army terms or acronyms.

Chapter 1

Human Resources (HR) Support

The HR community completed transformation in the execution and delivery of HR support that enabled a greater HR support capacity within the battalion and brigade manpower and personnel staff officer (S-1) sections. It continues to provide continuity of service and support to Soldiers whether they are deployed or at home station. This increased capacity allows for decentralized execution of HR support and provides the higher-level assistant chief of staff, personnel (G-1)/adjutant general (AG) the ability to focus on planning, analysis and less on the day-to-day management of the force. HR support is executed at tactical, operational, and strategic levels. It includes all activities and functions executed within the Army personnel development system life cycle management functions (structure, acquisition, distribution, development, deployment, compensation, sustainment, and transition) to man the force and provide personnel support and services to Soldiers, their families, military retirees, and Department of Defense (DOD) civilians and contractors who deploy with the force. Refer to AR 600-3, *The Army Personnel Development System*, for specific information regarding the personnel development system life cycle management functions.

OBJECTIVE

1-1. The objective of HR support is to maximize operational effectiveness of the total force by anticipating, manning, and sustaining military operations. HR support operations accomplish this by building, generating, and sustaining the force providing combatant commanders the required forces for missions and supporting leaders and Soldiers at all levels. The operational mission determines the relative weight of HR effort among the different HR core competencies as outlined in Army doctrine publication (ADP) 3-0, *Unified Land Operations*.

1-2. HR providers must understand the fluid nature of Army policies and procedures within the HR domain. As such, they must monitor and implement changes received through Army regulations, military personnel messages, all Army activities messages, and Headquarters, Department of the Army (HQDA) personnel policy guidance (PPG), and understand the intent of these changes in order to best support the force.

ENDURING PRINCIPLES

1-3. HR support uses a competency-based and performance-oriented strategy guided by HR enduring principles that assure a higher quality, more diverse and ready Total Army enabled by effective HR systems and agile policies. HR leaders have a responsibility to not only understand the importance of their efforts and unit mission, but also the missions of all their supported and supporting units. To meet the challenges of current and future operations, leaders are guided by six interdependent enduring principles of HR support that must be thoughtfully weighted and applied during the planning, execution, and assessment of missions. These six principles are:

- Integration. Integration maximizes efficiency by joining all elements of HR support (tasks, functions, systems, processes, and organizations) with operations ensuring unity of purpose and effort to accomplish the mission.

- Anticipation. Anticipation relies on professional judgment resulting from experience, knowledge, education, intelligence, and intuition to foresee events and requirements in order to initiate the appropriate HR support.

- Responsiveness. Responsiveness is providing the right support to the right place at the right time. It is the ability to meet ever-changing requirements on short notice and to apply HR support to meet changing circumstances during current and future operations. It involves identifying, accumulating, and maintaining sufficient resources, capabilities, and relevant information to enable commanders to make rapid decisions.

- Synchronization. Synchronization is ensuring HR support operations are effectively aligned with military actions in time, space, and purpose to produce maximum relative readiness and operational capabilities at a decisive place and time. It includes ensuring the HR operational process is planned, executed, and assessed.

- Timeliness. Timeliness ensures decision makers have access to relevant HR information and analysis that support current and future operations. It also supports a near real-time common operational picture (COP) across all echelons of HR support.

- Accuracy. Accuracy of information impacts not only on decisions made by commanders, but impacts Soldiers and their Families. For Soldiers, accurate information impacts their careers, retention, compensation, promotions, and general well being for family members, accuracy of information is critical for next of kin (NOK) notification if a Soldier becomes a casualty. HR providers must understand the dynamic nature of HR systems architecture and the fact that data input at the lowest level has direct impact on decisions being made at the highest level.

FOCUS OF HR SUPPORT

1-4. Meeting the goal of providing efficient and effective HR support relies on multi-functional HR leaders who focus their knowledge and skills in support of the Army's most important asset—its people. Only those who think strategically and work collaboratively, while inspiring and leading Army professionals, can achieve desired outcomes. In all areas, HR personnel should focus on the following:

- Agile and clear HR policies. HR policies must be clear, encompassing, and flexible enough to apply to the greatest number of personnel and address the widest range of circumstances. They must be adaptable enough to be able to guide and inform personnel in complex and changeable circumstances.

- Effective HR practices. HR practices that emanate from the policy-level should be streamlined, intuitive, and able to effect stable and predictable process results.

- Competency-based skills. HR personnel must be competent and able to accomplish HR core competencies and key functions. Competencies align the responsibilities, knowledge, skills and attributes needed to fulfill mission requirements.

- Outcome-oriented actions. In an environment that measures HR performance, the emphasis is on successful outcomes in fulfillment of mission priorities. While it is important to have effective HR processes and practices in place, it is critical that the ends drive the means.

- Self development. Self development is one of three domains of leader development and requires leaders to display discipline and a desire for excellence in lifelong learning. Using assessments, HR leaders must invest the time to become competent and confident in HR operations.

STRATEGIC HR SUPPORT

1-5. Strategic HR support involves the national-level capability to plan, resource, manage, and control the HR management life cycle functions for the Army. It involves integrating HR functions and activities across the Army staff, among the respective components, and among the Services. At the strategic level, the Army G-1; Chief, Army Reserve; and Director, Army National Guard (ARNG) manages HR support for their respective component. The Assistant Secretary of the Army (Manpower and Reserve Affairs) is responsible for civilian personnel policy, and the Civilian Human Resources Agency, a Field Operating Agency of the Army G-1, is responsible for civilian personnel operations. The Army G-1 develops Army policy for all HR systems and functions, while the U. S. Army Human Resources Command (HRC) applies and implements these policies for military personnel. The Installation Management Command (IMCOM) and the Military Postal Service Agency (MPSA) provide strategic support to the force for morale, welfare, and recreation (MWR) services and postal operations.

OPERATIONAL AND TACTICAL HR SUPPORT

1-6. HR policies and procedures developed at the national level translate into action at the operational and tactical levels. FM 7-15, Change 10, *The Army Universal Task List*, is a comprehensive, but not all-inclusive listing of Army tasks, missions, and operations.

1-7. Joint tasks are contained in the Universal Joint Task List. The Universal Joint Task List is a comprehensive collection of tasks in a common language and serves as the foundation for capabilities-based planning across the range of military operations.

FUNCTIONS OF HR SUPPORT

1-8. Figure 1-1 on page 1-4 depicts the four fundamental core competencies that HR personnel must accomplish in HR support operations. Each of the four competencies includes subordinate key functions which contribute to the success of the core competency. HR core competencies and their subordinate key functions are:

- Man the Force
  - Personnel Readiness Management (PRM)
  - Personnel Accountability (PA)
  - Strength Reporting (SR)
  - Retention Operations
  - Personnel Information Management (PIM)
- Provide HR Services
  - Essential Personnel Services (EPS)
  - Postal Operations
  - Casualty Operations
- Coordinate Personnel Support
  - Morale, Welfare, and Recreation Operations
  - Command Interest Programs
  - Army Band Operations
- Conduct HR Planning and Operations
  - HR Planning and Operations
  - Operate HR Mission Command Nodes

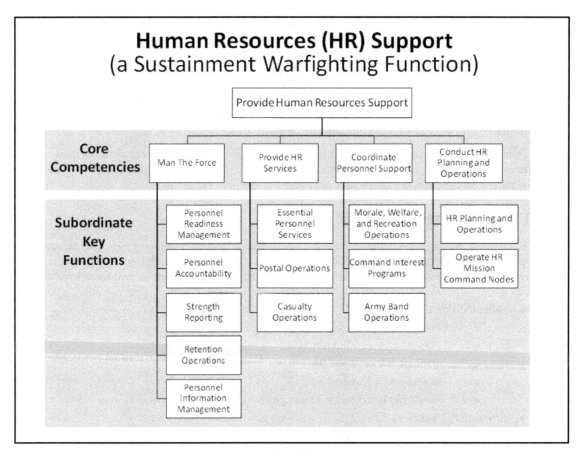

Figure 1-1. HR support

1-9.   HR units and staffs perform the core competencies and key functions at theater-level and below. Not all HR subordinate key functions are executed at each level of command. For example, PA is conducted at the S-1 level and monitored at division and above levels. Commanders and HR leaders should use FM 7-15 as a reference tool for developing general mission essential task lists, core capabilities mission essential tasks, operational orders, and standard operating procedures (SOPs).

CORE COMPETENCIES OVERVIEW

1-10. The following paragraphs provide an overview of the HR core competencies of man the force, provide HR services, coordinate personnel support, and conduct HR planning and operations.

MAN THE FORCE

1-11. *Man the Force* consists of all functions and tasks that affect the personnel aspects of building combat power of an organization. This includes PRM, PA, SR, retention operations, and PIM. The challenge is getting the right Soldier with the right qualifications to the right place at the right time.

1-12. Personnel readiness management involves analyzing personnel strength data to determine current combat capabilities, projecting future requirements, and assessing conditions of individual readiness. Personnel readiness management is directly interrelated and interdependent upon the functions of PA, SR, and PIM.

1-13. Personnel accountability is the by-name management of the location and duty status of every person assigned or attached to a unit. It includes tracking the movement of personnel as they arrive to, and depart from, a unit. For deployed units, this includes maintaining visibility of individuals as they enter, transit, and depart theater for reasons that range from normal rest and recuperation (R&R) to treatment at a medical treatment facility (MTF). Battalion and brigade S-1 personnel readiness teams (PR TMs) are at the tip of the spear for managing the automation systems that support Army-wide PA and require a team of HR professionals who are competent with automated HR systems and understand the PA process.

1-14. Strength reporting is turning by-name data into a numerical end product. Strength reporting is conducted at all levels of command (G-1/AG and S-1). The personnel SR process starts with by-name strength related transactions submitted at battalion or separate unit-level and ends with personnel database updates at all echelons of command. Strength reports reflect the combat power of a unit and are used to monitor unit strength, prioritize replacements, monitor deployable/non-deployable personnel, execute strength distribution, and make tactical and HR support decisions.

1-15. Retention operations objective is to improve readiness, force alignment, and maintain Army end-strength through the development and retention of Soldiers. While unit commanders and unit leaders are ultimately responsible for retaining Soldiers at their level, Career Counselors located at battalion and above organizations are technical experts charged with advising commanders on all aspects of the Army Retention Program. They also determine retention eligibility, retention options, and assist with eligibility for special commissioning programs consistent with published regulations and DA directives.

1-16. Personnel information management encompasses the collecting, processing, storing, displaying, reconciling, and disseminating of relevant HR information about units and personnel. Commanders, HR professionals, and planners rely on personnel information databases when performing their mission. Refer to AR 340-21, *The Army Privacy Program*, for specific recordkeeping requirements under the Privacy Act.

PROVIDE HR SERVICES

1-17. HR services are those functions conducted by HR professionals that specifically impact Soldiers and organizations and include EPS, postal operations, and casualty operations. Essential personnel services functions are performed by G-1/AGs and S-1s. Postal operations are performed by HR personnel in G-1/AGs, postal organizations, Military Mail Terminal (MMT) teams, Human Resources Sustainment Centers (HRSCs), and monitored within the Human Resources Operation Branches (HROBs). Casualty operations are performed by S-1s and HR unit personnel (e.g., HRSC, HROB, HR Company, and Casualty Liaison Team (CLT)) and monitored within the HROB.

1-18. Essential personnel services provides timely and accurate HR functions that affect Soldier status, readiness, and quality of life and allows Army leadership to effectively manage the force. Essential personnel services includes awards and decorations, evaluation reports, promotions and reductions, transfers and discharges, identification documents, leaves and passes, line of duty investigations, Soldier applications, and coordination of military pay and entitlements.

1-19. Postal operations provide mail and postal finance services within the deployed area of operations (AO). Processing mail involves receiving, separating, sorting, dispatching, transporting, and redirecting ordinary, official, insured, certified, return receipt, and registered mail; conducting multinational and international mail exchange; and handling official casualty, contaminated/suspicious, and enemy prisoner of war (EPW) mail. Postal finance services include selling postage stamps, cashing and selling money orders, mailing packages, providing insured/certified mail services and registered/special services (including classified up to SECRET level), and processing postal claims and inquiries.

1-20. Casualty operations management is the collecting, recording, reporting, verifying and processing of casualty information from unit level to HQDA. The recorded information facilitates next of kin (NOK) notification, casualty assistance, casualty tracking and status updates, and provides the basis for historical and statistical reports. This information is also shared with other DOD and Army agencies to initiate required actions. Accuracy and timeliness are critical components of casualty management, and depend on assured communications and reliable access to personnel information.

COORDINATE PERSONNEL SUPPORT

1-21. Coordinate personnel support functions normally require coordination by G-1/AGs and S-1s or generally fall under the G-1/AG and S-1 responsibility. These functions include MWR, command interest programs, and band operations.

1-22. Morale, welfare, and recreation operations include unit recreation, sports programs, and rest areas for military and deployed DOD civilian personnel. Morale, welfare, and recreation personnel provide these services and facilities in coordination with unit points of contact. G-1/AGs and S-1s coordinate MWR operations and plan for MWR operations. Morale, welfare, and recreation support includes coordinated Army and Air Force Exchange Service (AAFES) and American Red Cross (ARC) support.

1-23. Command interest programs are of general interest to organizations and Soldiers and include such programs as the equal opportunity program, Army voting assistance program, Army substance abuse program, Army body composition program, Army continuing education system, sexual harassment/assault response and prevention program, Army sponsorship program, family readiness, and other programs; however, this list is not all inclusive. All command interest programs have regulatory guidance or statutory requirements that S-1s must follow to ensure successful execution of the program.

1-24. Army band operations provide support to the deployed force by tailoring music support throughout military operations. Music instills in our Soldiers the will to fight and win, fosters the support of our citizens, and promotes our national interests at home and abroad. Detailed information on band operations is contained in Army tactics, techniques, and procedures (ATTP) 1-19, U. S. Army Bands.

CONDUCT HR PLANNING AND OPERATIONS

1-25. HR planning and operations are the means by which HR leaders envision a desired HR end state in support of the operational commander's mission requirements. It communicates to subordinate HR providers and HR unit leaders the intent, expected requirements, and desired outcomes in the form of an OPLAN or operations order, and the process of tracking current and near-term (future) execution of the planned HR support to ensure effective support to the operational commander through the following process (operations).

- Assessing the current situation and forecasting HR requirements based on the progress of the operation.
- Making execution and adjustment decisions to exploit opportunities or unforecasted requirements.
- Directing actions to apply HR resources and support at decisive points and time.

1-26. Operate HR mission command nodes is establishing, operating, and maintaining connectivity to HR data and voice communications nodes needed for HR operations. HR mission command nodes are required to enable HR personnel access to HR databases and should provide access across all commands and echelons, and to higher and lower elements.

THE ROLE OF THE ADJUTANT

1-27. HR transformation professionalized the S-1 sections of brigades and battalions, increasing their responsibilities and capabilities to improve the delivery of HR support. While much of this manual discusses the tactical and technical functions in terms of core competencies and subordinate key functions, HR professionals must take into careful consideration the art of how to execute them. The role of the adjutant goes beyond a set of additional duties assigned to the S-1 based on tradition or expediency. This most important tenant is found in the very root of the word adjutant which in its literal translation means to help. The help or assistance that is rendered to a commander by the adjutant is the foundation of one of the key command relationships that is formed. Commanders would rather have an officer with average technical skills who is practiced and brilliant in the art of HR support than a superior technocrat that cannot build and maintain relationships.

1-28. The adjutant is not a separate position or billet in an organizational structure but rather the dual role an individual fills. The function of the adjutant should not be confused with certain routine or specialized duties which may be performed. Routine duties may include clerical work, scheduling management, and correspondence management. Specialized duties are coordinating activities in support of the commander's programs and ceremonial duties historically assigned to the S-1. In each of these cases, the individual that performs these tasks is often referred to as the adjutant, but in fact, it is the senior principle staff officer for HR who serves as the trusted agent to the commander on all the most sensitive and delicate matters related to HR that is fulfilling the role of the adjutant.

1-29. The relationship established between the commander and the adjutant is critically important to the overall success of the HR mission. Each pairing is unique based on the commander's needs. The adjutant is the key advisor to the commander on all matters related to HR; must be able to connect in a deep and direct way, sense and stimulate reactions and desired interactions. The need for interpersonal skills and being perceptive cannot be overstated. The adjutant has the ability to discern deeper meaning; to determine the true significance of what is being expressed. To achieve these ends, the adjutant must have access to the commander. Having access often exposes the individual to the commander's unfiltered thoughts and feelings on sensitive and private personnel matters. Discretion, empathy and trust best describe the key attributes of any individual that fulfills this responsibility.

1-30. Since the skills and knowledge are complex and take time to master, it is important that senior HR professionals continuously coach, teach and mentor rising HR leaders in the art of HR support. This is especially important for HR leaders in geographically remote or austere locations. Anticipating the needs of an individual commander and then being able to act upon it with timely, accurate and relevant information can only be achieved through practice of the art. When the role is properly executed, the adjutant minimizes mission distracters, allowing commanders to better concentrate their efforts and decision-making on core mission objectives.

HR AND SUSTAINMENT RELATIONSHIPS

1-31. HR support is an element of personnel services and is aligned under the sustainment warfighting function. The *sustainment warfighting function* is the related tasks and systems that provide support and services to ensure freedom of action, extend operational reach, and prolong endurance (ADRP 3-0). The sustainment warfighting function consists of three major elements: logistics, personnel services, and Army health system support. All are necessary to maintain and prolong operations until successful mission accomplishment. As depicted in ADP 4-0, *Sustainment*, personnel services are sustainment functions that man and fund the force, maintain Soldier and family readiness, promote the moral and ethical values of the Nation, and enable the fighting qualities of the Army. Personnel services provide economic power at the operational and tactical levels. Personnel services complement logistics by planning for and coordinating efforts that provide and sustain personnel. Personnel services include:

- HR support.
- Financial management operations.
- Legal support.
- Religious support.
- Band support.

1-32. For HR support providers, sustainment leaders, and staffs, it is important to understand the HR and sustainment relationship as it relates to supporting and supported roles and responsibilities. Supported organizations include G-1/AGs and brigade and battalion S-1s. Supporting organizations are the HRSC, sustainment brigade expeditionary sustainment command (ESC) HROBs, and HR companies.

1-33. Mission command of all HR organizations is mission, enemy, terrain and weather, troops and support available, time available, civil considerations (METT-TC) driven and resides within the theater sustainment organizations. HR leaders provide mission command of HR organizations at company-level and below. At higher levels, HR organizations are aligned under sustainment units within the sustainment structure. For example, the HRSC is assigned to a theater sustainment command (TSC). The HR company, theater gateway personnel accountability team (TG PAT), and MMT Team are assigned to a sustainment brigade. This mission command alignment further enhances the ability of the HR unit to accomplish its mission set, as the sustainment commander has the sustainment assets and resources needed for non-HR related support.

1-34. Within the sustainment brigade, it is the individual sustainment brigade commander's decision which sustainment unit the HR organization is assigned or attached. There is no "right" mission command solution universal to every situation — commanders make task organization decisions based on the mission and the requirements. However, HR units are normally assigned to a special troops battalion (STB) of the sustainment brigade, but could be attached to a combat sustainment support battalion (CSSB) as mission dictates. Figure 1-2 on page 1-8 provides a schematic overview of the HR organizations and their relationship with sustainment units and supported units within a theater of operations.

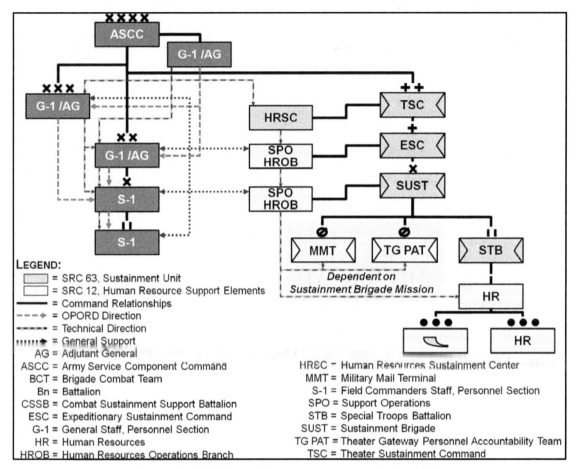

Figure 1-2. HR/sustainment structure relationship

Note: Standard requirements code (SRC) - 12 designations represent HR organizations while SRC-63 designations represent sustainment unit organizations.

1-35. Further mission command considerations should be made for the TG PAT and the MMT Team as they are led by an area of concentration-42 Lieutenant Colonel. While the teams are normally attached to a sustainment brigade, the commander of a sustainment brigade with a theater opening mission may elect to form a temporary task force for the purpose of carrying out a specific operation or mission associated with the TG PAT or MMT.

1-36. The role of the G-1/AG and S-1 section remains constant and they continue to be responsible for performing all HR core competencies and subordinate key functions. G-1/AGs and S-1s focus their support on providing internal HR support to their unit. External support is provided or coordinated by the supporting HROB in the sustainment brigade and ESC. Human resources organizations are responsible for executing postal, casualty, and PA missions. Commanders of sustainment organizations are responsible for the training readiness authority and mission execution of assigned or attached HR organizations.

HR SUSTAINMENT ROLES

1-37. Army service component command (ASCC). The ASCC G-1/AG is the senior Army HR representative/advisor in the theater of operations. The function of the ASCC G-1/AG is to enhance the readiness and operational capabilities of Army forces within the theater of operations and ensure HR support is properly planned, prioritized, and managed. This includes ensuring HR support is adequately resourced and executed through the operation order (OPORD) process and through direct communications between subordinate G-1/AGs and S-1s in accordance with (IAW) the ASCC commander's priorities, intent, and policies. Specific roles and responsibilities for the ASCC G-1/AG are contained in chapter 2 and subsequent chapters of this manual.

1-38. In today's operational environment, Army forces normally operate as part of a joint task force (JTF). As such, it is critical for the ASCC G-1/AG to coordinate closely with the JTF J-1, coalition forces land component commander (CFLCC) (if not part of the ASCC), or joint force land component commander (JFLCC) to ensure Army HR policies do not conflict with joint HR policies, procedures, and reporting requirements. JP 1-0, *Joint Personnel Support*, applies when operating as part of the joint force.

1-39. At the ASCC, Corps, and Division levels, the staff headquarters (HQ) is aligned with the warfighting functions as defined in ADRP 3-0, *Unified Land Operations*. Alignment with the sustainment directorate does not change the role and responsibilities of the G-1/AG. The G-1/AG retains its unique interrelationships with other staff elements and subordinate staff elements and serves as senior advisor to the commander on all HR matters.

1-40. The TSC is the senior sustainment organization for a theater of operations. The TSC is the key linkage between the ASCC G-1/AG and the HRSC. The TSC provides a centralized sustainment mission command of most deployed sustainment organizations and is responsible for planning, controlling, and synchronizing all operational-level sustainment operations for the ASCC or JTF during deployment, employment, sustainment, and redeployment. (Note: The TSC G-1/AG's focus is on TSC specific (internal) HR support, while the HRSC focus is theater-wide). Figure 1-3 depicts a TSC with an assigned HRSC. For more specific information on the mission and organization of the TSC, see ATP 4-94, *Theater Sustainment Command*.

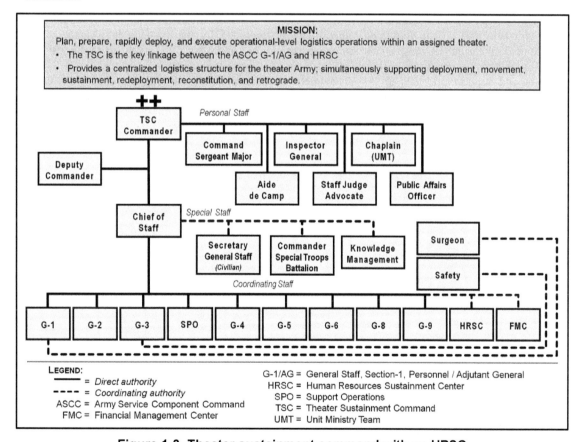

Figure 1-3. Theater sustainment command with an HRSC

1-41. The HRSC is a TSC staff element that provides theater-level HR casualty, PA, and postal support to Army forces within the theater IAW the policies, procedures, and priorities established by the ASCC. As a staff element of the TSC, the HRSC is the primary participant in the planning, integration, and execution of theater-wide HR support.

1-42. The role of the ESC is to provide forward-based mission command of sustainment forces. The ESC normally deploys to provide mission command when multiple sustainment brigades are employed or when the TSC determines that forward command presence is required. For more specific information on the mission and organization of the ESC, see ATP 4-94.

1-43. The sustainment brigade is a flexible, modular organization. Organic to the sustainment brigade are the brigade HQs and a STB. All other assets are task organized to the sustainment brigade to enable it to accomplish its sustainment warfighting roles and mission. Sustainment brigades provide sustainment support at the operational and tactical levels and are capable of providing mission command for theater opening and theater distribution missions. For specific information on the mission, organization and operations of the sustainment brigade, see ATP 4-93, *Sustainment Brigade*.

1-44. The HROB is an embedded element within each sustainment brigade and ESC support operations (SPO) section. The HROB has the mission to plan current and future operations, coordinate, integrate, and assess the emplacement and operations of HR elements executing the casualty, PA, and postal operations functions. This includes providing technical guidance and assistance to supported G-1/AGs and S-1s in casualty, PA, and postal missions. As part of the SPO, the HROB has the responsibility to coordinate the execution of non-HR related sustainment in support of HR operations.

1-45. The establishment of a close relationship between G-1/AGs, S-1s, and the supporting HROB is critical for timely support. HR support requirements for subordinate or supported organizations within the theater are established by the G-1/AG or the S-1 of the organization and forwarded to the sustainment brigade HROB. Once requests are received, the HROB evaluates the request against available resources and unit priorities. If the requested support can be provided by the sustainment brigade, then it is coordinated with the HR company. If the request cannot be supported, it is forwarded to the ESC HROB. HR organizations remain a constrained asset in the deployed theater; therefore, the HROB must recommend support priorities to the sustainment commander. Any HR support issues that cannot be resolved by the sustainment brigade or ESC/TSC are forwarded to the ASCC G-1/AG for prioritization and reconciliation. The ASCC G-1/AG, in coordination with the TSC (with the support of the HRSC), reconciles prioritization issues to ensure required HR support structure is available for the theater, within the ability of the Army to resource.

Chapter 2

HR Organizations and Staff Elements

This chapter discusses the mission, organization, and employment of HR organizations and staff elements. HR organizations and staff elements are designed to be tailorable, scalable, flexible, and capable of providing or sustaining HR support across the range of military operations.

HR organizations and staff elements responsible for providing HR support are:
- Army Human Resources Command (HRC)
- ASCC Sustainment Cell (G-1/AG).
- Corps Sustainment Cell (G-1/AG).
- Division Sustainment Cell (G-1/AG).
- Brigade S-1 section.
- special troops battalion (STB) S-1 section.
- Battalion S-1 section.
- Headquarters and Headquarters Battalion (HHBn) S-1 section.
- HR Operations Branch (HROB) (sustainment brigade and ESC).
- HR Sustainment Center (HRSC).
- Military Mail Terminal (MMT) Team.
- Theater Gateway Personnel Accountability Team (TG PAT).
- HR Company.
- Postal Platoon.
- HR Platoon.
- Army Bands.

ARMY HUMAN RESOURCES COMMAND (HRC)

2-1. The Human Resources Command is the functional proponent of the G-1 for military personnel management (except for the judge advocate general and the chaplain branches) and personnel systems. The HRC also supports the Director, ARNG and the Chief, Army Reserve, in their management of the Selected Reserve. The HRC mission is to execute career management, sustainment, distribution, and transition of personnel in order to optimize Army personnel readiness, enable leader development, and strengthen an agile and versatile Army that can prevent, shape, and win.

2-2. The major elements of HRC include: the Enlisted Personnel Management Directorate, which provides active and reserve enlisted Soldiers with career guidance and support; the Officer Personnel Management Directorate, which provides active and reserve officers with career guidance and support; The Adjutant General Directorate, which manages Soldiers' records, promotion boards, evaluation processing, and Veterans' support; the Personnel Information Systems Directorate, which provides information technology support to command functions; and various staff elements including G-3 Operations, Resource Management, Chief Information Officer, Surgeon, Inspector General, and Judge Advocate.

ARMY SERVICE COMPONENT COMMAND (ASCC) G-1/AG

2-3. The ASCC G-1/AG's primary function is to plan and prioritize HR support to assure a unity of purpose and effort that maximizes the readiness and operational capabilities of forces within the theater.

2-4.   The ASCC G-1/AG is an element of the ASCC operational sustainment directorate. The operational sustainment directorate combines the G-1/AG, assistant chief of staff, logistics (G-4), Assistant Chief of Staff, Financial Management (G-8), Surgeon, and Engineer into a single staff cell that provides oversight, policy, planning and synchronization of personnel services, logistics, and Army Health System support missions.   The ASCC G-1/AG relies on secure, continuous, survivable communications, and digital information systems.

2-5.   The ASCC G-1/AG primarily operates from the Main command post (CP), but has a two-person team within the Sustainment Cell of the Contingency CP.   This two-person team establishes and coordinates initial HR support operations for the theater and forms the basis for the G-1/AG's forward presence in the AO.   The Sustainment Cell of the Contingency CP may be augmented by other elements of the ASCC G-1 main staff sections or through individual augmentation.

2-6.   The ASCC G-1/AG does not exercise mission command of any HR organization.   The TSC ensures HR organizations (HRSC, MMT, TG PAT, HR Company) execute their HR missions IAW the policies, priorities, and timelines established by the ASCC G-1/AG.

2-7.   The ASCC G-1/Senior HR Technician role is to serve as a war-fighter, technical expert, trainer, and advisor to the command and S-1 on personnel issues.   The HR Warrant Officer administers, manages, maintains, operates, and integrates personnel systems across all levels throughout the Army structure.   As a result of the HR Warrant Officer's expertise and progressive levels of leadership, the HR Warrant Officer should be utilized in positions that supports the commander's mission and provides technical developmental opportunities.   The Senior HR Technician maintains external relationships and provides technical and functional oversight and support to sub-commands.

2-8.   The ASCC G-1/AG Sergeant Major (SGM) responsibilities are broad ranging, regardless of specific position or assignment.   In addition to the mission specific priorities and requirements by the senior commander and the G-1/AG, there are general requirements that the G-1/AG SGM must monitor and execute in order to ensure the health of organizations, and development and growth of future HR enlisted leaders.   The ASCC G-1/AG SGM advises the ASCC G-1/AG and organic Command Sergeant Major (CSM) on senior noncommissioned officer (NCO) movement/development across the footprint of responsibility.

2-9.   The ASCC G-1/AG SGM provides direct mentorship and training oversight to the Corps and Division G-1/AG SGMs in the geographic footprint of responsibility.   Due to the dispersed nature of senior HR NCOs, this requirement is critical in the plug and play nature of Army Force Generation (ARFORGEN) manning and unit structures, and goes beyond the boundaries of unit chains of command/assignment.   Like mentorship, ensuring HR Sustainment Training is conducted quarterly or as appropriate for a given mission/location, is vital to mission success and continuous development of HR Soldiers.   It also breaks the boundaries of unit chains of command/assignment.   Soldiers assigned in geographic locations deserve continuous technical development as part of Army leader development, in which, SGM/CSMs are key in overseeing this requirement.

2-10. The ASCC G-1/AG SGM maintains external relationships and provides readiness oversight. Partnering with IMCOM/Military Personnel Divisions (MPDs) to fill gaps in service to Soldiers and Families, depending on the structure of service and support locally, provides the continuous chain of support needed for optimum Soldier and Family care.   It also allows Soldiers the opportunity to perform EPS while in a garrison environment.   Partnering with the MTF to ensure nondeployable/profile data is transferred accurately and routinely through the medical/HR reporting systems ensures the Army mans units with capable Soldiers for a given assignment.

2-11. As depicted in Figure 2-1 on page 2-4, the ASCC G-1/AG is comprised of a HQs element and two branches: the Manpower Branch and the Plans and Operations, Programs, and Policy Branch.

2-12. The HQs section is responsible to:
- Monitor and manage inter-service agreements.
- Direct Army Force HR policy in accordance with (IAW) combatant command and Army policy.
- Coordinate with the Geographical Combatant Command J-1 and Service Personnel and Policy managers.

- Provide oversight of senior leadership responsibilities for the G-1/AG staff.
- Integrate HR related personnel services support within the theater.
- Direct military HR systems and systems to support deployed Civilians.
- Monitor and integrate HR systems.
- Coordinate HR command programs, as directed.

2-13. The Manpower Branch is comprised of three sections: the Awards and Actions section, individual augmentee (IA) Management section, and the Personnel Readiness section. The Manpower Branch is responsible to:

- Establish EPS policy and procedures for the theater.
- Process awards and decorations.
- Monitor theater personnel readiness.
- Advise the theater commander on personnel readiness.
- Collect and analyze personnel status (PERSTAT) report data.
- Monitor accountability of all theater personnel (military and deployed Civilians).
- Maintain theater and JTF personnel summary.
- Manage IAs for the Army Force/Combined Joint Task Force staff.
- Report all required manning data to the combatant commander, as directed.
- Coordinate and receive Joint augmentation.
- Prepare Commanding General casualty correspondence, as required.
- Monitor execution of casualty notification and assistance program.
- Monitor casualty database.
- Monitor line of duty (LOD) investigations.
- Monitor the deployed personnel database to ensure hierarchy reflects current task organization.
- Advise subordinate elements on new and changing HR automated system requirements that affect their ability to provide support. Note: This may include new versions of HR automated hardware and software, procedural changes within HR automated systems or implementation plans for new hardware/software.
- Manage personnel database roles and permissions for the theater staff and command group.
- Conduct liaison with the assistant chief of staff, signal (G-6) to resolve connectivity, security, and other systems issues, as necessary.

2-14. The Plans and Operations, Programs, and Policy Branch is comprised of three sections: the Current Operations section, MWR section, and a Postal section. Branch responsibilities are to:

- Monitor conditions and operations that might require reconstitution and regeneration.
- Assist the assistant chief of staff, operations (G-3) to determine manpower requirements for the theater HQs.
- Assess the progress of current HR support.
- Ensure casualty reporting is integrated in current operations tracking.
- Coordinate HR support requirements with the TSC.
- Produce annexes and commander's estimates in support of current and future plans.
- Coordinate with staff planners across functional areas.
- Develop and coordinate current and long-term operational HR policy.
- Establish and monitor policy execution of all theater-level HR support.
- Monitor postal support for the theater.
- Respond to postal investigation inquiries and approve Mail Cover requests.
- Identify a Postal Platoon to handle EPW mail.
- Manage command interest programs for the theater.
- Augment the current operations integration cell (COIC) as necessary for HR support.
- Track the COP ensuring HR support provides timely input to current operations.

- Interface with HQDA, ASCC, subordinate units, and multi-national partners, if serving as the J-1.
- Build, modify, and coordinate the personnel services portion of the task force deployment plan.
- Plan for the integration of Reserve Component (RC) assets.
- Plan and coordinate MWR support for the theater.
- Manage the leave and pass program, to include R&R.

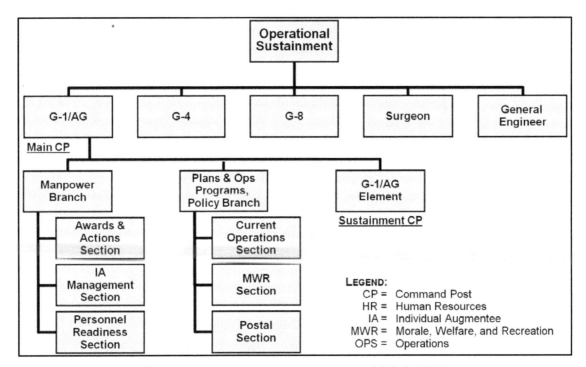

Figure 2-1. Organizational design – ASCC G-1/AG

CORPS AND DIVISION G-1/AG

2-15. Corps and Division G-1/AGs serve as the Assistant Chief of Staff for personnel and are the Corps and Division principal HR advisors. The Corps and Division G-1/AG are elements of the sustainment warfighting cell and operate from the Main CP. The sustainment cell consists of the G-1/AG, G-4, assistant chief of staff, financial management (G-8), Surgeon, and Engineer. At Corps-level, the G-4 serves as the chief of sustainment.

2-16. The Corps and Division Senior HR Technician role includes, but not limited to, overseeing the technical functionality and personnel systems associated with serving as the Division HR Operations/Casualty, Current Operations, EPS, PIM, or PRM officer-in-charge; Corps-level (or equivalent) HR Operations, COIC, Casualty Operations, HR Policy, EPS, PIM, or PRM officer-in-charge.

2-17. The Corps and Division G-1/AG SGM is a role with broad ranging responsibilities, regardless of specific position or assignment. In addition to the mission specific priorities and requirements by the senior commander and the G-1/AG, there are general requirements that the G-1/AG SGM must monitor and execute in order to ensure the health of organizations, and development and growth of future HR enlisted leaders. The Corps and Division G-1/AG SGM advise the Corps and Division G-1/AG and organic CSM on senior NCO movement/development across the footprint of responsibility. (Refer to paragraphs 2-7 and 2-8 for further information regarding the G-1/AG SGM). Some general responsibilities of the Corps and Division G-1/AG SGM include:

- Provide direct mentorship and training oversight to the senior HR NCO of each brigade and battalion in the geographic footprint of responsibility.
- Maintain external relationships and readiness oversight.

2-18. Corps and Division G-1/AG elements are multi-functional organizations with a responsibility to ensure HR support is properly planned, resourced, coordinated, monitored, synchronized, and executed for organizations assigned or attached. The Corps and Division G-1/AG have responsibility for the tasks below:

- Strength Reporting.
- Personnel Readiness Management.
- Personnel Information Management.
- Casualty Operations.
- Essential Personnel Services.
- Family and Morale, Welfare, and Recreation.
- HR Planning and Staff Operations.

2-19. G-1/AGs, as subject matter experts, have the responsibility for training and guiding subordinate HR elements assigned, attached or geographically co-located with the Corps or Division headquarters in all cases where the Corps or Division commander, acting as senior mission commander, has training resource authority for that subordinate organization. To effectively execute this responsibility, G-1/AGs may coordinate with sustainment organizations through the HRSC or appropriate level HROB to leverage HR assets in a coordinated effort to support the force. A list of recommended training activities is located in paragraph 2-95; however, this list is not all inclusive.

2-20. METT-TC determines the employment of the Corps G-1/AG. While the G-1/AG operates from the Main CP, the Corps HR COIC Support element and Division HR HQs Section Current Operations (HR COIC Support) may co-locate with the movement and maneuver COIC. Depending on the operational pace, other command post representation may be required. However, as the transformation of the HR structure limits manpower, consideration should be given to IAs to meet additional operating requirements.

2-21. The Corps and Division G-1/AG rely on non-secure, secure, continuous, and survivable communications and digital information systems. The G-1/AG depends on the availability of both secure and non-secure data systems and voice systems, requiring Non-Secure Internet Protocol Router Network (NIPRNET) and SECRET Internet Protocol Router Network (SIPRNET) connectivity with sufficient bandwidth to facilitate web-based applications. The G-1/AG relies on various HR automated databases to support operations.

2-22. The Corps may be designated to serve as the Army Force, JTF, Combined Joint Task Force, or as a Joint Force Land Component Command. If serving as part of any Joint Force, the J-1 (G-1/AG) has the responsibility to conduct or manage tasks outlined in JP 1-0. When serving in the position of Army Forces G-1/AG, the Corps G-1/AG is responsible for all functions and duties of the ASCC G-1/AG.

2-23. In some cases the division may be designated as the Army Force. If designated as the Army Force, the G-1/AG will be required to perform theater-level functions normally conducted by the ASCC G-1/AG. As the Army Force G-1/AG, the G-1/AG serves as the coordinating staff advisor responsible for the development of Army Force personnel plans, policies, and guidance on manpower and personnel issues.

2-24. As depicted in Figures 2-2 and 2-3 on page 2-8, the Corps G-1/AG staff section is comprised of a HQs element and seven sections and the Division G-1/AG staff section is comprised of a HQs element and six sections.

2-25. The HQs section of the Corps and Division G-1/AG is responsible to:

- Monitor and manage inter-service agreements.
- Direct Army Force HR policy IAW combatant command, Army, ASCC, and higher policy.
- Coordinate with the Geographical Combatant Command J1 and Service Personnel and Policy managers, if serving as the Army Force G-1/JTF J-1.
- Provide oversight of senior leadership responsibilities for the G-1/AG staff.
- Integrate HR related personnel services support.
- Direct military HR systems and systems to support deployed Civilians.
- Monitor and integrate HR systems.
- Monitor personnel readiness.

- Coordinate HR command programs, as directed.

2-26. The HR Operations section of the Corps and Division G-1/AG is responsible to:
- Monitor conditions and operations that might require reconstitution or regeneration.
- Assess the progress of current personnel support.
- Ensure casualty reporting is integrated in current operations tracking.
- Develop casualty estimation.
- Coordinate HR support requirements with supporting ESC and sustainment brigade.
- Produce annexes and commander's estimates in support of current and future plans.
- Augment the COIC, as necessary (Corps only).
- Track the COP ensuring HR support provides timely input to current operations.
- Interface with HQDA, ASCC, subordinate units, and multi-national partners, if serving as the J-1.
- Build, modify, and coordinate the personnel services portion of the task force deployment plan.
- Plan for the integration of RC assets.
- Coordinate with staff planners across functional areas.
- Plan and coordinate MWR support.
- Manage leave and pass program, to include R&R.
- Evaluate HR metrics.
- Provide HR guidance and training to S-1s.

2-27. The HR Policy section of the Corps G-1/AG and the HR Division of the Division G-1/AG are responsible to:
- Develop and coordinate current and long-term operational personnel policy.
- Provide technical oversight for policy execution of all HR support.
- Manage the IA program.
- Manage the rotation policy.
- Manage command interest programs.

2-28. The Essential Personnel Services section of the Corps and Division G-1/AG is responsible to:
- Establish EPS policy and procedures.
- Process awards and decorations.
- Monitor evaluations, promotions, reductions, and other EPS programs.
- Receive, process, and manage congressional inquiries and special actions.

2-29. The HR COIC support element of the Corps G-1/AG and the Current Operations section of the Division G-1/AG are responsible to:
- Monitor conditions and operations that might require reconstitution and regeneration.
- Assess the progress of current HR support.
- Ensure casualty reporting is integrated in current operations tracking.
- Coordinate HR support requirements with supporting ESC and sustainment brigade.
- Produce annexes and commander's estimates in support of current and future plans.
- Track the COP ensuring HR support provides timely input to current operations.
- Coordinate with staff planners across functional areas.

2-30. The Casualty Operations section of the Corps and Division G-1/AG is responsible to:
- Prepare all Commanding General casualty correspondence, as required.
- Develop Corps / Division casualty notification and assistance program policy, if required.
- Monitor casualty database.
- Monitor patient tracking and accountability through the surgeon.
- Monitor LOD investigations.

- Monitor duty status-whereabouts unknown (DUSTWUN), missing, prisoner of war, and missing-in-action (MIA) cases.
- Develop casualty estimation.
- Maintain liaison with CLTs, Mortuary Affairs (MA), postal units, medical commands, and MTFs.
- Coordinate and execute Civilian, Joint, and multi-national casualty actions as directed and augmented.
- Accept Liaison Officer Teams from Civilian agencies, and Joint, multi-national, and host-nation military Services.

2-31. The Personnel Information Management section of the Corps and Division G-1/AG is responsible to:
- Monitor the deployed personnel database to ensure hierarchy reflects current task organization.
- Execute HR automated systems requirements.
- Advise subordinate elements on new and changing HR automated system requirements that affect their ability to provide support. Note: This may include new versions of HR automated hardware and software, procedural changes within HR automated systems or implementation plans for new hardware/software.
- Manage personnel database roles and permissions for the Corps/Division, staff, and command group.
- Conduct liaison with G-6 as necessary to resolve connectivity, security, and HR systems issues.

2-32. The Personnel Readiness Management section for the Corps and Division G-1/AG is responsible to:
- Conduct PRM.
- Collect and analyze critical personnel readiness information.
- Collect and analyze PERSTAT report data.
- Prepare all required manning reports.
- Determine manpower requirements for the HQs.
- Determine manpower reporting requirements for subordinate elements.
- Monitor accountability of all personnel (military and deployed Civilians).
- Manage officer, warrant officer, enlisted, and deployed Civilian personnel, to include subordinate organizations, in coordination with HRC.
- Monitor personnel replacement requirements.
- Submit replacement requirements for key personnel.
- Maintain task force personnel summary.
- Recommend fill priority.
- Monitor in-transit visibility of incoming personnel.
- Report all required manning data to the combatant commander/ASCC, as directed.

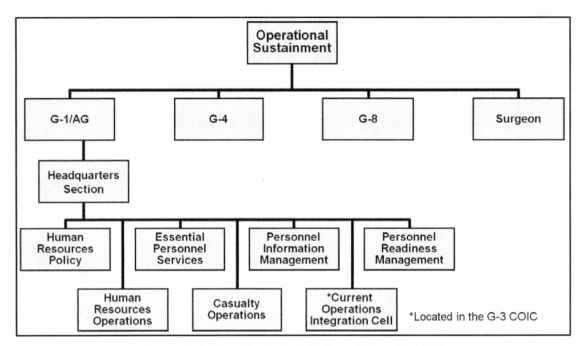

Figure 2-2. Organizational design - Corps G-1/AG

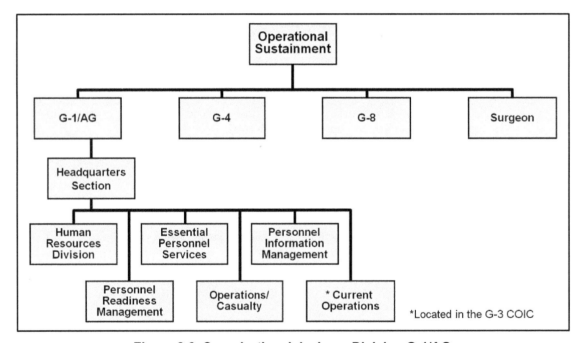

Figure 2-3. Organizational design – Division G-1/AG

BRIGADE S-1 SECTION

2-33. The function of the brigade S-1 section is to plan, provide, and coordinate the delivery of HR support, services, or information to all assigned and attached personnel within the brigade and subordinate battalions and companies. The brigade S-1 is the principal staff advisor to the brigade commander for all matters concerning HR support. The brigade S-1 may coordinate the staff efforts of brigade EO, Inspector General, and morale support activities. The brigade S-1 provides technical direction to subordinate unit S-1 sections. Figure 2-4 on page 2-10 depicts the organizational design of a brigade-level S-1 section. Refer to ATTP 1-0.1, S-1 Operations, for detailed duties and responsibilities of the brigade S-1 section.

2-34. Brigade-level S-1 sections include the TSC STB S-1 of General Officer-level organizations. These STB S-1 sections have the same capabilities and responsibilities of brigade-level S-1s. Units are responsible for their own EPS and other HR support as defined throughout this manual. General officer HQs, without an STB S-1 section or equivalent, must be augmented by their higher HQs in order to receive this support in a deployed area. G-1/AG sections of these HQs do not have the authority, personnel, or equipment to provide this internal STB S-1 support.

ORGANIZATION

2-35. The brigade S-1 section normally organizes personnel functionally (assigns specific personnel to an area of responsibility), then cross-trains within the section for continuity and consistency IAW METT-TC. The brigade S-1 section includes a leadership section consisting of the S-1, a warrant officer, and a noncommissioned officer in-charge with two ad-hoc teams: a PR TM and a HR Services Team. The S-1 leadership performs the Conduct HR Planning and Operations core competency and supervises the execution of all other HR mission essential tasks within the brigade.

2-36. The brigade PR TM focuses on Man the Force and Provide HR Services (Casualty Operations only) core competencies. The PR TM is responsible for executing PRM and strength distribution. The brigade strength manager is responsible for supervising all PRM and strength distribution actions, and is the leader of the PR TM. The brigade HR Technician serves as the principal advisor to the brigade S-1 on all aspects of HR management. The brigade HR Technician is responsible for the synchronization of HR support and sustains brigade readiness through the supervision of personnel readiness, strength accounting and management, EPS, mailroom operations, and financial support. The HR Technician manages the integration and utilization of HR enabling systems. The brigade S-1 noncommissioned officer in-charge provides direction for enlisted PRM and interfaces with the brigade CSM. The brigade CSM normally plays an active role in managing enlisted personnel; however, the S-1 has ultimate responsibility for the enlisted PRM process.

2-37. The brigade PR TM manages the brigade Distribution Management Sub-level (DMSL) for both officer and enlisted strength distribution. The PR TM coordinates the call forward of brigade replacements and executes the personnel portion of the unit status report (USR) process. The PR TM uses the electronic Military Personnel Office (eMILPO) or other systems that feed into the Total Army Personnel Database (TAPDB), Defense Casualty Information Processing System (DCIPS), Deployed Theater Accountability Software (DTAS), and Common Operational Picture Synchronizer (COPS) to execute brigade PRM and the Battle Command Sustainment Support System (BCS3) for limited PERSTAT functions.

2-38. The HR Services Team focuses on Provide HR Services and Coordinate Personnel Support core competencies. Subordinate key functions include EPS, Postal, MWR, Command Programs, and Customer Service. EPS functions are the primary focus of the team and are processed via authoritative personnel systems such as eMILPO, Regional Level Application Software (RLAS), and the Standard Installation/Division Personnel System – Army National Guard (SIDPERS-ARNG). This section provides common access cards (CAC) and Identification (ID) Tags to all brigade personnel. In some cases, the brigade S-1 also provides area support to contractors authorized to accompany the force (CAAF) and DOD Civilians for common access cards/Tags.

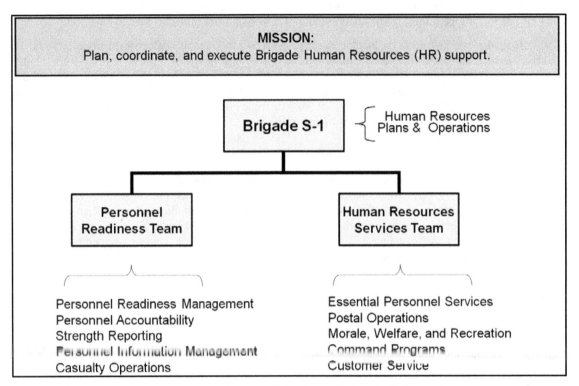

Figure 2-4. Organizational design – Brigade S-1 section

BRIGADE S-1 POSITIONING

2-39. The brigade S-1 section relies on non-secure, secure, and continuous digital information systems. Their success depends on the availability of both secure and non-secure data and voice systems which requires close coordination with the brigade signal staff officer (S-6). NIPRNET connectivity is provided by either very small aperture terminal (VSAT), Combat-Service-Support Automated Information Systems Interface (CAISI), or with the Joint Network Node. The brigade S-1 section requires access to the Force XXI Battle Command Brigade and Below (FBCB2), Blue Force Tracker, and similar systems that provide a COP through the Army battle command system (ABCS) infrastructure.

2-40. Brigade S-1 sections normally operate as an element of the Sustainment Cell in the brigade Main CP. When the S-1 section separates, the HR Services Team moves to the Brigade Support Battalion/STB CP with either the HR Technician or the senior HR NCO leading the split section. The majority of PRM, PA, and SR actions are performed at the brigade Main CP, while the majority of EPS and mailroom functions are performed in the brigade support area. Digital connectivity and the advent of enablers like the digital signature and forms content management better facilitate split-based operations. Casualty operations are conducted at both locations. It is critical that the split section maintains tactical voice, NIPRNET, and SIPRNET data connectivity with the remainder of the S-1 section at the brigade Main CP and the battalion S-1 sections.

BATTALION S-1 SECTION

2-41. The battalion S-1 section plans, provides, and coordinates the delivery of HR support, services, and information to all assigned and attached personnel within the battalion. The battalion S-1 is the principal staff advisor to the battalion commander for all matters concerning HR support. The battalion S-1 is the coordinating office for command interest programs, medical, and morale support activities. Refer to ATTP 1-0.1 for detailed duties and responsibilities of the battalion S-1 section.

2-42. The battalion S-1 section organizes within specific functional areas in order to synchronize personnel management activities and manage current and plan future operations. NIPRNET connectivity may be provided by VSAT and the CAISI Connect-the-Logistician system by connecting the battalion S-1 CAISI either through the Forward Support Company's VSAT, or the brigade S-1 VSAT. SIPRNET connectivity is coordinated through the battalion S-6. The S-1 ensures the S-6 includes DTAS in the battalion SIPRNET bandwidth requirement. Secure voice data is critical to remain linked to subordinate companies and the brigade S-1. Additionally, the S-1 section requires access to FBCB2, Blue Force Tracker, or similar systems to allow secure text capability with subordinate companies. The battalion S-1 section generally operates from the Main CP and may be collocated with the brigade S-1.

2-43. Battalion S-1 sections include the HHBn S-1 of General Officer-level organizations. HHBn S-1 sections have the same capabilities and responsibilities of battalion-level S-1s. They are responsible for their own EPS and other HR support as defined throughout this manual. G-1/AG sections of these headquarters do not have the authority, personnel, or equipment to provide this HHBn S-1 support.

2-44. The battalion S-1 section normally organizes personnel functionally (assign specific personnel to an area of responsibility), then cross-trains within the section for continuity and consistency. (Note: The battalion S-1 section size varies based on the size of the supported population.) The battalion S-1 section includes a leadership section consisting of the S-1 and the S-1 noncommissioned officer in-charge, and two ad-hoc sections or teams: a PR TM and an HR Services Team. The S-1 leadership team performs the HR Planning and Operations core competency, as well as supervises the execution of all other HR core competencies within the battalion. Figure 2-5 on page 2-12 depicts the organizational design for a battalion S-1 section. (Note: The battalion S-1 section also includes a Paralegal Specialist who normally works in the battalion or brigade Legal Section. Typically, the S-1 does not exercise control of the Paralegal Specialist.)

2-45. The battalion PR TM focuses on the Man the Force core competency. The PR TM is responsible for executing PRM and strength distribution under the supervision of the PR TM Chief, a 42A Staff Sergeant. While the battalion strength manager is responsible for supervising all PRM and strength distribution within the battalion, the general focus is on enlisted PRM and interface with the battalion CSM. The battalion CSM normally plays an active role in managing enlisted personnel; however, the S-1 has ultimate responsibility for the enlisted PRM process. The PR TM coordinates battalion replacement operations and uses various HR systems fed by TAPDB to execute battalion-level PRM. The PR TM executes error reconciliation and deviations to ensure consistency between TAPDB, eMILPO, RLAS, and SIDPERS-ARNG.

2-46. The HR Services Team performs the Provide HR Services and Coordinate Personnel Support core competencies. Subordinate key functions include EPS, postal, and MWR. The EPS function is the primary focus of the team. Awards, evaluation reports, promotions (to include semi-centralized Sergeant and Staff Sergeant promotions), and personnel actions for all assigned and attached personnel are executed by the HR Services Team. The HR Services Team processes replacements and maintains and updates Soldier records, including the Soldier's Army Military Human Resource Record (AMHRR). The AMHRR is defined as a collection of documents maintained as a single entity that pertains to a particular Soldier's career. The AMHRR includes, but is not limited to, the Official Military Personnel File, finance related documents and non-service related documents deemed necessary to store by the Army. A list of documents required for filing in the AMHRR can be found in AR 600-8-104, Army Military Human Resource Records Management.

2-47. The battalion section S-1 depends on the availability of both secure and non-secure voice and data systems requiring NIPRNET and SIPRNET connectivity with sufficient bandwidth to facilitate web-based applications. The S-1 section uses various HR systems for automated HR support, as well as for coordinating military pay, legal, and postal services for the battalion. All HR systems, with the exception of DTAS, operate in NIPRNET. Battalion S-1 sections should have CAISI for NIPRNET connectivity. Connectivity requirements direct that at least an element of the section be within line of site (3-5 km) of the VSAT in the Forward Support Company providing sustainment support for the battalion S-1 or to the brigade S-1 section, which also has VSAT capability. The battalion S-1 updates the DTAS daily. Company First Sergeants and executive officers can make daily strength reports or updates to the battalion S-1 via FBCB2.

2-48. The battalion S-1 section can operate from multiple locations. If operating from multiple locations, it is common for a small element and the S-1 officer to be located at the Combat Trains Command Post in proximity to the battalion Tactical Operations Cell, with the S-1 linked to the Tactical Operations Cell via FBCB2. The remainder of the section is either in the Task Force Support or Brigade Support Area in proximity to the Forward Support Company's VSAT or the brigade S-1 section VSAT. Elements of the S-1 section could also be located in the battalion Main CP or Tactical Operations Cell.

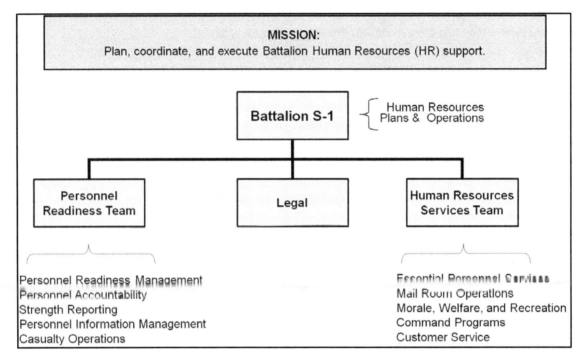

Figure 2-5. Organizational design – Battalion S-1 section

HUMAN RESOURCES SUSTAINMENT CENTER (HRSC)

2-49. The HRSC is a multi-functional, modular HR organization (staff element), and theater-level center assigned to a TSC that integrates and executes PA, casualty, and postal functions throughout the theater and as defined by the policies and priorities established by the ASCC G-1/AG. The HRSC provides support to the ASCC G-1/AG in the accomplishment of their PRM and PIM missions. They provide planning and operations technical support to the TSC Distribution Management Center. HRSC's flexible, modular, and scalable design increases the director's ability to recommend HR support requirements based upon the number of units and Soldiers supported and METT-TC. The HRSC also provides theater-wide technical guidance and training assistance for PA, casualty, and postal functions performed by the TG PAT, MMT Team, HR companies, platoons, and the HROB in the sustainment brigade and ESC.

2-50. The HRSC has the ability to tailor its organization to support the TSC theater-wide HR mission, as well as supporting other theater-level organizations such as a Combined Joint Task Force HQs. However, providing HRSC teams to other Army or Joint organizations should only be considered after a detailed analysis and should only be temporary in nature until IAs for the organization arrives in theater. The HRSC is capable of providing selected theater-level HR support simultaneously from the deployed location as well as from home station, through increased connectivity and the increased abilities of theater-level HQs to operate virtually.

2-51. The HRSC, in coordination with the TSC, has a defined role to ensure that the theater HR support plan is developed and then supported with available resources within the TSC. This includes collaborating with the ASCC G-1/AG and TSC to ensure appropriate HR support relationships are established and properly executed through the OPORD process. As the senior Army HR organization within the theater, the HRSC serves as the technical link and advisor to theater G-1/AGs, S-1s, HROBs, and HR companies for PA, casualty, and postal operations. The HRSC, in conjunction with the ASCC G-1, operates and manages the theater personnel database (DTAS) , the Postal Directory Address Database, and provides other theater-wide assistance for database issues and access.

2-52. The HRSC Modified Table of Organization and Equipment structure provides the capability to conduct split-based operations in support of the TSC. This capability supports the HRSC's ability to support the ESC during theater opening operations when they are the senior sustainment command. METT-TC analysis drives task organization. In cases where the TSC remains at home station, or during early entry operations when the TSC has not yet deployed, the HRSC may be required to deploy forward to establish theater capabilities for PA, PRM, PIM, and postal and casualty operations.

2-53. The HRSC, as the senior HR element responsible for executing PA, casualty, and postal missions, has a responsibility for providing technical guidance to theater HR organizations executing these missions. This technical guidance is provided by the various divisions of the HRSC and is passed to the ESC and sustainment brigade SPO HROBs, who then pass the information to the HR organizations assigned to sustainment units. The HRSC also provides technical guidance and support to the MMT and TG PAT. HR companies and platoons receive both technical and operational guidance from the supporting HROB.

2-54. The HRSC receives HR policy guidance from the ASCC G-1/AG, Army PPG, and in some areas HRC and other national-level HR organizations (Reserve Component). The HRSC receives employment and operational guidance from the TSC or the ESC commander. The HRSC receives life support from the TSC, or if conducting split based operations, the ASCC STB.

2-55. The HRSC, a staff section assigned to the TSC, is dependent upon the TSC STB for administrative support, to include company-level Uniform Code of Military Justice, religious, medical, legal, HR, administrative services, quarters and rations, logistics, unit maintenance of organic equipment, supplementary transportation support, and military pay. The HRSC relies on non-secure, secure, continuous, and survivable communications and digital information systems.

2-56. The HRSC consists of an Office of the Director and five divisions: Plans and Operations Division, PA/PRM/PIM Division, Casualty Operations Division (COD), Personnel Accountability (PA) Division, and Postal Operations Division (POD). Each division is further divided into teams for theater mission support. Figure 2-6 on page 2-14 depicts the organization of an HRSC. Since the HRSC is a modular unit, the HRSC Director has the capability to task organize teams to provide support as the mission dictates. Refer to Army techniques publication (ATP) 1-0.2, Theater-level Human Resources Support, for specific duties and responsibilities of the HRSC.

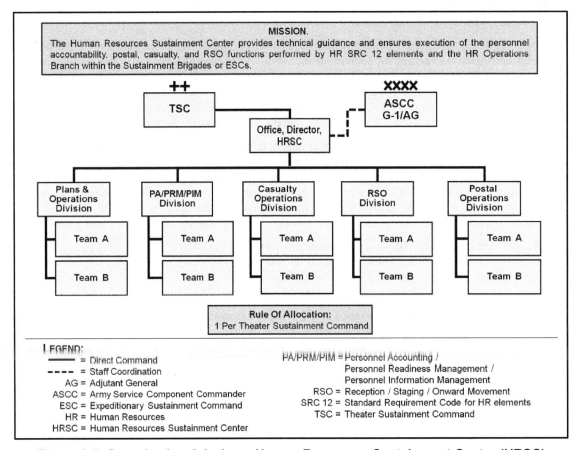

Figure 2-6. Organizational design – Human Resources Sustainment Center (HRSC)

HUMAN RESOURCES OPERATIONS BRANCH (HROB)

2-57. The HROB is a subordinate branch of the SPO within the sustainment brigade and ESC. The branch is responsible for the planning, coordinating, integrating, and synchronizing and allocation of PA, casualty, and postal operations missions and HR assets within the sustainment brigade and ESC area of operations. Refer to ATP 1-0.2 for detailed duties and responsibilities of the HROB. Figure 2-7 provides the recommended standardized structure for the HROB.

2-58. Critical functions of the HROB are to:
- Serve as integrator between the HRSC and assigned or attached HR organizations (HR Company, MMT Team, and TG PAT) for execution of HR support.
- Serve as integrator between supported units (G-1/AG and S-1) and the sustainment organizations for the execution of external HR support.
- Synchronize non-HR support requirements with other sustainment elements and organizations (e.g., transportation, billeting, and feeding for transient personnel).
- Plan, project, and recommend HR support requirements for current and future military operations – military decisionmaking process (MDMP).
- Ensure the emplacement and displacement of HR support organizations are in synchronization with the concept of support plan for PA, casualty, and postal operations.
- Deploy as part of the sustainment brigade or ESC early entry element to assist in establishing the initial theater PA, Casualty Assistance Center, and postal operations, if required.

2-59. The HROB receives technical guidance from the HRSC and operational guidance from sustainment mission command channels. Technical guidance includes mission analysis, determining the best method of support, and passing the requirement to the HR element for execution. If Noncombatant Evacuation

Operations occur within an area that the HROB is overseeing, they should coordinate with their assigned HR companies to assist in operations (e.g., PAT support) and provide technical guidance and coordination with the local brigades to ensure accountability of noncombatants. For further guidance on Noncombatant Evacuation Operations, refer to JP 1-0 and JP 3-35, Deployment and Redeployment.

2-60. To enhance the effectiveness and understanding of how HR support is an integrated element of sustainment, it is highly encouraged that HR officers serving in the HROB complete the Support Operations Course, either by correspondence or through an Intermediate-Level Education program.

2-61. Select members of the HROB are included as part of the early entry element of the SPO, focusing on the establishment of the PA portion of the reception, staging, onward movement, and integration (RSOI) process. Early entry element personnel also ensure initial postal support and casualty operations are established.

2-62. The HROB requires voice, SIPRNET and NIPRNET connectivity to communicate with the HRSC, subordinate HR organizations, supported organizations, and with other HROBs. The HROB requires access to ABCS, BCS3, FBCB2, COPS, Force Requirements Enhanced Database, and other systems fielded in the deployed AO. Refer to Chapter 3 for more information on HR automation systems.

2-63. It is critical for the ESC and sustainment brigade commander to ensure support relationships are clear to supported and supporting organizations. This is especially important for specialized support relationships the HRSC has with HR units.

2-64. The HROB tracks key performance indicators and is the sustainment brigade's element responsible for ensuring HR operations are fully integrated into overall sustainment operations. The HROB ensures a sufficient number of HR organizations are available to provide HR area support, monitors support provided by HR organizations, and manages HR support within the AO. The HROB provides technical guidance and resources to HR organizations (supporting units) and ensures they have the capability to provide the required PA, casualty, and postal support directed in the HR concept of support. They provide a supported/ supporting relationship with G-1/AGs and S-1s within the AO. To effectively manage HR support, the HROB must communicate and coordinate with supported and supporting HR elements. The HROB uses HR planning considerations to develop performance indicators to ensure HR operations are integrated into the overall sustainment plan. Refer to ATP 1-0.2 for detailed information on HROB performance indicators.

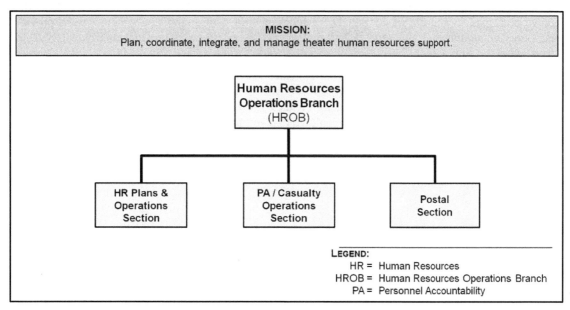

Figure 2-7. Organizational design – HR Operations Branch (HROB)

MILITARY MAIL TERMINAL (MMT) TEAM

2-65. The MMT Team provides postal support to an AO by establishing an MMT which coordinates, receives, and processes pro-grade mail, and dispatches retro-grade mail to destinations worldwide. Refer to ATP 1-0.2 for detailed duties and responsibilities of the MMT Team.

2-66. The MMT Team is initially employed in the theater opening mission as an element of an sustainment brigade with a theater opening mission to establish the joint military mail terminal (JMMT) or MMT. It is augmented with an HR Company HQs with four postal platoons. It establishes and provides the Army component of a JMMT at the inter-theater aerial port of debarkation (APOD). As the theater matures the MMT Team and supporting HR Company transitions to the theater distribution mission. The MMT Team receives technical guidance from the HRSC POD. The MMT does have mission command of the JMMT or MMT and provides all technical guidance to the HR company commander. It is normally employed as an assigned or attached element of a sustainment brigade STB.

2-67. The MMT Team provides specialized postal expertise and experience and limited augmentation manpower. The modular structure allows the commander to add the necessary level of seniority and experience appropriate for a JTF-level mission and to consolidate the necessary specialty equipment to do this bulk mission. The main function of this team is to process incoming mail and dispatch mail to the continental United States (CONUS) at the APOD.

2-68. The MMT Team consists of a HQs section, Operations section, and two Postal Squads. The MMT Director becomes the senior Army postal leader for all technical matters. The HQs section provides a direct link with other Services for operating space at the terminal, flight schedules, and ground transportation of mail. The HQs section also provides a single joint operations area (JOA)-level executor with the expertise and experience to support the ASCC G-1/AG and TSC commander. Figure 2 8 depicts the organizational design of an MMT Team.

2-69. The Operations section is the vital link for all theater postal operations planning and implementing all necessary input from the other Services and guidance from MPSA and DA Postal into the operating plan. It is the operational interface between the MMT and sustainment brigade SPO HROB sections which coordinates the distribution of mail within their AO.

2-70. Equipment is crucial to the success of MMT functions. All heavy postal equipment for the AO is associated with the MMT Team. The team has a Rough-Terrain Container Handler and 10-k forklifts to move bulk mail in and out of the APOD. Satellite phones, radios, and CAISI connectivity provide the necessary communication link to track unit movements and control mail movements from CONUS to and throughout the AO.

2-71. The MMT Team receives operational guidance and directives from the sustainment brigade SPO HROB and technical guidance from the ESC SPO HROB and the HRSC POD. The MMT is dependent upon the sustainment brigade for religious, medical, legal, HR, administrative services, quarters and rations, logistics, unit maintenance of organic equipment, and supplementary transportation support, and military pay. The MMT relies on secure and non-secure, continuous, and survivable communications and digital information systems in order to perform its theater-level postal mission.

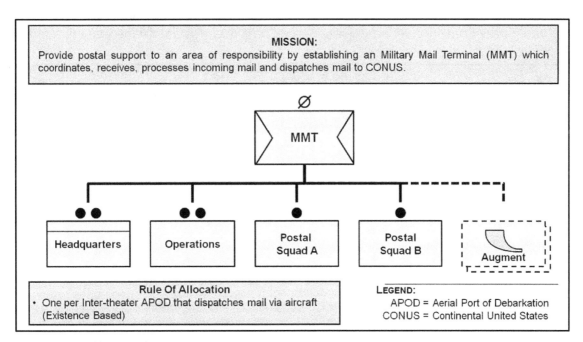

Figure 2-8. Organizational design – Military Mail Terminal (MMT) team

THEATER GATEWAY PERSONNEL ACCOUNTABILITY TEAM (TG PAT)

2-72. The TG PAT provides PA support to the theater of operations by coordinating and providing PA operations and database inputs as personnel enter, transit, and depart the theater at the inter-theater APOD and executes tasks supporting the PA task. The TG PAT operates as an element of the inter-theater APOD performing PA tasks and associated supporting tasks under the control of the sustainment organization responsible for the operation of the inter-theater APOD, normally a CSSB. Refer to ATP 1-0.2 for detailed duties and responsibilities of the TG PAT.

2-73. The TG PAT deploys and establishes a theater-level TG PAT Center with augmentation of an HR company HQs with two HR platoons at the primary inter-theater APOD. The TG PAT receives technical guidance from the supporting HROB and the HRSC, Personnel Accountability Division. The TG PAT requires a capability to communicate digitally through web and voice, both secure and non-secure, to Personnel Accountability Team (PAT) elements, G-1/AG sections, logistical support elements, and other branches of Service. It is employed as an assigned or attached element of a sustainment brigade STB. Operational guidance and directives are initiated by the TSC (HRSC) and should be issued in OPLAN or OPORD format. To support unit S-1s during RSOI and redeployment operations, the TG PAT has the capability to perform limited EPS (e.g., common access cards and ID tags, DD Form 93 (Record of Emergency Data), and SGLV Form 8286 (Servicemembers' Group Life Insurance Election and Certificate).

2-74. A TG PAT Center is an organization in the sustainment brigade and may be employed in a theater opening mission to establish a JOA TG PAT Center. As the JOA matures the TG PAT, and the augmenting HR Company, transitions to the JOA Distribution Mission.

2-75. The TG PAT, with a supporting HR company, is capable of supporting a population including other Services, multi-national forces, contractors, deployed DOD civilians, and U. S. government agencies when directed by Army Support to other Services and Joint Force Command orders. The TG PAT provides specialized PAT expertise and experience to oversee the entire spectrum of PAT functions from large scale unit reception missions (RSOI) during theater opening to labor intensive R&R missions in sustainment operations. The modular structure allows the commander to add the necessary level of seniority and experience appropriate for a high visibility theater-level missions. The main functions of this team are to provide the supporting staff to conduct all necessary coordination, planning, and implementation for a large scale PAT mission during the various stages of an operation. The TG PAT consists of a HQs and Operations section as depicted in Figure 2-9.

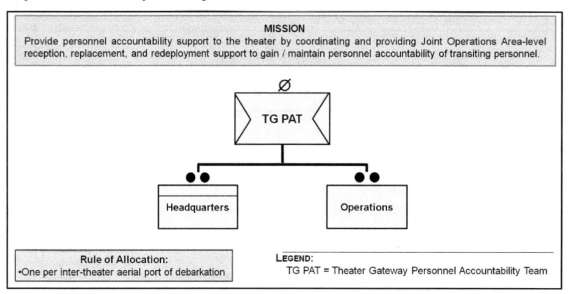

Figure 2-9. Organizational design – TG PAT

HR COMPANY HEADQUARTERS

2-76. The HR Company HQs provides mission command, planning, and technical support to all assigned or attached HR and Postal platoons. The HR Company HQs delivers HR area support for casualty, PA, and postal operations in the deployed AO. It is tailored for a CLT, PAT, postal, and/or combined mission by task-organizing the company HQs with specialized casualty, PA, or postal operation teams. Refer to ATP 1-0.2 for detailed duties and responsibilities of the HR Company HQs. The HR Company HQs has both long and short range capability for:

- PA, casualty operations, and postal planning.
- Current and future operations management.
- Database integration.
- Establishing CLTs and PATs.
- Leadership and oversight of three to seven platoons.
- Transportation coordination.

2-77. The HR Company HQs consists of a Command section, Plans and Operations section, and HQs Support section as depicted in Figure 2-10. The Command section exercises mission command over assigned HR or Postal platoons based on restricted operations areas and METT-TC; administers discipline and Uniform Code of Military Justice and assumes operational control (OPCON) over attached and co-located HR elements; and coordinates external support functions such as life support, personnel protection, logistics, and transportation.

2-78. The Plans and Operations section provides policy review and direction for HR operations; coordinates the consolidation of critical wartime function reports for the commander; and advises and coordinates with higher, lateral, and subordinate organizations on personnel matters. This section provides long and short range planning and guidance during the execution of current operations, and coordinates with the HR commander, the sustainment brigade, and ESC HROBs for all related operations. This section also prepares OPLANs and OPORDs, exercises control, and provides guidance regarding PA, casualty, and postal operations.

2-79. The HQs Support section manages personnel actions, ammunition, and limited supply (petroleum, oils, and lubricants, subsistence, billeting), energy conservation, sanitation, and transportation for assigned and attached personnel. Personnel perform integrated materiel maintenance for automotive and ground support equipment including tactical wheeled and general-purpose vehicles.

2-80. The HR Company requires capability to communicate by both secure and non-secure voice and data to supported platoons, STB and CSSB, sustainment brigade and ESC HROB, supported G-1/AG and S-1 sections, HRSC, MMT, TG PAT, and other sustainment and Joint elements.

2-81. The HR Company will be employed to support an MMT and TG PAT, or with a sustainment brigade providing area support. When deployed, the HR Company may be attached to an STB or CSSB. Specific attachment is dependent upon METT-TC analysis, the operating environment, and the sustainment brigade commander preference. The HR Company relies on the supporting sustainment brigade for logistical, maintenance, and field feeding support to all assigned or attached platoons.

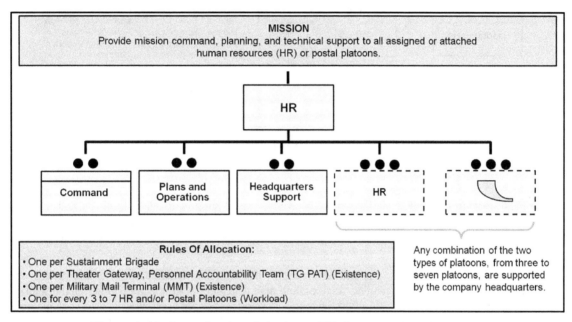

Figure 2-10. Organizational design – HR Company headquarters

HR PLATOON

2-82. A multi-functional platoon with the capability to provide casualty and/or PA support to all individuals and units in an assigned AO or to serve as a supporting element of the TG PAT. Refer to ATP 1-0.2 for detailed duties and responsibilities of the HR Platoon.

2-83. The HR Platoon accomplishes the casualty and PA functional mission with its capability to form teams from HR squads (CLTs and PATs) . This capability increases mission flexibility and its ability to support G-1/AG and S-1 sections by maintaining visibility and accountability of casualties and as personnel transit the theater.

2-84. During RSOI, HR Platoons are assigned to the TG PAT with responsibility for executing the PA portion of the RSOI mission. The ESC/sustainment brigade HROB are responsible for coordinating the execution of logistics and other non-HR support requirements with the supporting CSSB.

2-85. The HR Platoon requires the capability to communicate, secure and non-secure, to the HROB, TG PAT, HR Company HQs, HR Company Plan and Operations section, PATs, CLTs, supported HRSC, G-1/AG and S-1 sections, and logistics support elements (e.g., Airfield Arrival or Departure Control Group or Movement Control Team).

2-86. The Platoon HQs section provides technical guidance, leadership, logistical support, and mission command for each squad. The platoon operates according to METT-TC. Further, the team tracks emergency leaves, inter-theater and intra-theater transfers as dictated by METT-TC. Figure 2-11 on page 2-20 depicts the organization of an HR Platoon.

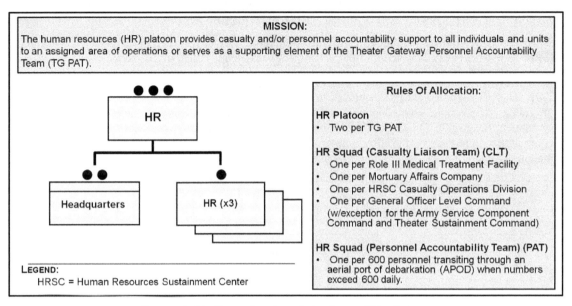

Figure 2-11. Organizational design – HR platoon

POSTAL PLATOON

2-87. The mission of the Postal Platoon is to provide postal support to all individuals and units in an assigned AO or to serve as an element of an MMT. Postal platoons operate in conjunction with Plans and Operations teams within HR companies. Refer to ATP 1-0.2 for detailed duties and responsibilities of the Postal platoon.

2-88. The Postal platoon deploys to the AO and provides modular, scalable, and flexible postal support including postal financial management, services, and mail distribution. It is a multi-functional organization providing postal support for up to 6,000 personnel at one location or serving as one of four platoons in support of an MMT Team. This universal modular platoon is capable of performing the complete spectrum of postal functions from postal service and postal finance to postal operations. It includes processing pro-grade mail, coordinating mail transportation to forward platoons, and processing retro-grade to CONUS. The platoon requires capability to communicate digitally for both secure and non-secure access and via voice to the HR Company HQs, G-1/AGs, and S-1 sections of units in the supported area.

2-89. As depicted in figure 2-12, the postal platoon consists of a HQs section, Postal Finance section, and two postal squads. The HQs section provides mission command, leadership, and resourcing. The Postal Finance section provides retail services at the same level of support that is provided by the United States Postal Service (USPS) in CONUS, and current level of support in garrison. Each postal squad has the capability to perform operations or services missions or to perform independently as needed as a mobile mail team. In addition to these functions, each postal squad (mobile mail team) has the ability to train, test, and certify unit mail clerks and inspect each unit mailroom at least quarterly. The platoons are equipped with variable reach forklifts to provide efficient mail movement in whatever type of area the platoon is supporting.

2-90. The Postal platoon receives all technical guidance through the HR company HQs and the corresponding Plans and Operations Team. The HR Company HQs provides all mission command to the attached Postal Platoons.

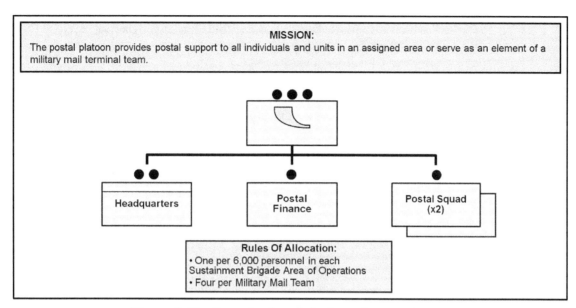

Figure 2-12. Organizational design – Postal platoon

PERSONNEL ACCOUNTABILITY TEAM (PAT)

2-91. To accomplish the PA function, the HR platoon forms PATs from HR squads. These teams provide PA at the aerial port of embarkation (APOE), APOD, sea port of debarkation (SPOD), sea port of embarkation (SPOE), and at intra-theater hubs where daily transit numbers exceed 600 personnel per day. The PAT provides PA of personnel entering, transiting, or departing the specific theater location. PATs rely on the supported organization for daily life support. Refer to ATP 1-0.2 for detailed duties and responsibilities of the PAT.

CASUALTY LIAISON TEAM (CLT)

2-92. CLTs are formed by HR squads within the HR Platoon to support the theater casualty operations mission. The CLT provides accurate casualty information (reporting and tracking) at MTFs, MA collection points, higher HQs G-1/AGs, General Officer commands, and other locations as specified by the HRSC. CLTs facilitate real-time casualty information for commanders. CLTs not only provide accurate casualty information, but they also act as a liaison for each affected commander. The CLT provides updated status reports to the affected unit and informs them if the Soldier is medically evacuated from theater. CLTs rely on the supported organization for daily life support. Refer to ATP 1-0.2 for detailed duties and responsibilities of the CLT.

2-93. Each CLT requires the capability to communicate digitally and via voice, secure and non-secure, to theater (HRSC COD), HR Platoon HQs, G-1/AGs, and S-1 sections of supported units. CLTs also require access to the Defense Casualty Information Processing System—Casualty Forward (DCIPS-CF) to send updates to the Casualty Assistance Center and Casualty and Mortuary Affairs Operations Center (CMAOC).

STANDARD REQUIREMENTS CODE (SRC)-12 UNITS AT HOME STATION RECOMMENDATIONS

2-94. SRC-12 units should maximize real-world training opportunities that focus on unit specific core functions, capabilities and technical roles to ensure their own unit preparedness to deploy and assist with the improvement of garrison HR operations. The following recommendations include:

- Real-World Training:
  - Process mail at Army post offices (APOs)/Retail APOs.

- Inspect installation mailrooms.
- Conduct mission readiness exercise (MRE)/mission rehearsal exercise (MRX) Reception operations.
  - Serve as a Casualty Assistance Center liaison.
  - Serve as Observer/Controller/Mentors.
  - Conduct installation manifesting.
  - Assist with installation PIM/PRM/PA/SR reconciliations.
  - Provide Soldier readiness processing (SRP) support.
  - Assist with installation staff assistance visits.
  - Provide eMILPO assistance and training to supported units, agencies, and the MPD.
  - Provide record updates for all on and off post units.
- Provide enlisted strength and Drill Sergeant management, reassignment processing, and classification / reclassification to supported units.
- Provide support in the areas of promotions, administrative separation actions, medical retentions, compassionate reassignments, officer candidate school applications, military testing, and voting assistance.
- Provide records accountability and maintenance, in and out processing of personnel, ID card and common access card issuance, Defense Enrollment Eligibility Reporting System (DEERS) enrollment, and installation mobilization activities.
- Provide transition support for all Active, ARNG, and U. S. Army Reserve (USAR) Soldiers separating from the military.

- Individual Capabilities·
  - Familiarize with systems functional guidance.
  - Train with live or training modules.
  - Create Unit Warrior Training Support Packages.
  - Attend installation training (e.g., S-1 Course; HR systems training).
  - Attend formal training (e.g., HR Plans and Operations Course; Brigade S-1 Course; Postal Course).
  - Utilize Forces Command, Soldier Support Institute, and Sustainment Center of Excellence Mobile Training Teams.
  - Attend SPO Phase I Course Online (e.g., recommend Leader Professional Development with an sustainment brigade Commander/SPO; recommend brown bag lunch).
  - Train and certify leaders. Apply to all trainers, evaluators, and leaders involved in unit training.
  - Conduct a rehearsal.
  - Conduct risk management.
  - Conduct troop-leading procedures.
  - Establish communications.
  - Receive an OPORD or fragmentary order and issue a warning order.
  - Conduct HR related mission analysis.
  - Analyze missions using METT-TC.
  - Identify specified, implied, and essential tasks.
  - Identify constraints (i.e., requirements for action and prohibition of actions for HR support).
  - Generate HR support options. Analyze course of actions (COAs), determine advantages and disadvantages, and compare COAs.

- Pre-deployment Training:
  - Incorporate sustainment brigade and ESC HROBs into training crosswalks.
  - Evaluate HR application of the MDMP.
  - Evaluate collaboration points.

- Evaluate individual and collective tasks.

- Establish mock APOs.

- Utilize non-HR specific systems (e.g., Command Post of the Future).

- Attend regional HR and Sustainment conferences.

- Attend regional multi-echelon, multi-component net centric MRE/MRXs in Active, USAR, and ARNG communities.

- Exercise Observer/Controller/Mentors.

- Provide sample situational training exercises to be used by leaders to develop training exercises for their units.

- Establish training and evaluation outlines to provide the training criteria for tasks that the unit must master to perform critical wartime operations. These training criteria orient on the levels of collective training executed by the unit. Each outline can be applicable to one or more operation.

ARMY BANDS

2-95. The mission of Army bands is to provide music to instill in our forces the will to fight and win, foster the support of our citizens, and promote our national interests at home and abroad. Army band units are designed to support Joint, interagency, and multi-national operations. This design provides flexibility to employ tailored music performance units in support of both deployed and home station mission requirements. Army bands support the Army through the provision of tailored music that enhances Warrior morale, supports Army recruiting efforts, provides comfort to recovering Soldiers, reinforces relations with host-nation populations, and maintains a connection with the American public and Army Families. Refer to ATTP 1-19, U. S. Army Bands, for detailed duties and responsibilities of Army bands.

2-96. Music Performance Teams (MPTs) are the modular building blocks of Army bands. They are designed to deploy separately from the band HQs in support of specific music missions for specified periods. MPTs can combine to form larger teams depending on mission requirements and unit capabilities. Each MPT is compact and designed for transport by air or ground assets. The MPT structure gives Army bands the flexibility to support concurrent musical missions in multiple geographical areas.

2-97. The modular structure of Army bands enables them to support both deployment operations and home station missions concurrently. This permits commanders to spread the positive impact of Army bands across the deployed force, international community, and the American public at home. Army bands based in the U. S. and its territories continue to provide music support of Army recruiting and public relations during overseas contingency operations.

2-98. Army bands are designated small, medium, or large according to the number of MPTs allocated. Figures 2-13 through 2-15 on page 2-24 and 2-25 reflect the organization of small, medium, and large bands. Army bands perform as a single unit (full marching band, large jazz ensemble, or concert band) or, when fully resourced, have concurrent MPT mission capabilities as outlined below. Each band employs the following MPTs as indicated:

- Ceremonial music ensemble (MPT B): Provides general military or patriotic music support for static ceremonies, protocol functions, defense support of civil authorities, and religious support activities.

- Large popular music ensemble (MPT C) – Army Band Large – (2): Provides general vocally driven contemporary music for troop support functions, protocol functions, and defense support of civil authorities. MPT C normally consists of percussion, bass, piano, guitar, trombones, saxophone, trumpet, a dedicated vocalist, and an audio engineer.

- Small popular music ensemble (MPT D) – Army Band Medium – (2): Provides general troop support functions, protocol functions, and defense support of civil authorities. MPT D normally consists of percussion, bass, piano, guitar, trumpet, and saxophone. MPT D may also include vocal and audio engineer as available and other musicians may be added when needed.

- Brass chamber music ensemble (MPT E) – Army Band Medium – (3); Army Band Large – (2): Provides general static ceremonies in smaller venues, protocol functions, defense support of civil authorities, and religious support activities. MPT E normally consists of tuba, trombone or euphonium, French horn, and trumpets.

- Woodwind chamber music ensemble (MPT F) – Army Band Large – (2); Army Band Small is not authorized MPT F: Provides general static ceremonies in smaller venues, protocol functions, defense support of civil authorities, and religious support activities. MPT F normally consists of French horn, bassoon, clarinet, oboe, and flute. Other musicians may be substituted as needed.

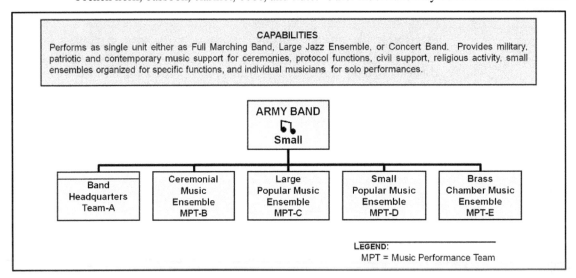

Figure 2-13. Organizational design – Army band small

2-99. Deployed bands may support the Rear Detachment with an MPT. In this circumstance, general support is provided for military or patriotic music for static ceremonies, protocol functions, family readiness group (FRG) functions, and religious and hospital support activities.

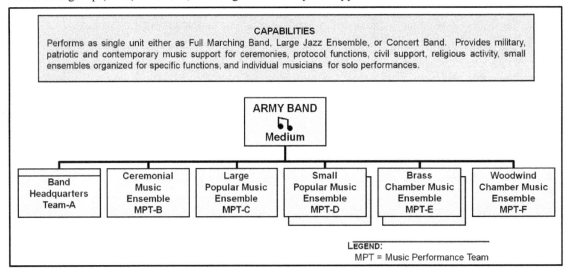

Figure 2-14. Organizational design – Army band medium

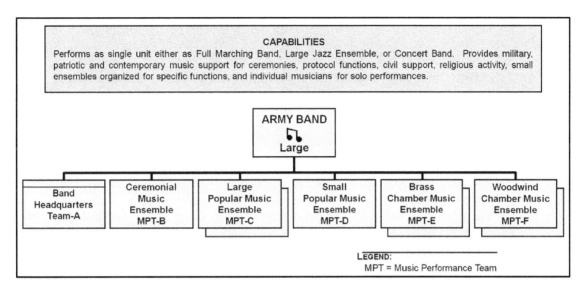

CAPABILITIES
Performs as single unit either as Full Marching Band, Large Jazz Ensemble, or Concert Band. Provides military, patriotic and contemporary music support for ceremonies, protocol functions, civil support, religious activity, small ensembles organized for specific functions, and individual musicians for solo performances.

ARMY BAND
Large

| Band Headquarters Team-A | Ceremonial Music Ensemble MPT-B | Large Popular Music Ensemble MPT-C | Small Popular Music Ensemble MPT-D | Brass Chamber Music Ensemble MPT-E | Woodwind Chamber Music Ensemble MPT-F |

LEGEND:
MPT = Music Performance Team

Figure 2-15. Organizational design – Army band large

HR REAR DETACHMENT RESPONSIBILITIES

2-100. One of the most important unit functions during deployment is the Rear Detachment. The Rear Detachment picks up the daily workload of the deployed unit and provides home station support for the unit. The Rear Detachment leadership maintains regular contact with the deployed unit and is responsible for the administrative operations of the Rear Detachment, including maintaining mission command, accounting for unit property and equipment, and managing personnel. Regardless of availability of HR personnel in the Rear Detachment, they are required to maintain these responsibilities IAW Army policy.

2-101. An important function of the Rear Detachment is serving as a vital communications link between the deployed unit and Family members. The deployed commander's goal is to accomplish the mission while keeping Soldiers safe so they can return home to their Families and communities. The Rear Detachment's goal works in tandem with that of the deployed commander to help Families solve their problems at the lowest level. This will avoid the problems and resulting anxieties from overflowing to the deployed Soldier or requiring the attention of the deployed commander. Throughout a deployment, the bond between the Rear Detachment and the FRG will determine the effectiveness of the Rear Detachment operation.

2-102. For deployments, Rear Detachments should be established at two levels (brigade and battalion) to perform the functions listed below. Normally, the brigade commander appoints brigade and battalion Rear Detachment commanders. However, the battalion appointment may be delegated to the battalion commander.

2-103. HR roles and responsibilities for Rear Detachments are to:
- Publish Rear Detachment assumption of command order.
- Establish and maintain two-way communication with forward deployed units to facilitate the flow of timely and accurate information, and to resolve issues that cannot be solved by the Rear Detachment.
- Provide HR support to brigade, battalion, and/or company Rear Detachments.
- Maintain accountability of non-deployed Soldiers and closely track casualties, Family issues, and wounded-warrior care.
- Maintain a Rear Detachment alert roster.
- Continue to execute, coordinate, or synchronize Rear Detachment HR operations and administrative matters.
- Maintain connectivity to HR systems and input/update Rear Detachment changes as needed.

- Provide custodian verification of emergency data (DD Form 93/SGLV Form 8286) as casualties occur.
- Provide HR support and services to Rear Detachment personnel.
- Coordinate installation support for Rear Detachment personnel and Familics of deployed personnel (e.g., ID cards, housing, and vehicle registration).
- Coordinate with the deployed S-1 and battalion or brigade operations staff officer (S-3) for call forward of personnel.
- Establish and maintain rating schemes for Rear Detachment personnel.
- Ensure hours of operation, procedures for accountability, and receipt of mail are adhered to.
- Provide HR support to Soldiers temporarily returned from deployment.
- Support planning for reception of unit personnel upon redeployment.
- Serve as coordinator between deployed HR elements, home station, and higher echelon HR support organizations.
- Maintain an FRG leader on appointment orders.
- Conduct or support casualty notification as defined in the unit SOP and IAW the installation Casualty Assistance Center.
- Coordinate with the ARC regarding emergency information on Soldiers and Family members. This includes logging, tracking, and processing Red Cross emergency messages and notifying the forward unit of impending ARC messages.
- Maintain a roster of Soldiers trained and certified for appointment as Casualty Notification Officers (CNOs) and Casualty Assistance Officers (CAOs) when a casualty occurs and monitor the performance of those Soldiers assigned as CNOs and CAOs.
- Ensure trained Soldiers are available for appointment as Summary Court Martial Officers (SCMOs) and LOD investigating officers as needed.

2-104. To ensure continuity of HR operations during deployments, it is crucial that Rear Detachments be established and operational, as far in advance of the deployment as possible. This not only ensures Rear Detachment HR operations are properly functioning prior to deployment, but enables deploying S-1 personnel to participate in unit pre-deployment training and be able to take advantage of unit block leave periods.

2-105. When considering which HR personnel should be part of the Rear Detachment, brigade and battalion S-1s must ensure selected personnel are familiar with HR operations. HR personnel designated to be members of the Rear Detachment should fully understand the HR relationships with FRG, installation HR support, and community resource activities. As HR personnel will likely be involved in casualty operations, it is recommended that the command select a senior NCO who demonstrates the professional characteristics of competence, character, and commitment as well as maturity and compassion. HR Rear Detachment personnel also deal with Family members, and as such, should have good leadership and communication skills and have some experience in dealing with Family support issues.

2-106. The key to successful HR operations are:
- Establish HR Rear Detachment operations early.
- Work as a team with the deployed S-1, Rear Detachment commander, and FRG.
- Know HR policies and be proficient with HR databases and systems required to perform the HR mission.
- Have strong communication, listening, crisis management, and people skills.
- Ensure individual roles and responsibilities are detailed in the Rear Detachment SOP (use HR checklist).
- Cross-train HR personnel.
- Maintain and foster genuine care and concern for Family needs.
- Ensure all Rear Detachment personnel are trained on casualty notification and assistance procedures.

Chapter 3

Man the Force

Man the Force is an HR core competency. The objective of the man the force strategy is to ensure the Army acquires and retains the best the Nation has to offer in sufficient volume and diversity of skills each year to ensure the right people are available in the right places with the right skills in sufficient volume and affordability for maximum flexibility to embrace change and provide commanders human resources necessary to be operationally adaptable. The Army HR inventory must be able to ensure a force that is agile, responsible, tailorable and capable of responding to any mission, anywhere, anytime. This requires diversity of human inventory, readiness, agility and availability of the Total Force—Active, Guard, Reserve, and Civilian each capable of being an indispensible member of the Joint Force. Properly manned units are vital to assuring the fulfillment of missions as a strategic element of national policy. It enhances predictability and ensures that leaders have the people necessary to perform assigned tasks.

GENERAL

3-1. Man the force impacts the effectiveness of all Army organizations, regardless of size, and affects the ability to successfully accomplish all other HR core competencies and subordinate key functions. Man the force is described as any action or function that impacts on strength or readiness of an organization. Man the force combines anticipation, movement, and skillful positioning of personnel so the commander has the personnel required to accomplish the mission.

3-2. HR providers rely on numerous HR databases and automated systems to accomplish man the force functions. The enduring principle of accuracy is paramount in man the force because data integration occurs at multiple levels with multiple systems used by decision makers at the National HR Provider level (e.g., HRC and Army G-1). HR providers must take ownership of data they control to eliminate or reduce errors that affect man the force functions.

3-3. Man the force includes five subordinate key functions:
- Personnel Readiness Management (PRM).
- Personnel Accountability (PA).
- Strength Reporting (SR).
- Retention Operations.
- Personnel Information Management (PIM).

3-4. Since the Army operates in simultaneous and complex environments, man the force is a critical function which can only be efficient and responsive to commanders and HR leaders if database changes are made as soon as they become known. This is especially important if skills, capabilities, and special needs of units continue to change to meet operational mission needs.

SECTION I – PERSONNEL READINESS MANAGEMENT (PRM)

3-5. Personnel readiness management involves analyzing personnel strength data to determine current combat capabilities, projecting future requirements, and assessing conditions of individual readiness. Personnel readiness management is directly interrelated and interdependent upon the functions of PA, SR, and PIM.

3-6.   During military operations, there are two HR communities that directly support PRM. They are HR units which execute theater HR operations and the G-1/AGs and S-1s who are responsible for executing and managing their command's readiness.

3-7.   Personnel readiness management standards for deploying units are established by the Army (HQDA) G-1, which uses authorized strength levels, target fill levels, Personnel Manning Authorization Document directed authorizations, and the operational (deployment) timelines established by the Army G-3.

3-8.   Personnel readiness management in brigades and battalions starts by comparing its organization's personnel strength against its required authorizations. By adding predictive analysis of manpower changes (non-deployable rates, projected casualty rates, evacuation policies, and replacement flows), units can assess the personnel readiness of the organization and determine replacement allocation priorities. As HRC has a direct linkage with brigade units, replacement decisions are streamlined and replacements arrive at the unit in a timely manner. This process also enables G-1/AGs and S-1s to more effectively manage unit personnel readiness, and when necessary, assist units in obtaining replacement personnel or changing the priority of replacement fills. Changing the priority of replacement fills should only be made based on operational input from the commander or the G-3/S-3.

3-9.   Personnel readiness management is a function that must be performed on a continuing basis. Units have little time to "peak" for combat operations and rely on the S-1 to execute its mission diligently, every day. Critical military occupational specialty (MOS) shortages or large numbers of non-deployable Soldiers, for example, cannot easily be overcome once a unit is alerted for movement. Battalion and brigade S-1s play a crucial role in the PRM process by ensuring duty status changes or non-deployability data is changed in DTAS (deployed duty status only), eMILPO, RLAS, and SIDPERS-ARNG, and posted to the AMHRR, if required. This may include submission of documents to RC home station HQs to update RLAS and/or SIDPERS-ARNG. Unforecasted losses, such as those that result from administrative or legal actions or which result from medical issues, can have a significant impact on unit readiness. If losses cannot be mitigated by initiating appropriate measures, such as cross-leveling personnel from the installation/unit or reorganizing unit personnel, then elevation of the issue to HRC is appropriate.

3-10.   In support of ARFORGEN, the National HR Provider (e.g., HRC and National Guard Bureau) determines replacement force packages based on forecasted losses and allocates to brigade-level IAW HQDA manning guidance. The replacement flow is depicted in Figure 3-1.

3-11.   Active Army replacement personnel arrive at the brigade's installation and are in-processed by the installation and unit. If unit replacements are assigned after the unit is deployed, they are called forward by the deployed unit. RC replacement personnel are processed through the CONUS Replacement Center (CRC) for all deployed RC units. Diversions from the original assignment should be by exception and only made to meet operational requirements. Deviations from the original assignment are coordinated directly with the National HR Provider that directed the assignment.

3-12.   The ASCC G-1/AG is responsible for developing replacement and casualty shelf requisitions, as part of the deliberate planning process. HRC assists Army commands in developing casualty requisition packages by using an enlisted targeting process casualty package generation methodology for current operations (Active Army). This captures casualties over a 12-month period to determine the average number of casualties that a Brigade Combat Team may incur during their deployment. Based on this, HRC develops a casualty package and applies the package to future Active Army Brigade Combat Team deployers during their respective latest arrival date (LAD)-6 through return time window.

3-13.   As soon as possible, the ASCC G-1/AG is responsible for developing pull packages, to support wartime operations, with an estimated number of replacements for anticipated casualty losses that need to be sent to the combatant command. When the ASCC G-1/AG is unable to do so due to operational circumstances, HRC works in concert with the forward element to get replacements off the installation for additional casualty replacements above the enlisted targeted casualty package. HRC replaces the installation location these Soldiers were pulled from if they are not over target strength.

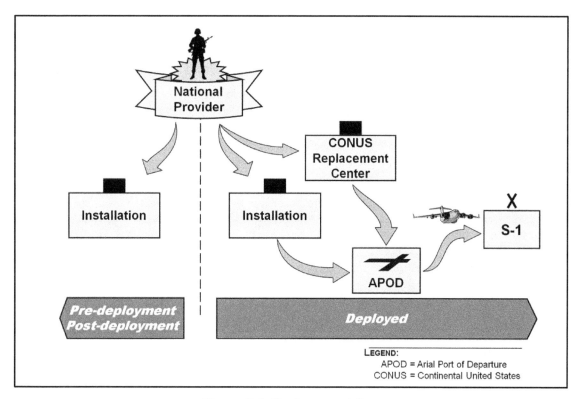

Figure 3-1. Replacement flow

RESPONSIBILITIES

3-14. The paragraphs below outline the personnel readiness management responsibilities at the various echelons of command.

ASCC G-1/AG

3-15. During the planning phase of operations, the ASCC G-1/AG identifies unit and personnel requirements, to include deployed CAAF and DOD Civilian personnel. During operational planning and execution, and if replacement or casualty shelves are used, the system delivers filler and casualty replacements to the theater to bring units to combat-required strength. HRC maintains a copy of the pre-established theater shelf requisitions and performs annual maintenance. HRC maintenance includes a review for consistency with HQDA manning guidance, MOS, and area of concentration structure changes. ASCC G-1/AG PRM responsibilities include:

- Develop theater PRM plans, policies, milestones, and priorities.
- Advise the commander on PRM.
- Monitor and assess the PRM (strength reports, projected gains, estimated losses, and projected numbers of personnel returning to duty) of theater units via DTAS and various HR systems that feed off TAPDB information.
- Monitor and maintain personnel readiness status of subordinate units.
- Coordinate reassignments to meet urgent operational requirements.
- Ensure PRM is included in OPLANs and OPORDs.
- Prepare casualty estimate in coordination with the National HR Provider.
- Establish and manage the personnel portion of reconstitution or reorganization efforts.
- Obtain return to duty (RTD) data from surgeon.

3-16. If shelf requisitions are implemented, the ASCC G-1/AG has the following additional responsibilities:

- Predict and validate personnel requirements based on current strength levels, projected gains, estimated losses, and the projected number of Soldiers and Army Civilians returning to duty from MTFs.
- Determine replacement priorities in coordination with the G-3.
- Monitor the theater replacement system.
- Monitor reassignments to ensure they meet operational requirements.

CORPS AND DIVISION G-1/AG

3-17. Corps and Division G-1/AGs maintain overall responsibility for PRM of subordinate elements. Corps and Division G-1/AGs maintain the responsibility to assist brigade S-1s and the National HR Provider in shaping the force to meet mission requirements. The Corps and Division G-1/AG continue to maintain a COP of unit-level strength and work with HRC for sourcing solutions. Corps and Division G-1/AG PRM responsibilities are to:

- Establish and ensure PRM SOPs are in synchronization with ASCC PRM policies and procedures.
- Manage PRM for subordinate units, to include task organized units in a deployed theater and home station.
- Advise the commander on PRM.
- Validate replacement priorities for displaced units.
- Determine replacement priorities (based on G-3 priorities to ensure personnel distribution management is executed by HRC and supports the operational plan). Coordinate diversions as required.
- Manage subordinate unit assignment priorities to ensure they meet the commander's guidance.
- Prepare casualty estimate.
- Coordinate and monitor RTD projections with the surgeon.
- Include PRM in OPLANs and OPORDs.
- Establish electronic link to HR systems.
- Manage PRM for non-deployed personnel, to include Rear Detachments.
- Participate in the personnel portion of reorganization or reconstitution efforts.
- Maintain and monitor the status of key combat leaders and request replacements when required.
- Cross-level Corps and Division assets as required.
- Direct brigade resets in coordination with G-3.
- Conduct assessment of PRM using strength reports, projected RTD reports, and information contained in various HR systems that feed off TAPDB information. Include gains, losses, and estimates not included in strength reports.
- Assess new equipment and weapons systems' impact on personnel requirements.
- Perform the duties of the ASCC G-1/AG if serving as the Army Force or JTF.

BRIGADE S-1/STB S-1 (GENERAL OFFICER-LEVEL HQS)

3-18. Brigade and STB S-1 sections are responsible for PRM. The brigade or STB S-1 has a direct link with HRC and maintains communication and coordination with the higher-level G-1/AG for the execution of its PRM responsibilities, which include:

- Establish a link with the HRC for replacement of key personnel.
- Confirm deployment operational timelines with HRC, G-3.
- Manage PRM for subordinate units.
- Establish and execute brigade/STB PRM and distribution fill plan, and coordinate with HRC on modifications based on operational requirements or commander's priorities.
- Distribute Soldiers to subordinate units and publish orders.

- Develop unit-level PRM policies and SOPs.
- Input timely and accurate Soldier personnel data, strength, and duty status transactions in the appropriate HR system of record (e.g., eMILPO, RLAS, and SIDPERS-ARNG) .
- Verify the accuracy of manning status in subordinate units.
- Provide feedback to HRC on issues of training, gender, additional skill identifier (ASI), special qualification identifier (SQI), and special instructions.
- Determine, in coordination with the S-3, replacement priorities based on current and forecasted readiness status and commander's intent.
- Monitor and advise the commander on the personnel readiness status (current and projected) of subordinate units to include: key leaders, critical combat squads, crews, and teams.
- Predict personnel requirements, based on current strength levels, projected gains, estimated losses, and the projected number of Soldiers and Army Civilians returning to duty from MTFs.
- Monitor losses (e.g., combat, non-combat, legal actions, medical, MOS Administrative Retention Review (MAR2), and Medical Evaluation Boards (MEBs)).
- Monitor and maintain visibility of non-available or non-deployable Soldiers, to include Rear Detachments.
- Coordinate the call forward of replacements.
- Coordinate and synchronize with the brigade logistics staff officer (S-4) on equipment for replacement personnel.
- Plan and coordinate the personnel portion of reorganization or reconstitution operations.
- Manage SRP to validate individual readiness and ensure visibility through updates to appropriate systems and databases.
- Manage Soldier utilization; distribute and properly slot Soldiers within the brigade/STB.
- Report critical personnel requirements to HRC for individual Soldiers and/or teams.
- Monitor and reconcile strength deviations.
- Prepare the personnel portion of the USR to ensure unit personnel readiness is accurately reflected, identifies critical shortages, and establishes manning expectations.
- Manage unit identification code (UIC) hierarchies through various databases to ensure an accurate readiness COP to the National HR Provider.
- Ensure PRM is included in all OPLANs and OPORDs.

BATTALION S-1

3-19. The battalion S-1 implements the priorities of fill established by the commander by conducting and executing PRM for the unit. This includes PA, SR, managing casualty information, monitoring projected gains and losses, and managing RTD Soldiers (in coordination with the medical platoon). Battalion S-1s directly impact PRM by ensuring the accuracy of a Soldier's status in the appropriate HR system of record (e.g., DTAS, eMILPO, RLAS, SIDPERS-ARNG) — PRM starts with complete, accurate, and timely Soldier data updates at the battalion. Battalion S-1 section responsibilities include:

- Develop unit-level PRM policies and SOPs.
- Ensure timely and accurate updates in the HR system of record for all required personnel data, strength, and duty status changes.
- Prepare the personnel portion of the USR to ensure unit personnel readiness is accurately reflected, identifies critical shortages, and establishes manning expectations.
- In coordination with the battalion S-3, determine replacement priorities based on current and forecasted readiness status and commander's intent.
- Monitor and report to the commander the personnel readiness status (current and projected) of subordinate units to include: key leaders, critical combat squads, crews, and teams.
- Predict personnel requirements, based on current strength levels, projected gains, estimated losses, and the projected number of Soldiers and Army Civilians returning to duty from MTFs.
- Monitor losses (e.g., combat, non-combat, legal actions, medical, MAR2s, and MEBs).
- Monitor status of non-available or non-deployable Soldier status, to include Rear Detachments.

- Coordinate and synchronize with the S-4 on equipment for replacement personnel.
- Plan and coordinate the personnel portion of reorganization or reconstitution operations.
- Manage the SRP to validate individual readiness and ensure visibility through updates to appropriate systems and databases.
- Manage Soldier utilization; distribute and properly slot Soldiers within the battalion.
- Report critical personnel requirements for individual Soldiers and/or teams.
- Prepare the personnel portion of the USR to ensure unit personnel readiness is accurately reflected.
- Ensure PRM is included in all OPLANs and OPORDs.

DISTRIBUTION PROCESS

3-20. The responsibility for PRM is an inherent responsibility of command and is accomplished by G-1/AGs and S-1s. G-1/AGs and S-1s rely on various HR systems and databases and DTAS for strength related information. Figure 3-2 depicts the distribution process. The Army has three distribution levels:

- Distribution management level. Management of division-level or two-star command equivalent organizations.
- Distribution management sub-level (DMSL). Management of brigade or Colonel command equivalent.
- Virtual Distribution Management Level. Management of grouped units that would otherwise take a combination of distribution management level and DMSL codes.

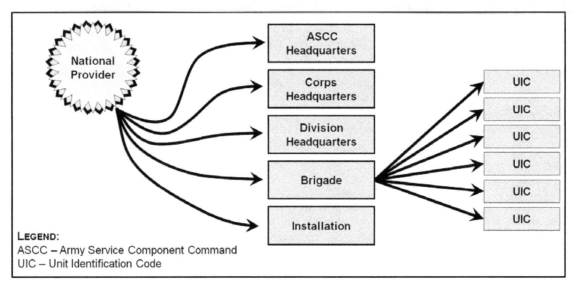

Figure 3-2. Distribution process

DETERMINING PRIORITIES

3-21. G-1/AGs and S-1s at all levels assist commanders in developing their personnel priorities. The use of automated HR systems provides G-1/AGs and S-1s a COP with the National HR Provider and allows them the ability to provide detailed analysis to the commander. Brigade S-1s work directly with the National HR Provider to fill authorized vacancies and develop distribution plans within their organization. G-1/AGs at all levels maintain situational understanding of competing priorities and assist brigades and the National HR Provider when shifting priorities, changes in operational plans, or other unforeseen events create situations where the personnel fill for an organization is no longer in synchronization with Army manning guidance. G-1/AGs are responsible for attempting to resolve subordinate command manning issues internally prior to involving HRC.

3-22. The distribution plan allows the G-1/AG and S-1 section to know where to assign incoming Soldiers. Based on the mission, a brigade S-1 may maintain different fill levels for subordinate units which may not be consistent with their authorized manning level. Key considerations for developing the distribution plan include:

- Commander's priorities.
- Unit personnel readiness reports, tactical SOPs, OPLANS, and related plans and reports.
- Replacement forecasts and casualty, filler, and RTD estimates. Lessons learned from deployments highlight the need for S-1s to manage these Soldiers as they often return from different roles of medical support, both within the theater and from locations outside the theater.
- Critical shortages by grade, ASI, SQI, area of concentration, and MOS.
- Changes to OPLAN/OPORD.
- Specific manning requirements for squads, crews, and teams.
- Timelines for exercises, train-up, and deployment (ARFORGEN process).

RECONSTITUTION

3-23. *Reconstitution* is defined as extraordinary actions that commanders plan and implement to restore units to a desired level of combat effectiveness commensurate with mission requirements and available resources (ADRP 4-0, Sustainment). It transcends normal day-to-day force sustainment actions. Reconstitution includes two methods of regenerating combat strength when a unit is not engaged; they are reorganization and regeneration. Though not executed very often, G-1/AGs and S-1s should be prepared to organize and execute either one of these actions.

REORGANIZATION

3-24. *Reorganization* is an action to shift resources within a degraded unit to increase its combat effectiveness (ADRP 4-0). Commanders of all types of units at each echelon conduct reorganization. Units reorganize before considering regeneration. Reorganization includes the following measures:

- Cross-leveling equipment and personnel.
- Matching operational weapons and systems with crews.
- Forming composite units (joining two or more units with high attrition rates to form a single mission-capable unit).

REGENERATION

3-25. *Regeneration* is the action of rebuilding a unit and involves rebuilding a unit requiring large scale replacement of personnel, equipment, and supplies (ADRP 4-0). Current manning practices have limited the ability of units to execute regeneration actions as the preferred approach has been to rotate entire units in and out of the theater. These units may then require further reorganization. Regeneration may involve reestablishing or replacing the chain of command. It also involves conducting mission-essential collective training to get the regenerated unit to standard with its new personnel and equipment.

UNIT RESET

3-26. Unit reset is an Army imperative to restore balance to the Army and systematically restore deployed units to a level of personnel and equipment readiness that permits units to resume training for future missions and is an integral element of the ARFORGEN model. It involves the reintegration of Soldiers and their Families, post-deployment medical assessments, professional education, restoring equipment readiness, and individual training.

3-27. Through on-time HR support, Unit Reset enables Army operations and achieves maximum personnel readiness. Unit Reset supports the success of overseas contingency operations and Army transformation, Soldier professional development, and individual Soldier preferences. Unit Reset decisions affect all Soldiers assigned to deployed units returning to home station.

3-28. Unit reset is the decision process that determines whether Soldiers assigned to units returning from deployment remain assigned to their current unit; are assigned to a different unit on the same installation; are placed on assignment instructions to another installation, or are returned to RC donor units.

3-29. Units are reset based on current HQDA manning guidance. Unit reset procedures and rules of engagement are provided to unit leadership by HRC. A number of Soldiers are selected to fill Army requirements to serve as drill sergeants, recruiters, and other special duty assignments. Assignment and school report dates are after deployment stabilization end dates. Soldiers with less than 24 months time on station at the end of the deployment stabilization period are stabilized unless required for higher priority mission requirements.

3-30. HQDA measures unit reset from return to deployment and tracks via the USR. Units have returned when 51% of their personnel (not equipment) have arrived at home station. The phases of the unit reset model are depicted in table 3-1.

Table 3-1. Unit reset model

Phase Name	Start Point	End Point
In-Theater	Return – 180 days	Return
Reset:		
Active Component	Return	Return + 180 days
Reserve Component	Return	Return + 365 days
Train/Ready:		
Active Component	Return + 181 days	Entry into ARFORGEN available Force Pool
Reserve Component	Return + 365 days	Entry into ARFORGEN available Force Pool

Legend: ARFORGEN = Army Force Generation

3-31. **Reset Phase.** Active Army brigade-sized units are C5 and have no readiness expectation for 180 days following return. However, units must continue to report their rating on the USR. This phase focuses on Soldier and Family reintegration. For Active Army units, HRC ensures that the unit's authorized field grade officers, warrant officers, company grade officers, and Master Sergeant/Sergeant First Class NCOs are either retained or replaced as soon as, and to the extent possible, after return from deployment. Successful accomplishment of these goals allows the unit to fill its company commander, key staff, and NCO leadership positions, and facilitate leader development, team building, and the completion of unit reset actions.

3-32. **Train-Ready Phase.** HRC mans units IAW HQDA manning guidance.

3-33. HRC manages all brigade-sized units IAW ARFORGEN Focused Manning. Under ARFORGEN Focused Manning, the Army applies the following principles to all Active Army brigade-size units:
- ARFORGEN Focused Manning is event-driven. The Army mans and prioritizes units based on deployment at the LAD, MRE/MRX, and redeployment (Return) dates. HRC coordinates with brigade-sized units to complete the Officer Personnel Disposition Roster and issues the enlisted rules of engagement required to plan and execute Personnel Reset.
- HRC establishes a manning goal IAW HQDA manning guidance.
- For units identified to deploy, manning standards vary by unit type but are tied to the MRE, MRX, and LAD. HRC assigns as many new Soldiers as possible with sufficient retainability to meet the timeline of the pending deployment. For units not identified to deploy, manning is based on available inventory IAW HQDA manning guidance.

PRE-DEPLOYMENT READINESS

3-34. Successful pre-deployment readiness for units begins with an SOP that outlines specific steps G-1/AGs and S-1s must complete prior to deployment. During the early phase of pre-deployment, or during unit reset is the time for G-1/AG and S-1s to plan unit and Soldier readiness activities. Pre-deployment readiness:

- Includes all subordinate units, even those that are not scheduled to deploy.
- Applies to individuals identified to support rear detachment or home station operations as they may be called forward.
- Includes the functions of PA, individual readiness, replacement of non-deployable personnel, and PRM. Also includes legal, financial, medical and dental, Family support, and Soldier well-being matters.

3-35. As part of the planning process, G-1/AGs and S-1s decide how to execute PRM in various deployment scenarios. Some of these factors include:

- Size of the deployed force.
- Size of the stay behind force and the Rear Detachment.
- Length of deployment.
- S-1 manning requirements.
- Availability of connectivity at the forward location.
- Number of replacements expected at home station.

3-36. The Soldier readiness program is outlined in AR 600-8-101, Personnel Processing (In-, Out-, Soldier Readiness, Mobilization, and Deployment Processing) and is the Army's program to ensure Soldiers meet readiness criteria for deployment. Each organization (brigade and battalion) should include SRP in their unit SOP. Units need to be aware that pre-deployment may vary even in the same brigade from deployment to deployment. Regardless of the approach, G-1/AGs and S-1s must clearly outline for their subordinate units the pre-deployment process and what commanders are expected to accomplish. Units should also advise their higher HQs and HRC of the process to ensure there are no conflicts.

3-37. Individual Soldier readiness is just as important as training and vehicle maintenance prior to deployment. HR leaders must learn they are the conduit for all matters that involve personnel readiness. This requires active discussion of issues and priorities with the commander, G-3/S-3, Chief of Staff, Executive Officer, and CSM. Failure to properly plan for HR support can seriously impact not only on the commander's ability to make manning decisions based on personnel, but can also impact the readiness and morale of the forces deployed.

3-38. Upon notification of deployment, initial efforts must be concentrated in the following areas:

- Accountability for assigned and attached personnel. This is crucial as personnel may be on temporary duty (TDY), attending school, or in authorized leave status. If required, the S-1 may recommend the commander recall personnel on TDY, attending non-DA sponsored schools, or in an authorized pass or leave status. Recall of personnel attending DA sponsored schools must be requested through the chain of command to HQDA.
- Verify the non-available status of all Soldiers and update required databases as required.
- Initiate reassignment actions for Soldiers who remain non-available for the duration of the deployment.
- Cross-level personnel within the unit as necessary.
- Coordinate RC cross-levels from external RC donor units to include the Individual Ready Reserve.

3-39. Other pre-deployment actions include:

- Support or coordinate PRM requirements for deploying units.
- Ensure HRC has the correct DMSL mapping for deploying units.
- Publish a unit SRP schedule and conduct SRPs.

- Complete the Train-up/Preparation stage of DA Form 7631 (deployment cycle support (DCS) checklist).
- Conduct a deployment brief for unit personnel and their spouses.
- Coordinate appropriately with the FRG leaders.
- Issue or coordinate the issuance of ID cards for DOD Civilian employees and CAAF prior to deployment.
- Request G-3 to establish derivative unit identification codes (DUICs) for PA of personnel not deploying. Units can also use the DUIC as an interim placement until replacement personnel are assigned to a specific unit.
- Ensure the Rear Detachment is fully capable of providing HR support during deployment. Under most circumstances, the G-1/AG and S-1 sections should leave sufficient Rear Detachment personnel to maintain accountability, process replacements, and provide essential personnel services.
- Ensure the Rear Detachment is granted access and permissions to the appropriate HR systems.
- Ensure all S-1 personnel are trained on eMILPO, RLAS, SIDPERS-ARNG, interactive Personnel Electronic Records Management System (iPERMS), DTAS, DEERS, Real-Time Automated Personnel Identification System (RAPIDS), Tactical Personnel System, and DCIPS.
- Coordinate with supporting medical and dental activities (e.g., medical records review for immunization requirements; verification that the panographic dental X-Ray and the deoxyribonucleic acid or DNA sample is on file; and verify profiles of medically disqualified personnel via the Medical Protection System).
- Verify Soldier financial readiness
- Update Soldier data elements that affect pay using the appropriate HR system.
- Review and update Soldier records, with particular attention to data elements that affect deployable status.
- Ensure DD Form 93 and SGLV Form 8286 are correctly reflected in iPERMS.
- Coordinate with the appropriate staff section for preparation of Isolated Personnel Reports.
- Verify security clearances of S-1 personnel.
- Identify evaluation reports that are required.
- Verify common access cards and ID tags; replace or reissue as required.
- Coordinate for legal services, wills, and powers of attorney.
- Ensure all Sergeant First Class through Sergeant Major, Chief Warrant Officer 2, and Captain through Colonel rear detachment personnel are trained and certified as CNOs and CAOs.

3-40. As deployment time nears, S-1s should provide S-3s with the unit's incoming gains roster to designate times and resources for theater specific individual readiness training. This coordination and successful execution prior to the LAD will directly affect a unit's deployed strength.

3-41. S-1s coordinate with the unit CSM and First Sergeants to ensure they are involved and monitor medical readiness programs closely. The non-deployable categories that increase the most prior to deployment are temporary and permanent profiles and referrals to MAR2/MEB/Physical Evaluation Board (PEB). S-1s should reinforce to unit commanders the need for them to monitor their Soldiers to ensure they complete their regular birth-month medical checks—Physical Health Assessments. These checks are a precautionary step in identifying medical conditions and fixing them prior to the LAD. S-1s should encourage commanders to make decisions on Soldiers who are "borderline" for deployment as early as possible. If deployability decisions are made just before deployment, there is insufficient time for brigade S-1s to work backfills with HRC distribution managers prior to deployment. Below are the common medical boards and programs that S-1s are involved with:

- MOS Administrative Retention Review. A MAR2 is an administrative board held to determine if Soldiers with permanent profiles (P3/P4) meet retention standards in their current primary MOS. Soldiers who are issued permanent profiles (P3/P4) must be processed IAW MAR2 (unless the Soldier is referred directly to the MEB/PEB process by the medical profiling officer due to the Soldier not meeting medical retention standards).

- Medical Evaluation Board. The MEB is an informal process comprised of at least two medical officers who evaluate the medical history of the Soldier and determine if the Soldier meets medical retention standards. If Soldiers are determined not to meet medical retention standards, they are referred to a PEB. If Soldiers are determined to meet medical retention standards, they are RTD. However, if the MEB was generated from a MAR2 referral, regardless of its findings, the case is forwarded to a PEB.

- Physical Evaluation Board. The PEB is comprised of an informal board and a formal board presided over by a three member panel which makes a determination for the purpose of a Soldier's retention, separation, or retirement.

- Warrior Transition Unit. Personnel undergoing medical care and rehabilitation may be assigned or attached to a Warrior Transition Unit. Warrior Transition Units are for Soldiers with complex medical needs requiring six months or more of treatment or rehabilitation. Commanders must clear Uniform Code of Military Justice actions, other legal actions, investigations, property/hand receipt issues, and LOD determinations prior to transferring Soldiers to a Warrior Transition Unit.

- Community Based Warrior Transition Unit. The Community Based Warrior Transition Unit functions as a Warrior Transition Unit for Soldiers who receive medical care in their community at DOD or Department of Veterans Affairs health care facilities. Community Based Warrior Transition Units primarily provide outpatient care management and transition services for USAR and ARNG Soldiers who do not need day-to-day medical management provided by Warrior Transition Units on Army installations. Community Based Warrior Transition Units perform mission command functions, and provide administrative support, medical case management, and medical processing for assigned Soldiers. Regular Army Soldiers may be attached to a Community Based Warrior Transition Unit on a case-by-case basis.

3-42. Maintaining Personnel Readiness. To minimize the number of non-deployable personnel, S-1s must take the following steps:

- Intensively manage physical profiles and the MAR2, MEB, and PEB processes. The earlier in a unit's deployment cycle that these determinations and referrals are made the better it allows HR leaders the ability to dialogue with National Provider distribution managers to work reassignment/backfill actions.

- Aggressively execute SRP requirements and allocate time to conduct regular reoccurring Soldier personnel readiness maintenance events. Specific time should be allocated on a reoccurring basis for leaders to manage the readiness of their personnel.

- Input status changes to DTAS, eMILPO, RLAS, and SIDPERS-ARNG of individuals as they become known. This permits strength managers at HRC to update information on the unit and facilitates dialogue with National Provider distribution managers when working reassignment/backfill actions.

- Actively engage with the National Provider distribution manager for each specific unit. Active and regular communication with National Provider distribution managers is essential in obtaining timely reassignment/backfill actions of identified "hard" unchangeable non-available and non-deployable Soldiers.

3-43. As directed by AR 220-1, Army Unit Status Reporting and Force Registration – Consolidated Policies and Department of the Army pamphlet (DA PAM) 220-1, Defense Readiness Reporting System-Army Procedures, Army units report their combat readiness each month on the USR. This document identifies the current status of personnel, supply, equipment, and training readiness. It informs HQDA of current factors that degrade the unit's readiness and helps commanders at all levels to allocate resources, determine trends, and identify authorizations versus the unit's wartime requirement. The personnel data portion reflects the unit's assigned strength percentage, available strength percentage, available senior grade percentage, available MOS qualified strength, personnel turnover rate percentage, total non-available personnel by category, and the unit's overall personnel rating.

3-44. Management of DUICs. DUICs are used in HR systems for identification of units and their modular teams, as well as split-unit elements that are associated with a parent organization (battalion or brigade units). UICs and DUICs must be included in the Defense Readiness Reporting System-Army; otherwise, S-1s will not be able to view authorization reports.

- Split-unit elements are physically located away from the parent organization. Modular teams may or may not be located with the parent organization. DUICs also have a PRM replacement function. HRC assigns incoming personnel replacements directly to a UIC that is associated with a brigade, and in some cases to separate and disperse battalion units as needed. Brigades in turn assign these incoming personnel to subordinate units.

- DUICs are also used to 'place' personnel who remain in the Rear Detachment during a deployment in a different UIC from the parent unit. If DUICs are used, the unit should have two DUICs to place Soldiers. One DUIC should hold Rear Detachment cadre who do not deploy forward with the unit and will conduct Rear Detachment operations. The second DUIC should hold Soldiers that are neither deploying, nor are Rear Detachment cadre.

- Under modularity, brigades have a greater responsibility for self managing the use of their own DUICs. HR leaders and S-1s must in turn reconcile all UICs and DUICs on a monthly basis, ensuring Soldiers are assigned to the correct location.

SECTION II – PERSONNEL ACCOUNTABILITY (PA)

3-45. Personnel accountability is the by-name management of the location and duty status of every person assigned or attached to a unit. It includes tracking the movement of personnel as they arrive at, and depart from, a unit for duty. The Army's PA system is designed to account for:

- Soldiers.
- Army Civilians.
- CAAF.
- Joint, interagency, intergovernmental, and multi-national personnel when directed.

GENERAL

3-46. PA is one of the most important functions a battalion or brigade S-1 performs on a continuing basis regardless of location or environment. Data accuracy is critical to the PA process. Promptly entering PA changes allows HR leaders at all levels to have timely and accurate PA data and enables S-1s to balance MOSs within brigades, battalions, and companies. PA is the key factor used for conducting strength reporting.

3-47. PA includes the by-name recording of specific data on arrivals and departures from units (e.g., unit of assignment and location), duty status changes or grade changes, assignment eligibility and availability codes, and MOS/specialty codes. Battalion and brigade S-1 Personnel Readiness sections are at the "tip of the spear" for Army-wide PA execution and require a team of HR professionals who are competent with automated HR systems and understand the PA process. S-1 section leaders need to ensure their Soldiers are trained to work in a deployed or austere environment. Figure 3-3 depicts the PA reporting process and the PA flow for data and individuals.

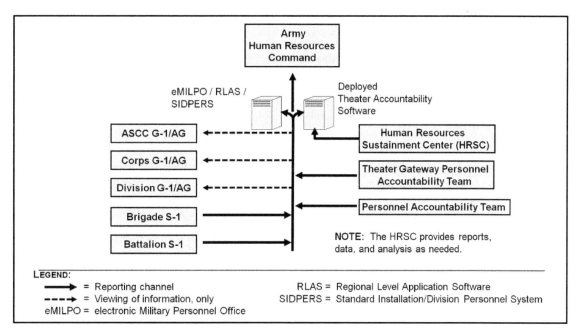

Figure 3-3. Personnel accountability reporting process

3-48. For accountability of CAAF and other theater designated contractor personnel, the Synchronized Pre-deployment and Operational Tracker (SPOT) is designated as the Joint Enterprise contractor management and accountability system. SPOT maintains by-name accountability for all CAAF and theater designated contractors. The CAAF Coordination Cell, attached to the Army field support brigade (AFSB), assists in establishing and maintaining the tracking and accountability of all CAAF and other contractors as directed. The AFSB Logistic Branch uses SPOT and the Joint Asset Movement Management System (JAMMS) to accomplish their CAAF accountability and tracking missions, and incorporates contractor numbers in their reports to the HRSC and ASCC G-1/AG. The ASCC G-1/AG is responsible for developing PA and reporting policies for contractors. The HRSC, G-1/AGs, and S-1s execute these policies. G-1/AGs monitor the accountability process to ensure subordinate units are executing it properly. See ATP 4-91, Army field support brigade and ATTP 4-10, Operational Contract Support, for additional information on SPOT.

3-49. Army commanders maintain accountability of Army Civilians, CAAF, AAFES employees, and ARC workers assigned or attached in support of contingency operations. These personnel are entered into DTAS upon arrival in theater.

3-50. The PA process is crucial to the Army's entire PIM system and impacts all HR core competencies. PA is not only maintained by units, but must be maintained as personnel enter, transit, and depart the theater. The HR Authorization Report (formerly known as the unit manning roster) serves as the source document for battalion and brigade S-1s, reflecting the slotting of assigned personnel. Other PA tasks include:

- Account for military personnel individually in DTAS, eMILPO, RLAS, and SIDPERS-ARNG.
- Collect, process, and sort critical information about Soldiers, units, CAAF including other theater designated contractor personnel, and DOD Civilians.
- Track and account for transiting personnel in DTAS, especially as R&R operations and redeployment operations commence.

3-51. The Army has an automated PA software package (DTAS) for use in a deployed theater. In the event DTAS is not available (due to lack of bandwidth or other issues) manual reports can be used such as the PERSTAT, personnel summary (PERSUM), and Personnel Requirements Report (PRR).

RESPONSIBILITIES

3-52. The following paragraphs outline the personnel accountability responsibilities at the various echelons on command, including the SRC 12 supporting structure.

ASCC G-1/AG

3-53. The ASCC G-1/AG Manpower Division has the following responsibilities:

- Deploy individuals as part of the early entry element to manage and monitor PA as part of the early entry module.
- Establish personnel reporting plans, policies, and timelines reflecting detailed reporting procedures and responsibilities (who reports to whom), in coordination with the J-1 combatant command.
- Monitor HR systems of record to obtain PA information.
- Establish connectivity with HRC, RC Personnel Offices, rear detachments (as required), appropriate joint HQ/other Services/federal agencies, and CRC.
- Collect, reconcile, correlate, analyze, and present critical PA information to the ASCC commander and personnel readiness managers.
- Establish and provide oversight for CLTs at MTFs in the AO (executed by the COD of the HRSC).
- Conduct reassignments to meet operational requirements (coordinate with subordinate G-1/AG and S-1s and HRC).
- Assist with a directed Personnel Asset Inventory for any subordinate unit when the unit's strength imbalance between eMILPO, RLAS, SIDPERS-ARNG, and TAPDB is 2% or more or when DTAS and unit PERSTATs are out of balance IAW theater policy.

CORPS AND DIVISION G-1/AG

3-54. The Corps and Division G-1/AG PA responsibilities include:

- Monitor deployed PA system to ensure compliance with ASCC guidance and timelines.
- Resolve corps and division PA issues (in coordination with the HRSC, brigade S-1, and appropriate HROB).
- Ensure the synchronization of timely vertical flow of automated personnel information from battalions, brigades, and separate units.
- Coordinate with the HRSC to establish an automated PA system that aligns assigned and attached element UICs with supporting S-1s.
- Ensure arriving battalions and separate units provide copies of their flight or sea manifests to the appropriate TG PAT at the port of debarkation.
- Perform those responsibilities of the ASCC G-1/AG when serving as the Army Force.
- Maintain liaison and flow of PA information from CLTs at Corps and Division MTFs and hospitals.
- Notify subordinate G-1/AGs and S-1s of all pending and potential task organization changes.

BRIGADE S-1/STB S-1

3-55. The brigade and STB S-1 PA responsibilities include:

- Operate a manifesting cell at ports of embarkation, collect manifest data at ports of debarkation, and enter those personnel into the theater database.
- Maintain 100% accountability for assigned or attached personnel, to include replacements, RTD Soldiers, R&R personnel, individual redeployers, Army Civilians, CAAF including other theater designated contractor personnel, and multi-national personnel, as required.
- Ensure the brigade/STB meets higher HQs PA policies and timelines.

- Collect, summarize, analyze, update, and report by-name personnel strength information using SIPRNET or NIPRNET, in the directed format.
- Ensure the Rear Detachment maintains accountability of non-deployed personnel and that their deployment non-available codes and duty status changes are promptly entered into eMILPO, RLAS, and SIDPERS-ARNG.
- Process and monitor assignment eligibility and availability code information for assigned and attached personnel.
- Process duty status change information (i.e., present for duty (PDY) to wounded-in-action (WIA), killed-in-action (KIA), and MIA), and update appropriate databases and HR systems.
- Process information on replacements and RTD personnel, as required, into the appropriate database.
- Track transiting unit personnel (e.g., leave and R&R), and local changes in location/base camp.
- Reconcile manual with automated strength information; identify and resolve discrepancies by submitting the appropriate transaction.
- Update automated AO DTAS, as required.
- Coordinate CLTs, MA, hospitals, and military police for information on casualties, patient tracking, and stragglers and update the database as appropriate.
- Coordinate connectivity for secure and non-secure voice and data systems with the battalion S-6 and brigade S-1, where appropriate.
- Manage HR databases and systems access for the brigade.
- Ensure S-1 personnel have the appropriate security clearances, access, and permissions to the appropriate HR databases and systems required to perform their mission.

BATTALION S-1 SECTION

3-56. Battalion S-1 PA responsibilities include:
- Maintain 100% accountability for assigned or attached personnel, to include replacements, RTD Soldiers, R&R personnel, Army Civilians, CAAF including other theater designated contractor personnel, and multi-national personnel, as required.
- Collect, summarize, analyze, update, and report by name personnel strength information using SIPRNET or NIPRNET, in the directed format.
- Ensure all personnel are entered into the theater database on entry or departure from the theater.
- Process and monitor assignment eligibility and availability code information for assigned and attached personnel.
- Process duty status change information (i.e., PDY to WIA, KIA, and MIA), and update appropriate databases and HR systems.
- Ensure the Rear Detachment maintains accountability of non-deployed personnel and that their deployment non-available codes and duty status changes are promptly entered into eMILPO, RLAS, and SIDPERS-ARNG.
- Process information on replacements and RTD personnel, as required, into the appropriate database.
- Track transiting unit personnel (e.g., leave and R&R).
- Reconcile manual with automated strength information; identify and resolve discrepancies by submitting the appropriate transaction.
- Coordinate with CLTs, MA, hospitals, and military police for information on casualties, patient tracking, and stragglers and update HR databases and systems as appropriate.
- Coordinate connectivity for secure and non-secure voice and data systems with the battalion S-6 and brigade S-1, where appropriate.
- Ensure S-1 personnel have the appropriate security clearances, access, and permissions to the appropriate HR databases and systems required to perform their mission.
- Ensure PA is included in the unit tactical SOP.

HRSC

3-57. The HRSC has the following PA responsibilities:

- Deploy a PA team/section with the early entry module to establish the theater deployed personnel database prior to Soldiers' arrival.
- Execute theater PA operations IAW the ASCC G-1/AG policies, plans, timelines, and other guidance.
- Establish and maintain the DTAS theater database and ensure connectivity to the DTAS enterprise server.
- Ensure required data is entered into the database to generate a joint personnel status (JPERSTAT) report.
- Operate the automated theater PA management system servers.
- Conduct data reconciliations and quality control checks (this is critical as personnel accountability information is the basis for SR).
- Inform the ASCC G-1/AG when a theater unit's percent of strength imbalance between DTAS and the daily PERSTAT exceeds theater policy.
- Ensure adequate resources and training is available for database.
- Ensure the database for mobile units is synchronized at the Personnel Processing Center (PPC) for reception operations.
- Provide guidance and oversight for accountability cells at ports of embarkation and debarkation in JOA.
- Coordinate with the appropriate HROB and S-1 to resolve any PA issues or problems.
- Provide training and guidance to theater units.

THEATER GATEWAY PERSONNEL ACCOUNTABILITY TEAM (TG PAT)

3-58. The TG PAT has the following PA responsibilities:

- Establish the initial theater PPC during early entry operations.
- Input and account for all personnel by date as they enter into, transit, or depart the theater.
- Plan and coordinate the execution of logistics support (e.g., billeting and transportation) of transiting personnel as necessary.
- Identify proposed theater locations for placement of other PATs (in coordination with HRSC and the sustainment brigade (HROB)).
- Ensure PATs have the necessary access to HR databases.
- Coordinate PA issues with the HRSC and supporting sustainment brigade HROB.

HROB

3-59. The HROB has the following PA responsibilities:

- Participate in the planning, deployment, sustainment, and redeployment process for current and future PA operations.
- Ensure TG PAT personnel are included as part of the early entry element for theater opening.
- Monitor PA activities to ensure they meet the policy, guidance, and timelines from the theater G-1/AG and HRSC.
- Assist the TG PAT in obtaining adequate facilities needed to conduct PA.
- Assist in the coordination of logistics and services to support TG PAT operations. (Note: This includes support of non-HR related tasks such as transportation to and from aircraft, transporting personnel to the PA processing center, transportation for transiting personnel, billeting, feeding, and storage of equipment or arms).
- Ensure HR Company and /or HR Platoon augmentation to the TG PAT is adequate.
- Monitor the establishment and operations of PATs at forward locations.
- Monitor the number of personnel processing through the TG PAT and at PAT locations.

- Provide and coordinate PA training for PA activities.
- Receive, resolve, and forward PA issues received from supported units (G-1/AGs and S-1s).
- Coordinate customs support for TG PAT.
- Provide PA advice and guidance as needed.
- Maintain voice and data communications with the HRSC, HROB, and supporting HR Company.

HR COMPANY

3-60. The HR company has the following PA responsibilities:
- Provide supporting HR platoons and PATs to support the TG PAT mission.
- Provide PATs at locations designated by the HRSC, TG PAT, or HROB of the supporting sustainment brigade. Teams should be located at all forward operating bases that have a transit population of 600 personnel per day.
- Provide data integration support for all personnel transiting the TG PAT or at intra-theater processing point where a PAT is located.
- Coordinate PA issues with the HROB of the supporting sustainment brigade.
- Manage and plan PA support for current and future PA operations.
- Ensure all PATs have the necessary access to HR database systems.
- Maintain voice and data communications with the HROB and subordinate platoons and teams.

SECTION III – STRENGTH REPORTING (SR)

3-61. Personnel strength reporting is a numerical end product of the accountability process. It is achieved by comparing the by-name data obtained during the PA process (faces) against specified authorizations (spaces or in some cases requirements) to determine a percentage of fill. Strength data reflects a unit's authorization and required base-line strength. It starts with strength-related data submitted at unit-level and ends with an updated database visible at all echelons, to include HRC. Personnel strength reporting is a command function conducted by G-1/AGs and S-1s to enable them to analyze manning levels and readiness, which provide a method of measuring the effectiveness of combat power. As strength reports may impact tactical decisions, the timely and correct duty status of individuals are critical to the SR process.

3-62. Personnel SR include reporting all personnel who deploy with the force. This includes Soldiers, military personnel from other Services, DOD civilians, and CAAF including other theater designated contractor personnel.

3-63. The SR process begins by unit S-1s processing strength related transactions into various HR automated systems that update the HR COP at all levels and ends with the production of a PERSTAT report (JPERSTAT in a Joint environment) . This report can be either manual or automated. Greater accuracy in the strength reporting process can be gained by generating reports from automated systems that perform PA functions. These automated reports reduce error by treating each entry as a record versus a data element that requires separate update. Additionally, automated processing is capable of simultaneous versus sequential reporting, which provides greater responsiveness to HR providers and their commanders. The strength reporting process is shown at figure 3-4 on page 3-18.

3-64. The strength reporting process provides commanders with a snapshot of the personnel component of their combat power and capabilities. Every level of command develops their requirements for data elements reflected on the strength report. At a minimum, commands should report strengths by unit, location, component, category (e.g., military, DOD civilians, and CAAF including other theater designated contractor personnel), and duty status. Internally, commanders may use additional data elements that provide a better snapshot of actual capabilities by weapon system, cohort (officer/warrant/enlisted), MOS, ASIs, and language ratings. Unit G-1/AGs and S-1s should develop strength reports that best represent the personnel component of combat power for their organizations. Within a deployed theater, the ASCC G-1/AG establishes PERSTAT reporting requirements for unit strengths to include required "as of" times.

When operating in a joint environment, the JPERSTAT requires the same data elements as the PERSTAT. An example of the JPERSTAT report is depicted in figure 3-5.

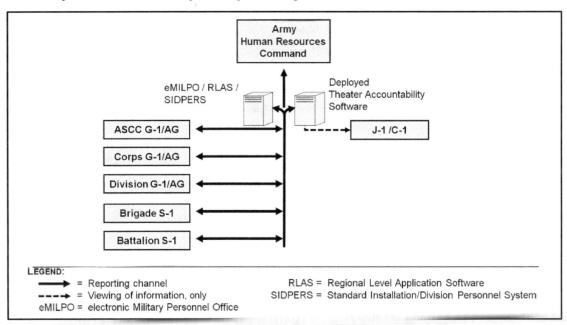

Figure 3-4. Strength reporting process

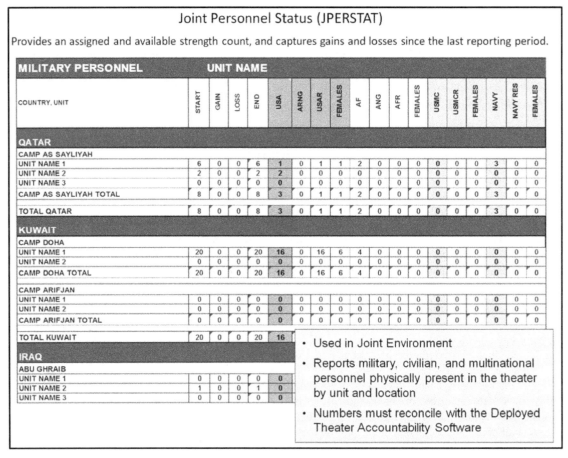

Figure 3-5. Sample joint personnel status (JPERSTAT)

3-65. The PERSTAT/JPERSTAT captures only military and civilian personnel who are PDY, Soldiers on R&R (only 12 month deployments) or emergency leave, and those TDY in CONUS. It should not include local nationals, foreign national contractors (unless specifically theater designated as CAAF), or detainees. The PERSTAT/JPERSTAT provides "boots on the ground" numbers and reflects all civilians (DOD and CAAF including other theater designated contractor personnel) and all military personnel from each Service assigned, attached, or are under OPCON and present in the theater of operations at the time of the report.

3-66. HR providers must understand command relationships. Unless stated otherwise in orders, SR requirements follow along administrative control lines. G-1/AGs and S-1s must be a part of all decisions to change task organizations to ensure SR requirements are communicated to subordinate commands.

KEY TERMINOLOGY

3-67. Key terms commonly used in personnel SR are described below:

- Task Force Organization—Lists military forces, units, and individuals temporarily grouped under one command for the accomplishment of a specific operation or assignment.
- Personnel Summary—This report displays a unit's personnel strength in aggregate numbers, as of a given time. It reports strength by personnel category (officer, warrant, enlisted, and Civilian), gains, losses, and duty status changes since the last report. Commanders and personnel readiness managers use the report to assess organizational combat power and set priorities.
- Personnel Requirements Report—HR managers report personnel requirements through a PRR. This report lists unit personnel replacement requirements by grade and MOS, and is based on comparison of authorized versus assigned strength.
- Required Strength—Unit wartime requirements, which can normally be found on a unit's Modified Table of Organization and Equipment or an RC unit's mobilization/deployment order; normally the same as authorized strength.
- Authorized Strength—Unit peacetime requirements; the number against which personnel assignments are made and can normally be found on a unit's Modified Table of Organization and Equipment or an RC unit's mobilization/deployment order, may be directed by the Personnel Manning Authorization Document.
- Operating Strength—Soldiers who are available to deploy as compared to authorizations. This relates to available strength on the USR and does not include Soldiers who are non-deployable or not available.
- Assigned Strength—Includes all Soldiers currently assigned on orders to the unit; however, the Soldier's duty status may vary.
- Attached units and Soldiers are included in the personnel strength report of the gaining commander (attached units are fed; housed; armed; receive replacements; mail; and so forth, by the gaining commander). Commanders (S-1s) of attached units provide the gaining HQs personnel data on their Soldiers, normally in an electronic format. The next higher HQs that own both units provide the attachment orders.
- Administrative Control—When commanders establish command relationships, they determine if the command relationship includes administrative control. Administrative control is the direction or exercise of authority over subordinate or other organizations in respect to administration and support (e.g., control of resources, personnel management, readiness, mobilization, and demobilization).
- Operational Control (OPCON)—Unit strength is included in the personnel strength report of the parent unit of assignment. OPCON relationships are normally temporary in nature and are directed by task organization for a specific operational mission. Generally, OPCON units are not logistically supported (fed, housed, armed, receive replacements, or mail) by the gaining unit. When an OPCON unit is receiving those services, clarification of command relationships needs to be made through detailed instructions initiated by the higher HQs of both organizations. Generally, a unit receiving services is attached. Although the gaining commander does not include the strength of an OPCON unit in his or her strength report, its personnel readiness is operationally important to the gaining commander. OPCON Soldiers may be reported by the

task force they are operating under by annotating in the remarks section of the personnel status report of the parent and gaining organization.

- Direct support and general support or any other term that defines support relationships does not determine command relationships. Personnel SR is guided by command relationship, not support relationship.

3-68. The use of command and support relationships in personnel SR operations must be clearly understood by the losing and gaining S-1 section, to ensure there is no "double counting" of task organized units. The most common discrepancy with SR is the double counting of units the day of a change in task organization. Effective date and time groups for task organization changes are critical to reporting timelines and the "as of" data reflected in strength reports. Battalion and brigade S-1 sections maintain operational awareness for task organization changes and ensure SR reflects task organization changes. S-1s must communicate laterally to ensure gaining and losing S-1s are clear on reporting conditions.

RESPONSIBILITIES

3-69. The strength reporting responsibilities are explained in detail in the following paragraphs.

ASCC G-1/AG

3-70. The ASCC G-1/AG Manpower Division has the following responsibilities:

- Establish personnel SR plans and policies reflecting detailed reporting procedures, timelines, formats and responsibilities (who reports to whom), in coordination with the JTF/Joint Force Land Component Command/Combined Force Land Component Command J-1.
- Manage and maintain ASCC personnel SR information.
- Prepare and maintain PERSTAT/JPERSTAT reports.
- Monitor DTAS to obtain SR information.
- Assist with a Personnel Asset Inventory for any subordinate unit when the unit's strength imbalance between DTAS and the daily PERSTAT exceeds theater policy.
- Establish connectivity with HRC, RC Personnel Offices, Rear Detachments (as required), appropriate Joint HQ/other Services/federal agencies, and CRC.
- Monitor, analyze, and validate unit strengths to determine personnel requirements and priorities.
- Prepare and maintain PERSUMs and PRRs.
- Predict and validate personnel requirements based on current strength levels, projected gains, estimated losses, and the projected number of Soldiers and Army Civilians RTD.
- Recommend replacement priorities to the G-3 (if replacement shelves are created).
- Develop theater personnel distribution plans and manage the theater replacement system (if replacement and casualty shelves are used).
- Conduct reassignments to meet operational requirements (coordinate with subordinate G-1/AGs, S-1s, and HRC).

CORPS AND DIVISION G-1/AG

3-71. The Corps and Division G-1/AG has the following responsibilities:

- Perform ASCC personnel SR responsibilities when serving as the Army Force.
- Establish and enforce SR requirements for subordinate units.
- Notify subordinate G-1/AGs and S-1s of all pending and potential task organization changes.
- Ensure reports reflect the latest task organization.
- Consolidate and submit PERSTATs, PERSUMs, and PRRs, as required.
- Coordinate with the HRSC, if necessary, to establish an automated PA system that aligns assigned and attached element UICs with supporting S-1s.
- Conduct personnel SR quality control checks.
- Coordinate with the G-3 for replacement priorities.

BRIGADE S-1/STB S-1 (GENERAL OFFICER-LEVEL HQS)

3-72. Brigade and STB S-1 responsibilities include:
- Collect, summarize, analyze, update, and report personnel strength information to G-1/AG or higher HQs.
- Monitor duty status change information (i.e., PDY, WIA, KIA, MIA), and update personnel database and HR management systems.
- Process information on replacements, RTD Soldiers, DA Civilians, multi-national personnel, as required.
- Perform error reconciliation and correct deviations in strength between eMILPO, RLAS, SIDPERS-ARNG, and TAPDB, and between DTAS and the manual PERSTAT.
- Update DTAS daily.
- Submit personnel status reports (e.g., PERSTAT and JPERSTAT) to higher HQs.
- Submit PERSUMs and PRRs when required by higher HQs.
- Coordinate with the Rear Detachment, appropriate staff sections, and external agencies for information on casualties, patient tracking, and stragglers and ensure battalion S-1s update the database.
- Plan and coordinate for connectivity for secure and non-secure data systems, as well as access to secure voice communications systems.
- On order or in support of, operate a manifesting cell at ports of embarkation, collect manifest data at ports of debarkation, and enter those personnel into the theater database.
- Ensure arriving battalions and separate units provide copies of their flight or sea manifests to the appropriate PAT at the port of debarkation.

BATTALION S-1

3-73. Battalion S-1 responsibilities include:
- Collect, summarize, analyze, update, and report personnel strength information, using secure or non-secure data systems in the directed format with the proper enabling HR system.
- Perform error reconciliation between the manual PERSTAT and DTAS when required.
- Process information on replacements, RTD Soldiers, Army Civilians, and multi-national personnel as required.
- Submit personnel status reports (e.g., PERSTAT and JPERSTAT) to the brigade S-1.
- Submit PERSUMs and PRRs by unit SOPs or established procedures from higher HQs.
- Coordinate with appropriate agencies for information on casualties, patient tracking, and stragglers and update the database as appropriate.
- Coordinate for connectivity for secure and non-secure voice and data systems with the battalion S-6 and brigade S-1, where appropriate.
- Ensure deploying members of the PR TM have been granted clearances and accesses to the appropriate HR systems.
- Provide copies of flight or sea manifests to the appropriate PAT at the port of debarkation and maintain copy at unit-level.

BATTLEFIELD FLOW

3-74. Prior to arriving in theater, the ASCC G-1/AG or Army Force G-1/AG establishes theater policy for personnel SR to include reporting standards and timelines. Coordination with the G-6 is necessary to ensure access to NIPRNET and SIPRNET is established for required HR databases and automated systems. During initial entry, strength managers must be prepared to operate with limited or no connectivity.
- The early entry element of the HRSC establishes the DTAS and initiates database hierarchy management.
- The TG PAT, supported by an HR Company, establishes theater PA operations at theater reception points (APOD/SPOD).

- The TG PAT ensures all personnel and units arriving in theater are accurately entered into DTAS. For units, the S-1 normally provides a copy of their unit's database which the TG PAT then uploads into DTAS.
- The HR Company establishes PATs at the APOD and other designated locations to maintain accountability and tracking of personnel as they transit the theater of operations.

3-75. All arriving personnel (Soldiers, DOD Civilians, and CAAF) and units must be accurately entered in the system to ensure accurate personnel SR throughout the duration of the theater-level operation. As units and individuals arrive in theater, the PAT, which directly impacts the effectiveness of deployed personnel SR operations, records their arrival in theater.

3-76. HR PAT elements capture and record data into DTAS information on Soldiers and units who can be tracked as they enter, transit, and depart the theater. PATs are only placed at locations where the personnel flow equals 600 or more per day. S-1 sections complement this system by performing PA tasks within their elements for small-scale movements conducted within the brigade AO and in movement to the intra-theater APOD where no HR organization assets are assigned.

SECTION IV – RETENTION OPERATIONS

3-77. The Army Retention Program plays a continuous role during military operations. Army retention is a program that ensures all Soldiers, regardless of the operation, have access to career counseling and retention processing. Army Career Counseling is the fundamental element of the Army Retention Program which provides commanders the internal command climate knowledge needed to adjust their individual Retention Programs to ensure the needs of the Soldiers and Families are met without jeopardizing the manning requirements necessary to provide for the defense of the Nation. Army Retention affects unit strength.

3-78. Commanders are the Retention Officers for their respective commands and CSMs are the senior Retention NCOs for their units. To be truly effective, the Army Retention Program requires enthusiastic command involvement and dedicated expert advice to retain high quality Soldiers. Retaining quality Soldiers who are certified in competence, character, and commitment ensures the stability of the Army's future force.

3-79. While unit commanders and leaders are ultimately responsible for retaining Soldiers at their level, Career Counselors located at battalion and above organizations are technical experts charged with advising commanders on all aspects of the Army Retention Program. Career Counselors, due to their advisory role to the commander, are placed on his or her Special Staff. They also determine retention eligibility, retention options, and assist with eligibility for Special Commissioning Programs consistent with published regulations and DA directives. See AR 601-280, Army Retention Program, for more detailed information on the Army Retention Program.

CAREER COUNSELOR'S ROLE IN PREPARATION FOR DEPLOYMENT

3-80. The Army Retention Program is the long-term answer for maintaining end strength. At the center of this program is the career counselor. Retention operations are functions that are conducted at home station and during military operations. While career counselors are not Table of Organization and Equipment (TOE) assets in most organizations, they play an important role not only during pre-deployment, but while deployed. Unit leaders need to ensure career counselors are included as part of the deployment force and included in operational orders and contingency plans. Retention operations should be included in unit SOPs.

3-81. At home stations, career counselors accomplish unit specific retention missions consistent with goals of the Army Retention Program. While deployed, career counselors continue to implement the Army Retention Program through reenlistment and other retention initiatives. Stop-movement efforts do not eliminate the requirement for career counselors to deploy. It is only a temporary tool used to maintain Army end strength.

3-82. During deployments, unit commanders need to ensure adequate career counselor support is available to Rear Detachment or non-deployed personnel. This can be accomplished via a memorandum of understanding or agreement between units or with the post retention office.

3-83. When planning for deployment operations, the following actions must be accomplished:

- Screen all Soldier records not serving on indefinite status to ensure they are entered into the Reenlistment, Reclassification, and Assignment System, and complete a DA Form 4591 (Retention Data Worksheet) for all non-indefinite status Soldiers with a current enlisted records brief.
- Coordinate with unit G-6/S-6 for telephone and network connectivity into required databases and automated systems.
- Obtain sufficient office equipment and supplies (e.g., laptop computer, appropriate software, scanner, printer, digital sender, U. S. flag, storage containers, necessary forms, and digital camera).

3-84. During pre-deployment processing, career counselors should brief Soldiers on deployment extensions and the stop-movement program, if necessary. Additional duty Reenlistment NCOs must be identified and trained for continual retention support, especially for geographically dispersed units.

RESPONSIBILITIES

3-85. The unit responsibilities in the retention operations process are explained in the paragraphs below.

ASCC/CORPS/DIVISION

3-86. ASCC/Corps/Division Career Counselor responsibilities include the following critical tasks:

- Oversee all operations, actions, and incidences to ensure compliance with established standards and regulatory guidance.
- Include retention operations in all OPLANs, OPORDs, and SOPs.
- Monitor subordinate units to ensure retention programs are staffed with MOS qualified Career Counselors.
- Assist Career Counselor as needed in obtaining equipment and assets.
- Maintain and publish statistics on Army Retention Program eligibles, missions, and accomplishments.
- Ensure subordinate commanders accomplish missions, functions, tasks, and responsibilities.
- Analyze and report retention impacting trends to the command and higher HQs.
- Establish retention awards and incentive programs for the command.
- Accomplish retention missions consistent with goals of the Army Retention Program.
- Maintain communications with subordinate units and higher echelons.
- Conduct staff assistance visits and training for all subordinate units.
- Establish and monitor quality control for all pertinent Soldier data and retention related contractual documents.
- Establish and manage attrition management controls (i.e., Bars to Reenlistment and Declination Statements to Continued Service).
- Manage and monitor Soldiers in the MAR2 process.
- Update expiration term of service dates on medical extensions IAW current applicable messages and policies.
- Maintain communication with the MPD, Actions Section on approved medical extensions.

BRIGADE

3-87. Senior Career Counselor responsibilities include the following critical tasks:

- Oversee operations, actions, and incidences of subordinate units to ensure compliance with regulatory guidance and directives.

- Maintain and publish statistics on command retention eligibles, missions, and accomplishments.
- Establish retention awards and incentive programs for the brigade.
- Conduct staff assistance visits and training for all subordinate units.
- Coordinate with staff principals to ensure subordinate units have all required equipment, software, and supplies needed for retention operations at all levels of readiness.
- Ensure units have screened all Soldiers' records.
- Include retention in unit SOPs.
- Ensure Soldiers not on an indefinite reenlistment status are entered in the Reenlistment, Reclassification, and Assignment System.
- Accomplish retention missions consistent with goals of the Army Retention Program.
- Oversee and assist retention efforts of subordinate units.
- Establish and monitor quality control for all pertinent Soldier data and retention related contractual documents.
- Establish and manage attrition management controls (i.e., Bars to Reenlistment and Declination Statements to Continued Service).
- Coordinate with the brigade S-3/S-6 to ensure communications (network) are available to support retention mission.
- Verify Career Counselors and unit leadership locations.
- Locate and contact local finance, HR services, and other supporting agencies and establish working procedures.
- Establish a communication and distribution system with rear detachment retention elements.
- Ensure workspace is secured.
- Manage and assist Soldiers in the MAR2 process.

BATTALION

3-88. Career Counselor responsibilities include the following critical tasks:
- Oversee operations, actions, and incidences of subordinate units to ensure compliance with regulatory guidance and directives.
- Maintain and publish statistics on battalion retention eligibles, missions, and accomplishments.
- Establish a retention awards and incentive program for the battalion.
- Conduct staff assistance visits and training for subordinate units.
- Coordinate with staff principals to ensure subordinate units have all required equipment, software, and supplies needed for retention operations at all levels of readiness.
- Ensure units have screened all Soldiers' records.
- Include retention in unit SOPs.
- Ensure Soldiers not on an indefinite reenlistment status are entered in the Reenlistment, Reclassification, and Assignment System.
- Accomplish retention missions consistent with goals of the Army Retention Program.
- Oversee and assist retention efforts of subordinate units.
- Establish and monitor quality control for all pertinent Soldier data and retention related contractual documents.
- Establish and manage attrition management controls (i.e., Bars to Reenlistment and Declination Statements to Continued Service).
- Coordinate with the battalion S-3/S-6 to ensure communications (network) are available to support retention mission.
- Verify career counselors and unit leadership locations.
- Locate and contact local finance, HR services, and other supporting agencies and establish working procedures.
- Establish a communication and distribution system with rear detachment retention elements.

- Ensure workspace is secured.
- Manage and assist Soldiers in the MAR2 process.

COMPANY

3-89. Company Retention NCO responsibilities include the following critical tasks:
- Accomplish retention missions consistent with goals of the Army Retention Program.
- Include retention operations in unit SOPs.
- Coordinate with staff principals to ensure subordinate units have all required equipment, software, and supplies for retention operations at all levels of readiness.
- Maintain career counselors and unit leadership locations.
- Coordinate bonus entitlement payments, including Selective Reenlistment Bonus, anniversary payments, and payments of accrued leave through the servicing career counselor.
- Provide reports as required.
- Coordinate transportation to Soldiers' locations.
- Ensure workspace is secured.
- Counsel Soldiers on how current Army policies, bonus incentives, and opportunities in the RC affect retention options.
- Establish and monitor quality control for all pertinent Soldier data and retention related contractual documents.
- Establish and manage attrition management controls (i.e., Bars to Reenlistment and Declination Statements to Continued Service).
- Assist Soldiers in the MAR2 process.

SECTION V – PERSONNEL INFORMATION MANAGEMENT (PIM)

3-90. Personnel Information Management is a process to accurately collect, protect, process, store, display, reconcile, validate, and disseminate information about Soldiers, their Family members, DOD civilians, military retirees, and other personnel as required. PIM supports the execution of all HR core competencies. This information can be in the form of data, pictures of data, or documents. Data from documents are input into the Army database and shared with the Department of Defense IAW DoDI 8320.02. The AMHRR is an administrative record as well as the official permanent record of military Service belonging to a Soldier. The creation of a Soldier's AMHRR begins with the first commitment by the government to the individual and commitment by the individual to the government (point of contract) during the Acquire process and updated during the complete HR lifecycle IAW AR 600-8-104. The information provided by PIM assists leaders at all levels from tactical to strategic in their decisionmaking process for HR functions and functions calculated using HR data. Documents are transmitted and stored via iPERMS for AMHRRs. Properly managed, PIM satisfies the Army's legal obligation to retain historical information about veterans, retirees and DOD civilians who deploy with the force. Pictures of data reflected in iPERMS should match the data in the HR database and vice versa; however, updating an HR database or automated system does not eliminate the requirement to ensure the most up to date sources documents are present in the AMHRR.

3-91. Every decision or action taken by the Army is based on information. Information management is included as part of all military operations and the operations process (planning, preparation, execution, and continuous assessment). PIM supports the life cycle management of Soldiers (Access/Retain, Assign, Sustain, Evaluate/Promote, and Separate).

3-92. The goal of PIM is to provide timely and accurate personnel data used to:
- Provide accurate personnel information to support the execution of functions and actions.
- Provide relevant and accurate personnel information to assist commanders in their decision-making process for HR functions and actions.
- Provide personnel information for developing essential elements of friendly information.
- Provide personnel information data required in the execution of the warfighting function of sustainment.

3-93. PIM information is contained displayed or processed using the NIPRNET for unclassified information and SIPRNET for sensitive PIM information. As PIM systems are web-based, access to the web is required. Effective PIM is critical to enable timely PRM which maintains unit personnel combat power.

RESPONSIBILITIES

3-94. The paragraphs below explain the roles and responsibilities of the various individuals and units in the personnel information management process.

SOLDIERS/DOD CIVILIANS

3-95. Soldiers and DOD Civilians have a responsibility to ensure PIM self-service items and other essential personnel data are correctly and promptly entered into appropriate database when changes occur.

COMMANDERS

3-96. Commanders at all levels are responsible for taking active or pro-active actions that protect and defend PIM data and documents to ensure that actions requiring their attention or processing are conducted in a timely, accurate, and prompt manner. Commanders are responsible for including inspection and oversight strategies to ensure any of their decisions or their staff's actions result in timely submission in the PIM. Special commander emphasis will be given to disciplinary actions, readiness status and commitment to the government or change in commitment to the government by the individual or vice versa. Commanders will ensure protection of documents and data pertaining to enlistment, appointment, duty stations, assignments, training, qualifications, performance, awards, medals, disciplinary actions, insurance, emergency data, separation, retirement, casualty, administrative remarks and any other personnel actions covered in AR 600-8-104.

ASCC G-1/AG

3-97. The ASCC G-1/AG is responsible for all PIM policies in their operational area. Specific responsibilities include:

- Manage PA and SR using the appropriate HR system of record.
- Establish and manage policies and procedures that affect PIM for subordinate units and the theater.
- Publish implementing instructions for personnel policies and programs for supported units.
- Establish, operate, and maintain ASCC deployed theater personnel database.

CORPS AND DIVISION G-1/AG

3-98. The Corps and Division G-1/AG indirectly manage and monitor PIM on all assigned units. Corps and Division G-1/AGs exercise these responsibilities primarily in their role of coordinating EPS and managing the casualty reporting system for the Corps and Division. Corps and Division G-1/AGs PIM responsibilities include:

- Monitor personnel information on all assigned and attached personnel with particular attention to information that updates specific HR databases and automated systems.
- Manage PA and SR using the appropriate HR system of record.
- Manage personnel files and records IAW governing regulations and policies.
- Establish and manage policies and procedures that affect PIM for subordinate units.

BRIGADE S-1/STB S-1 (GENERAL OFFICER-LEVEL HQS)

3-99. The brigade/STB PR TM (HR Technician (420A) and two 42A personnel) is normally responsible for PIM within the brigade/STB Personnel Processing Activity. PIM managers at brigade should anticipate an implied PIM mission during contingency operations, to include Joint and multi-national personnel. During stability and defense support of civil authorities, brigade S-1s may assist host-nation security forces with the development of their own PIM system, as security partnerships are formed and transfer of security responsibilities occur.

3-100.   PIM responsibilities include:
- Establish local PIM SOPs.
- Manage brigade/STB Personnel Processing Activity.
- Manage subordinate unit access to PIM systems (e.g., determine user roles and grant access, manage permission levels to HR systems, resolve and reconcile discrepancies in databases, and manage PIM hierarchy).
- Provide direct oversight of subordinate units on maintenance of Soldier personnel data. This fundamental change provides brigade commanders the ability to gather and analyze personnel data to assist in decision making.
- Manage personnel information/deviations for the brigade/STB.
- Update eMILPO, RLAS, SIDPERS-ARNG, DTAS, and other required automated systems as required
- Ensure the following key automation enablers are accessed and updated in a timely manner: DEERS, iPERMS (posting of DD Form 93(s) and SGLV form-series in particular), DTAS, and DCIPS-CF.
- Manage personnel files IAW governing regulations and policies.
- Provide technical assistance on all HRC operated personnel automation systems to supported users.

BATTALION S-1

3-101. The battalion S-1 is the starting point for personnel information updates. Battalion S-1 PIM responsibilities include:
- Establish battalion PIM SOP.
- Update strength-related information in automated databases to include gains, losses, grade changes, and duty status changes.
- Manage personnel information (manual and/or electronic) on assigned and attached personnel that update the following systems: eMILPO, RLAS, SIDPERS-ARNG, DTAS, DCIPS-CF, iPERMS, and others as required.
- Manage personnel files IAW governing regulations and policies.
- Coordinate with the brigade/STB to obtain and manage access and permissions to PIM systems.

HRSC

3-102. The HRSC PA/PRM/PIM Division manages theater-wide PIM. It maintains and operates the PIM database for the theater. Specific responsibilities include:
- Assist, maintain, and operate personnel database with ASCC G-1/AG.
- Manage personnel information (manual and/or electronic) on assigned and attached personnel that updates the following systems: eMILPO, RLAS, SIDPERS-ARNG, DTAS, DCIPS-CF, and others as required.
- Manage user access, roles, and permissions within DTAS.
- Reconcile differences between DTAS and other HR automated databases and systems as required.
- Manage unit hierarchy in DTAS for all theater units.
- Manage theater PA.
- Manage personnel files and records IAW governing regulations and policies.
- Provide technical guidance for PIM to HROB, G-1/AGs, and brigade/STB S-1s.
- Publish implementing instructions for personnel policies and programs for support units and the theater.
- Provide technical assistance to supported units on all personnel automated systems in theater.

HR AUTOMATION SUPPORT

3-103. HR systems are essential in accomplishing Army-wide PIM execution and require a team of HR professionals who are competent with automated HR databases and systems and understand how HR functions and tasks are processed and conducted. It is critical to ensure personnel are cross-trained on all HR systems and processes. The following paragraphs briefly describe HR databases and HR automation systems used by HR professionals and organizations, and other automation support and equipment needed to perform HR missions. Refer to ATTP 1-0.1 and ATP 1-0.2 for more detailed information on HR automation support.

DATABASES

3-104. **Automated Military Postal System (AMPS)**. The AMPS connects military post offices (MPOs) and other military postal activities around the world directly to the MPSA via the world-wide web. Instead of relying on telephone messages, e-mails, or other secondhand communication methods, AMPS users can view the information about their MPOs on their own desktops and make changes or corrections to the information themselves. AMPS provides the deployed MPO with the capability to process Postal Service Form 2942As (Military Mail AV7s), finance business, postal net alerts, product tracking services, and monitors voting information.

3-105. **Defense Casualty Information Processing System – Casualty Forward (DCIPS-CF) and DCIPS - Casualty Report (DCIPS-CR)**. The DCIPS-CF/CR is an automated system used to record and report casualty data. This system is employed by HR units; typically CLTs, brigade and brigade-level STB S-1 sections, and G-1/AGs performing casualty reporting missions. It is capable of producing automated casualty reports. While not required, battalion S-1s may utilize DCIPS-CF to submit their casualty reports to higher HQs. It is important to understand that DCIPS-CF/CR can operate in both the NIPRNET and SIPRNET modes. Classified casualty reports forwarded to the theater of operations Casualty Assistance Center may require reentry into an unclassified system prior to forwarding to CMAOCBrigade, brigade-level STB S-1s, and G-1/AGs are required to coordinate with the HRC, and when deployed, the HRSC ensures they have access to DCIPS-CF/CR.

3-106. **Defense Enrollment Eligibility Reporting System (DEERS)** . The DEERS is a database that maintains personnel and benefits information for Active, Retired, and Reserve uniformed Servicemembers; eligible Family members of active, retired, and reserve uniformed Servicemembers; DOD personnel; and DOD contractors requiring logical access. DEERS verifies eligibility when producing common access cards and supports benefit delivery including medical, dental, educational, and life insurance. In addition, DEERS enables DOD e-business, including identity management, reduces fraud and abuse of government benefits, and supports medical readiness.

3-107. **Deployment and Reconstitution Tracking Software.** The Deployment and Reconstitution Tracking Software application provides a standardized suite of software for Active Army units and mobilizing RC units to conduct DCS and complete DA Form 7425 (Readiness and Deployment Checklist). The application validates each of the functional areas during SRP. The Deployment and Reconstitution Tracking Software receives personnel readiness and unit data from various Army information systems, including the Reserve Component Automation System, Mobilization Planning Data Viewer, Medical Protection System, eMILPO, Global Command and Control System – Army, and the Department of the Army Mobilization Processing System. Active Army unit and personnel data is transmitted from eMILPO to the Deployment and Reconstitution Tracking Software based on a request from the installation specifying the UIC(s). It is the only approved automated system to support SRP.

3-108. **Integrated Total Army Personnel Database**. The Integrated Total Army Personnel Database integrates individual records from the five physical TAPDB databases into a single physical database. Ownership rules determined by the three Army components are applied, so the database shows which component "owns" the Soldier at the time the records are loaded.

3-109. **Real-Time Automated Personnel Identification System (RAPIDS) - Deployable**. The deployable RAPIDS workstation is a laptop version of a fixed RAPIDS workstation designed for use in both tactical and non-tactical environments. It provides DEERS updates and issues CACs to Soldiers at home station or in a deployed environment. The deployable workstation also provides the user with a

CAC/personal ID number reset capability. This system works only when connected to DEERS and has the same operational capability as the standard desktop version of the RAPIDS workstation.

3-110. **Tactical Personnel System.** The Tactical Personnel System is a stand-alone database that provides an ad hoc ability to create a temporary system to account for unit personnel. The system has limited ability to perform robust PA or SR. HR professionals use it primarily to create manifests for transportation by air. The Tactical Personnel System is capable of producing automated manifests that can be loaded in Air Force manifesting systems and DTAS.

3-111. **Theater Force Tracker.** The Theater Force Tracker provides a database of all units that are or have been deployed to theater and is available on SIPRNET. It is a web-based application supporting United States Army Central, the Army's component of United States Central Command. It is a developed application that provides a picture of units and detachments supporting the United States Central Command's theater of operations. Theater Force Tracker leverages data from authoritative Army databases to provide a comprehensive inventory of the units supporting the mission. This information allows the command to monitor force assignments and plan for unit rotations to ensure the command has the right forces in theater to perform the United States Army Central's mission.

3-112. **Total Army Personnel Database (TAPDB).** The TAPDB is the Army's corporate HR database. It is implemented as five separate databases: TAPDB—Guard for the HQs, National Guard; TAPDB—Reserves; TAPDB—Active Enlisted; TAPDB—Active Officer; and TAPDB—Civilian.

HR AUTOMATION SYSTEMS

3-113. **Army Disaster Personnel Accountability and Assessment System.** The Army Disaster Personnel Accountability and Assessment System is the Army's official tool for reporting the status of PA subsequent to a natural or man-made catastrophic event. The Army Disaster Personnel Accountability and Assessment System is a web-based, user friendly system to determine the status and whereabouts of Soldiers, DOD civilians, outside the continental United States (OCONUS) CAAF, and Family members. The Army Disaster Personnel Accountability and Assessment System is designed to meet the policy requirements outlined in the DOD Instruction (DODI) 3001.02, Personnel accountability in conjunction with Natural or Manmade Disasters, and Chairman of the Joint Chiefs of Staff Manual 3150.13C, Joint Reporting Structure – Personnel Manual, which requires each Service component to provide the most expeditious accountability of designated personnel categories following a disaster.

3-114. **Army Records Information Management System.** The Army Records Information Management System is a system for identifying, arranging, and retrieving Army records for reference and disposition according to a directive, usually an AR or DA PAM, which prescribes their creation, maintenance, and use. It focuses on the management of long-term and permanent records and allows the business process to manage short-term records. The Army Records Information Management System addresses only the record copy of information; all other copies of the same information may be disposed of when no longer needed for business not to exceed the time that the record copy is kept. The Army Records Information Management System simplifies recordkeeping, shifts retention and disposition burdens to record holding areas, improves records processing for deployed units in contingency operations, and provides a host of support services and automated tools on the web.

3-115. **Common Operational Picture Synchronizer (COPS).** The most powerful PIM enabling system available to Active Army brigade S-1s is COPS, which allows a common view of authorized unit strength and Personnel Manning Authorization Document authorizations. COPS is a web-based tool designed to give HR strength managers and commanders the capability to view officer and enlisted strength and authorization data; this data can also be viewed by DMSL managers at HRC. The common operational picture synchronizer provides a drill down capability to information at the specialty, grade, ASI, and SQI level of detail. In addition, it also provides the capability to drill down assigned strength to the individual Soldier level. COPS compares strength data acquired from the TAPDB and authorization data from the Total Army Authorization Documentation System, and provides a manning view of assigned versus authorized strengths by UIC level of detail. COPS further emphasizes the need for S-1s to ensure eMILPO, and other automated systems that update personnel readiness statuses (e.g., Medical Protection System), are maintained and monitored on a continual basis.

3-116. **Department of the Army Mobilization Processing System.** Subsequent to the attacks of September 11, 2001, the Army Operations Center initiated development of an automated mobilization process resulting in the Department of the Army Mobilization Processing System, which is the current system used to mobilize units and individuals. The Department of the Army Mobilization Processing System electronically processes and tracks mobilization request packets through all necessary approval levels and stages enabling the rapid issuance of mobilization orders and improving the Army's ability to account for and track units and individuals throughout the mobilization process. It is an Army mobilization resource that is essential for the timely expansion and sustainment of military forces.

3-117. **Deployed Theater Accountability System (DTAS).** The DTAS establishes and maintains PA in a JOA. It is a classified system fielded to all HR commanders, personnel, and organizations. DTAS provides a tool to accurately account for and report military and civilian personnel. This capability is critical for immediate and future operations.

3-118. **Electronic Joint Manpower and Personnel System.** The Electronic Joint Manpower and Personnel System supports the Joint Manpower and Personnel Program and is a management information system that provides an automated method to coordinate manpower changes and track personnel at the Joint Staff, combatant commands, Chairman of the Joint Chiefs of Staff-Controlled Activities, and other Joint activities. The system allows the Joint Staff, combatant commands, Chairman of the Joint Chiefs of Staff-Controlled Activities, and other Joint activities to maintain, review, modify, and report manpower requirements while providing a personnel database using manpower as the hierarchy. Additionally, the system provides an interface to the Joint Duty Assignment Management Information System for Joint officer management. Capabilities of the Electronic Joint Manpower and Personnel System are contained in the Electronic Joint Manpower and Personnel System User's Guide.

3-119. **Electronic Military Personnel Office (eMILPO).** The eMILPO is a web-based application which provides the Army with a reliable, timely, and efficient method for performing personnel actions, PA, and SR. eMILPO is utilized by S-1s at all levels and is the mechanism for updating active duty Soldier information at the top of the system. eMILPO transactions establish or update the TAPDB and ultimately (daily) the Integrated Total Army Personnel Database at HRC. eMILPO modules allow users, HR managers, and commanders visibility of the location, status, and skills of their Soldiers from HQDA-level down to unit-level.

3-120. The Enterprise Datastore (commonly referred to as Datastore) provides snapshots of personnel data across the eMILPO database to support logical and decision-making needs for users within the total Army hierarchy. Daily updates ensure the data is accurate, reliable, and available in a timely manner.

3-121. **Enlisted Distribution and Assignment System (EDAS).** The Enlisted Distribution and Assignment System is a real-time, interactive, automated system which supports the management of the enlisted force. Assignment and distribution managers at HRC use this system to create requisitions and process assignments, to create and validate requisitions, and to add or modify requisitions. It also provides enlisted strength management information. Installations primarily use eMILPO to update data on TAPDB—Active Army Enlisted. Field users use the Enlisted Distribution and Assignment System to create requisitions and to read data that they are authorized (e.g., information on Soldiers assigned to their commands and incoming personnel.

3-122. The web-based system provides access to the same source information provided to the Army personnel community in the Enlisted Distribution and Assignment System. The information is static and updated on a daily basis. The system provides access to summary reports, requisition reports, personnel information, assignment information, and a data dictionary lookup function.

3-123. **Human Resources Command User Registration System.** The Human Resources Command User Registration System is a web-based application used by unit administrators to request access to HRC controlled databases and automated systems (does not support requests for eMILPO access).

3-124. **Installation Support Modules.** Installation Support Modules consists of four standardized, web-based, custom-developed applications packaged into functional modules that integrate day-to-day installation business practices and processes. Three of the modules support HR business functions (In/Out-Processing, Transition Processing, and Personnel Locator); while the fourth module, Central Issue Facility, supports key logistics business functions. Installation Support Modules operate in a web environment that uses a single centralized database to store all module-associated Army data. The database and web/application servers provide a multi-mastered database environment that allows for an Enterprise view of data worldwide. Data replication (almost immediate) between two master sites provides for continuity of operations and back-up and recovery. Key customers include commanders, personnel managers, and logistics personnel at installation and higher-levels of command throughout the Army. Installation Support Modules enable commanders to train, equip, sustain, deploy, and transition Soldiers to meet ARFORGEN ready pool requirements.

3-125. In/Out-Processing provides automation support for quickly in-processing Soldiers into their gaining installations (i.e., welcoming and bringing individual Soldiers and their Family members "on board") and providing information on their deployment eligibility to gaining unit commanders. Out-processing provides automation support for rapidly out-processing Soldiers who are departing an installation to separate from active duty, transferring to another duty station, or departing for temporary duty of 90 or more days at a different location.

3-126. Transition Processing provides an automated, integrated method of data collection and document processing to support transitioning Soldiers from active duty status to retirement, discharge, or release from active duty.

3-127. The Personnel Locator provides automated support for tracking installation military personnel, unit of assignment, and phone numbers. It also provides mail directory service for personnel who have departed an installation or who have recently arrived.

3-128. **Interactive Personnel Electronic Record Management System (iPERMS).** The iPERMS is the repository of AMHRR file legal artifacts for all components.

3-129. **Interactive Web Response System**. The Interactive Web Response System provides information to a variety of users (individuals, S-1s, HR managers, and commanders) to facilitate an effective evaluation system. The system reflects administrative information on officer evaluation reports, regardless of component, and noncommissioned officer evaluation reports on Active Army and RC NCOs. The Interactive Web Response System allows visibility of evaluation administrative information for officer and noncommissioned officer evaluation reports once received at HRC using a variety of report formats. Examples of report formats include individual look up by social security number, senior rater reports, evaluation statuses by UIC, Personnel Services Battalion code, command, State, and late officer evaluation reports. Reports are sorted by the date received at HRC.

3-130. **Regional Level Application Software (RLAS)**. The RLAS is used by the USAR and is a client-server web-enabled application for the management of personnel and resources. RLAS shows overall readiness posture of the unit by Soldier and generates TAPDB—Reserves transactions and electronically transmits the data to HRC.

3-131. **Reserve Component Automation System**. The Reserve Component Automation System is an automated information system that supports commanders, staff, and functional managers in mobilization, planning, and administration of the Army's RC forces. It is primarily a National Guard system, but the USAR uses some mobilization modules. It is a web-based information system that provides visibility of personnel management data, tools for retirement points accounting, and mobilization planning. Unit-level personnel can view all data for Soldiers assigned. The Reserve Component Automation System is populated by SIDPERS-ARNG daily; however, system changes do not update SIDPERS-ARNG.

3-132. **Reserve Component Line of Duty (LOD) Module**. Provides a web-accessible comprehensive, user-friendly tool for use at units, Joint Force Headquarters, Regional Support Commands, United States Army Reserve (USAR) Command, National Guard Bureau, and CMAOC to administer and manage LOD determinations, incapacitation pay, medical care, and safety programs. The LOD Module helps the user organize materials needed to complete the electronic DA Form 2173 (Statement of Medical Examination and Duty Status) or DD Form 261 (Report of Investigation Line of Duty and Misconduct Status), transfer forms electronically to the next step, and track LOD investigation actions. Information available via the Medical Operating Data System pre-populates data fields where appropriate. Improved security occurs with the digital signature of specified data elements using a CAC.

3-133. **Retirement Point Accounting System.** Supports commanders, staff and other HR personnel in supporting members and former members of the Ready Reserve, Standby, Retired Reserve and Officer Active duty Obligor with tools for retirement point accounting mandated by Title 10, United States Code and DODI 1215.07, Service Credit for Reserve Retirement. The system generates a retirement point statement which should be reviewed by current members and USAR units annually. The Retirement Point Accounting System is used for the recording and maintenance of retirement points earned by a Ready Reserve Soldier during his or her career for a non-regular retirement and 1405 time for a regular retirement. The system also maintains grade advancement and survivor benefit information for the certification of non-regular retired pay.

3-134. **Soldier Management System.** The Soldier Management System Integrated Web Services is a web-based collection of data, applications, and tools to assist career managers and other HR personnel in supporting Active Army, ARNG, USAR Soldiers, veterans, retirees, Family members, and other stakeholders. The principal integrated web service application is the Soldier Management System. To access the Soldier Management System, HR personnel must have a common access card and a security role set up and approved by HRC.

3-135. **Standard Installation/Division Personnel System-ARNG (SIDPERS-ARNG).** The SIDPERS-ARNG performs functions similar to those performed in eMILPO for the Active Army. It is the National Guard's database of record for personnel, in which, each of the 54 States and Territories maintains its own database. Each State transmits their updates to the National Guard Bureau who loads these State-level changes into TAPDB—Guard.

3-136. **Total Officer Personnel Management Information System II.** Brigade and battalion S-1s use the Total Officer Personnel Management Information System II for officer and warrant officer information retrieval and data query functionality. It has two subsystems: The Total Officer Personnel Management Information System II and electronic Total Officer Personnel Management Information System. The Total Officer Personnel Management Information System is a Microsoft Windows based program, intended to provide the user with friendly point and click screens, and easy access to data. The system, with its web-based interface, allows user's real-time access via the Internet from any location world-wide. The system also updates all officer and warrant officer records for selected data points. Deploying units must ensure Soldiers have requested access from HRC and that they have received the prerequisite training on the Total Officer Personnel Management Information System. Assignment and distribution managers at HRC use this system to create and validate requisitions and process assignments. It is also used by HQDA, Army Commands, and Installations to manage officer strength and distribution of officers and to maintain officer record data on the TAPDB-Active Army Officer.

3-137. The electronic Total Officer Personnel Management Information System is a read-only system and also requires access clearance. The electronic system allows users the opportunity to pull officer and warrant officer information, such as officer records briefs, promotion orders, and request for orders. Additionally, users are able to retrieve senior enlisted promotion orders from this system.

OTHER AUTOMATION SYSTEMS AND EQUIPMENT

3-138. **Army Battle Command System (ABCS).** The ABCS integrates the mission command system found at each echelon, from ground force component commanders at the theater or Joint-level to the individual Soldier or weapons platform. ABCS supports the mission by integrating the automation systems and communicates with the functional link at strategic and tactical HQs.

3-139. **Battle Command Common Services.** The Battle Command Common Services is a suite of servers that forms the hub for the network of ABCS systems. It provides the tactical mission command and enterprise servers, services, and large-volume data storage for commanders and staffs at battalion through ASCC levels, and attaches to the tactical local-area network via Ethernet and Joint network node topologies. Essential enterprise services include e-mail, asynchronous collaboration and file storage, and data-basing. Data residing on the tactical local-area network is stored in a fabric attached storage device that is part of the Battle Command Common Services server suite.

3-140. **Battle Command Sustainment Support System (BCS3).** The BCS3 is the Army's logistics mission command automation system. It aligns sustainment, in-transit, and force data to aid commanders in making critical decisions. This system capability provides operators the common operating picture in the form of total asset visibility to quickly and efficiently see the status of selected critical items. The BCS3 provides a visual of the operational area through a map centric display. The system's software is capable of running on classified or unclassified networks. It provides the ability to plan, rehearse, train, and execute on the same system. The system provides sustainment and movement information for command decisions by displaying current status and the tools to determine future projections of fuel, ammunition, critical weapons systems, and personnel. It integrates actionable data from numerous available ABCS and the standard Army management information system (STAMIS) to support mission command. BCS3 is fielded at every echelon from theater through brigade and supports predictive sustainment based on the impact of dues-in and the status of combat essential items such as fuel, ammunition, weapons systems, and personnel. BCS3 has four main functional features which, together with medical and movement information, encompass the overall logistics common operating picture.

3-141. **Coalition-Local Area and Coalition-Wide Area Networks.** Coalition networks establish support coordination and collaboration among U. S. and non-U. S. forces in an operational environment. Coalition-Local Area and Coalition-Wide Area Network services support planning and execution of operations involving multinational forces. Coalition-Local Area and Coalition-Wide Area Networks operate at both unclassified and classified levels. They may operate as local or limited regional entities, or they may connect to and extend the services of the combined enterprise regional information exchange system which is a standing classified-capable coalition network.

3-142. **Combat Service Support Automated Information Systems Interface (CAISI).** The CAISI accepts information from automation devices interfacing over military communication networks (e.g., satellite communications, Defense Data Network, Defense Switching Network, VSAT, U. S. public switched networks, and commercial communications systems of Nations with which the U. S. has defense agreements). It provides connectivity for the STAMIS through a 12 port 10Base2 multi-port wireless device module. The two CAISI components are: Bridge module and a System Support Representative. It is a high data rate, sensitive but unclassified wireless local area network.

3-143. **Command Post of the Future.** First introduced as a transformational technology in support of Operation Iraqi Freedom, Command Post of the Future is a software capability hosted on a computer system that currently provides collaboration and visualization for Army division and brigade commanders and staff. The Command Post of the Future software provides a collaborative operating environment, voice over internet protocol, a highly intuitive, graphical user interface and enhanced briefing capabilities. The Command Post of the Future allows commanders from battalion-level and higher to feed real-time situational understanding into the system and have that information available in text and graphic representation immediately by fellow commanders and staffs at all levels. The system is a valuable planning and management tool that allows commanders to access real-time situational understanding.

3-144. **Defense Connect Online.** Defense Connect Online provides web conferencing and instant messaging capability. The Defense Connect Online major components are the Defense Connect Online Portal, Adobe's Acrobat Connect web conferencing tool, and Jabber Instant Messaging with presence and awareness. Connect meetings with screen-sharing, white boarding, integrated voice over internet protocol, and multi-person video help with information dissemination and shared situational understanding. Participants collaborate in an informal, highly interactive manner with shared screens, applications, images, and documents.

3-145. **Director's Personnel Readiness Overview.** An ARNG web-based analysis tool that provides an accurate picture of a State or unit's strength posture with drill-down capability.

3-146. **Force XXI Battle Command, Brigade and Below (FBCB2).** The FBCB2 is a suite of digitally interoperable applications and platform hardware. The FBCB2's design provides on-the-move, real-time, and near-real-time situational understanding as well as mission command information to sustainment leaders from brigade to the platform and Soldier-level. FBCB2 is a mission essential sub-element and a key component of the ABCS. FBCB2 feeds the ABCS common database with automated positional friendly information and current tactical battlefield geometry for friendly and known or suspected enemy forces. Common hardware and software design facilitates training and SOPs.

3-147. **Force Management System Website.** The official repository for Army (NIPRNET/CAC access) decisions on mission, organizational structure, personnel and equipment requirements, and authorizations for Army units and Army elements of Joint organizations for the current year through the first program year. The Force Management System Website maintains HQDA approved authorization documents (modified TOE, Table of Distribution and Allowances (TDA), and Common Tables of Allowance) and staffing documents for review and coordination with commands, installations, and units.

3-148. **Force Requirements Enhanced Database.** The Force Requirements Enhanced Database is a historical database for mobilized units. It is the system by which all United States Central Command Units Request for Forces are submitted, reviewed, approved, disapproved, deleted, and sourced. It provides the sourced unit's mission statement, capabilities, LAD, boots on ground, UIC, passengers, and location.

3-149. **Gateway Tracking System.** The TG in the United States Central Command AO utilizes a stand-alone, local Oracle Software Database, known at the Gateway Tracking System, to maintain visibility of passengers transiting theater.

3-150. **Global Air Transportation Execution System.** The Global Air Transportation Execution System is an Air Mobility Command aerial port operations and management information system designed to support automated cargo and passenger processing, the reporting of in-transit visibility data to the Global Transportation Network, and provides the billing to the Air Mobility Command's financial management directorate. It is a peripheral system to the Army PA systems and one of several systems managed under the Gates Enterprise Management System, a flight tracking system. The system docs not allow read-only rights, thus the reason the U.S Air Force limits access.

3-151. **Global Combat Support System-Army.** The Global Combat Support System-Army replaces several of the Army's current STAMISs. The system tracks supply chain, maintenance equipment and financial transactions related to logistics for all Army units. It operates in conjunction with other key systems such as BCS3, and provides support personnel detailed information required by the Soldier and the current availability of needed materiel, to include items in the distribution system. The system addresses the Army's current automation dilemma of having stove-piped systems, that is, systems that do not share information horizontally among different functional areas. It employs state-of-the-art technology to include client-server technology designed to take full advantage of modern communications protocols and procedures. The design allows the maximum amount of communications capability and flexibility so that it can take advantage of any available communication systems to include commercial or military, terrestrial, or space-based. The Global Combat Support System-Army complies with the defense information infrastructure, common operating environment and technical and data element standards. The system is also the first Army logistics system which maintains a daily interface with an Army HR system (i.e., eMILPO).

3-152. **Global Command and Control System-Army.** The Global Command and Control System-Army is the Army link for ABCS to the GCCS. The system provides a suite of modular applications and information and decision support to Army strategic and operational theater-level planning for theater operations and sustainment. The Global Command and Control System-Army supports the apportionment, allocation, logistics, and deployment of Army forces to the combatant commands. Functionality includes: force tracking, host-nation and civil military operations support, theater air defense, targeting, military information support operations, mission command, logistics, medical, provost marshal, counter-drug, and personnel status. The system is primarily deployed from Corps to Division.

3-153. **Information Management and Reporting Center System.** A tool used by the ARNG for education and incentive tracking; includes tracking of bonuses.

3-154. **Joint Asset Movement Management System (JAMMS).** The JAMMS is a stand-alone automation system designed to capture movement and location information about deployed forces, U. S. government employees, and CAAF (including other designated contractor personnel) in specified theaters of operation at transit locations. JAMMS has no direct connectivity to local area networks or servers. The system consists of a laptop computer, bar code (CAC) scanner, and ancillary equipment.

3-155. **Joint Capabilities Requirement Manager.** The Joint Capabilities Requirement Manager is the principal DOD tool used by Global Force Managers to capture force capabilities, develop force requirements, and coordinate Global Force Provider Activities.

3-156. **Joint Personnel Accountability Reconciliation and Reporting**. The Joint Personnel Accountability Reconciliation and Reporting develops a process for obtaining personnel visibility of all U. S. forces in a geographic combatant commander's AO using automation. It leverages existing Defense Manpower Data Center systems and HR expertise of personnel tracking systems. It provides reconciliation and reporting of personnel from multiple DOD sources.

3-157. **Maneuver Control System**. The Maneuver Control System consists of a network of computer workstations that integrate information from subordinate maneuver units with those from other mission command system battlefield functional areas to create a joint common data base referred to as the COP. Tactical information products, such as situation maps and reports, allow the display and manipulation of this information. The system also provides a means to create, coordinate, and disseminate operational plans and orders. It also supports the MDMP.

3-158. **Medical Protection System.** In addition to the HR systems listed previously, S-1s need access to the Medical Protection System. It is a medical system which provides S-1s and their commanders with a real-time, world-wide system to monitor and assess the medical readiness and deployability for Soldiers in their respective units. The Medical Protection System is accessible to brigade surgeons to assist in planning and executing Army Health System operations and to provide commander's with medical situational understanding. S-1s can use the system to track the DOD individual medical readiness requirements, and provide commanders with comprehensive reports to assess medical readiness for their Soldiers.

3-159. System reports are color coded as red, amber, and green to provide commanders with an immediate glance as to the readiness of their units. A particular key module for S-1s to utilize is the USR Report Tool module. The Medical Protection System USR tool assists commanders and staff with completing the USR. S-1s use the report and data tool when preparing the USR and turn in with the USR as supporting documentation of the unit's medical readiness. Users can access the system for read-only or read and write capability. Individuals who only require read-only access can request a logon and password from the Medical Protection System home page.

3-160. **Net Unit Status Reporting**. Net Unit Status Reporting is a web-based Army Readiness input tool that enables HR users to import current readiness, status information, and data on their unit(s) from official sources and assists HR users in preparing and submitting readiness status reports into the Defense Readiness Reporting System-Army. The Defense Readiness Reporting System-Army is a "Commander's Report" that provides enhanced features that directly links users to respective Army authoritative databases and provides user-friendly web-based input tools to ease report submission.

3-161. **Non-Secure Internet Protocol Router Network (NIPRNET)**. The NIPRNET is a network of government-owned internet protocol routers used to exchange sensitive unclassified information. It provides access to specific DOD network services and supports a wide variety of applications such as e-mail, web-based collaboration, information dissemination, and connectivity to the world-wide internet. Access to the NIPRNET is obtained through a standardized tactical entry point site or teleport and is then distributed through an unclassified theater network. NIPRNET enables a myriad of other reach functions from deployed forces to the sustaining base and lateral collaboration among deployed elements.

3-162. **SECRET Internet Protocol Router Network (SIPRNET)**. The SIPRNET supports critical mission command applications and intelligence functions. It operates in a manner similar to the NIPRNET, but as a secure network. As with NIPRNET, SIPRNET provides access to many web-based applications, as well as the ability to send and receive classified information up to Secret. These applications and capabilities enable the effective planning and execution of plans in a secure environment. SIPRNET also enables a myriad of reach logistics functions from deployed forces to the sustaining base and lateral collaboration among deployed elements.

3-163. **Secure and Non-Secure Voice**. Secure and non-secure voice remains a significant user requirement in all networks. Switched voice service allows connections between and among home station and theater locations. The service includes long haul switched voice, facsimile, and conference calling. Secure voice connections may also be used for facsimile traffic. More networks are now incorporating and employing secure voice over internet protocol instead of the traditional switched circuit requirements. Non-secure voice provides the essential day-to-day connections used in common, routine business, but also includes requirements to provide connectivity to Civilian telephone networks in the sustaining base and host-nation. Additionally, the non-secure voice network and defense switched network can be extended to Joint and multi-national subscribers.

3-164. **SharePoint.** SharePoint is a web platform developed by Microsoft for small to large organizations. The design is a centralized replacement for multiple web applications, and supports various combinations of enterprise website requirements. SharePoint is highly scalable and is capable of supporting multiple organizations on a single server farm.

3-165. **Single Mobility System.** The Single Mobility System is a web-based computer system that provides visibility of air, sea, and land transportation assets and provides aggregated reporting of cargo and passenger movements. The system does this by collecting plane, ship, and truck movement data from other computer systems such as the Global Transportation Network, Consolidated Air Mobility Planning System, Global Defense Support System, Joint Air Logistics Information System, Air National Guard Management Utility, and the Defense Transportation Tracking System.

3-166. **Synchronized Pre-Deployment and Operational Tracker (SPOT).** The SPOT is the Joint Enterprise Contractor Management and Accountability System. The SPOT generated CAAF accountability data is provided to the HRSC and ASCC G-1/AG per local command policy. The ASCC G-1/AG is responsible for developing mission specific CAAF accountability and reporting policies. The HRSC, G-1/AGs, and S-1s execute these policies. G-1/AGs monitor the accountability process to ensure subordinate units are properly executing the accountability process. See JP 4-10, AR 715-9, Operational Contract Support Planning and Management, and ATTP 4-10, Operational Contract Support Tactics, Techniques, and Procedures, for additional information on SPOT.

3-167. **Transportation Coordinator's Automated Information for Movement System II.** The Transportation Coordinator's Automated Information for Movement System II is a Joint automated information system for unit moves, installation transportation office, and transportation management office functionality. It provides an integrated traffic management capability and supports deployment, redeployment, and sustainment of U. S. Forces. The system ultimately integrates with unit, installation, and depot-level supply systems to manage inbound and outbound movement, shipment, documentation, and requisition information. The system provides the TSC with an automated capability to forecast the arrival of personnel and inter-theater cargo and containerized shipments, and to maintain visibility of command interest cargo en route to the theater. Thereby enhancing TSC capabilities to maintain the intra-theater segment of the distribution system in balance and operating efficiently.

3-168. The Transportation Coordinator's Automated Information for Movement System II provides TSC distribution managers the capability to coordinate and provide transportation services to shippers, carriers, and receiving activities located throughout the theater. Automated functions include documenting transportation movement requests, tasking mode operators, forecasting, and reporting container and cargo movements throughout the distribution system. Other capabilities include scheduling and de-conflicting convoy movements, maintaining unit personnel location manifesting data, and maintaining in transit cargo and asset movement visibility. The system provides mode operators an automated capability to receive commitments, conduct mission planning, task available assets, and maintain fleet asset status data.

3-169. **TRANSCOM Regulating and Command and Control Evacuation System.** The TRANSCOM Regulating and Command and Control Evacuation System provide inpatient visibility and capture those casualties not reported through normal channels. The system combines transportation, logistics, and clinical decision elements into a seamless patient movement automated information system. It is capable of visualizing, assessing, and prioritizing patient movement requirements, assigning proper resources, and distributing relevant data to deliver patients efficiently. The TRANSCOM Regulating and Command and Control Evacuation System automate the processes of medical regulations (assignment of patients to suitable MTFs) and aero medical evacuation during peace, war, and contingency operations.

3-170. **Trusted Associate Sponsorship System.** The Trusted Associate Sponsorship System is a web-based tool used to gather information to verify eligibility for issuing common access card to authorized contractors. Contractors who must complete the CAC application can access the data from any computer providing that the trusted agent or trusted agent security manager has issued the contractor a system generated user name and password. This provides increased control in who may apply for a common access card, eliminate data re-entry, and provide real-time information about DOD contractors. (Note: There is a distinction between contractors eligible for the common access card and others needing physical access when issuing local contractor ID cards).

3-171. **Very Small Aperture Terminal (VSAT).** The VSAT is a software-driven, small-dish, transportable, satellite terminal used for reliable connectivity. Used in conjunction with CAISI, it permits the receipt and transmission of data and voice over internet protocol via the NIPRNET from anywhere in the world to anyplace in the world. Together with CAISI, VSAT has given the TSC the communication asset it needs to manage and maintain mission command sustainment support across the theater. VSAT provides forward deployed sustainment units a communication capability for sustainment automated systems that is substantially the same as in the garrison environment.

3-172. **Video Teleconferencing.** A mainstay collaboration tool in deployed environments. It provides the best available technical alternative to face-to-face meetings that provide users with human-factor feedback and interaction when they must collaborate from separate locations. Video teleconferencing also better facilitates online collaboration and coordination with various automation tools and applications.

This page intentionally left blank.

Chapter 4

Provide HR Services

HR services are those functions which directly impact a Soldier's status, assignment, qualifications, financial status, career progression, and quality of life which allows the Army leadership to effectively manage the force. HR services include the functions of EPS, postal, and casualty operations. To ensure the effectiveness and promptness of HR services it is critical that actions which impact Soldiers be processed or routed promptly by the chain of command and HR technicians. Many HR services are available through self-help, web-enabled applications.

SECTION I – ESSENTIAL PERSONNEL SERVICES (EPS)

4-1.   Essential personnel services functions are initiated by the Soldier, unit commanders, unit leaders, G-1/AGs and S-1s, or from the top of the HR system (HRC). Table 4-1 below and continued on page 4-2 depict the responsibilities for EPS functions. The majority of EPS actions are processed via eMILPO, RLAS, and SIDPERS-ARNG, with documentation added to the AMHRR. However, there are some actions that must be processed separately by the commander or S-1 (e.g., congressional inquiries, customer service, and participation in boards) . Typical actions initiated by Soldiers are requests for DA Form 4187 (Personnel Action), requests for leave or pass, updates to family member information for record of emergency data or life insurance elections, and updates to allotments, savings bonds, and/or direct deposit. Typical actions initiated by commanders include request for awards or decorations, promotions, reductions, and bars to reenlistment. Evaluation reports are normally initiated by the supervisor at all levels.

Table 4-1. Essential personnel services (EPS) responsibilities

Function/Task	Responsible Agencies					
	BN	BDE	DIV	CORPS	ASCC	IMCOM
Develop EPS Policy/Timelines/SOP	✓	✓	✓	✓	✓	✱
Awards and Decorations	✓	✓	✓	✓	✓	
Evaluation Reports	✓	✓	✓	✓		
Promotions	✓	✓	✓	✓		✱
Transfers/Discharges	✓	✓	✓	✓	✓	✓
Leaves and Passes	✓	✓	✓	✓	✓	
Military Pay/ Entitlements	✓	✓				

Table 4-1. Essential personnel services (EPS) responsibilities

Function/Task	Responsible Agencies					
	BN	BDE	DIV	CORPS	ASCC	IMCOM
Officer Accessions	✓	✓				✓
Personnel Action Requests	✓	✓	✓	✓	✓	✱
Line of Duty Investigations	✓	✓	✓	✓	✓	✱
AR 15-6 Investigations Appointment	✓	✓	✓	✓	✓	
Bars to Reenlistment (Flag Input)	✓	✓				
Issue Identification Cards/Tags		✓				✱
Citizenship/ Naturalization	✓	✓				✱
Deletions/Deferments		✓	✓	✓	✓	✱
Reassignments	✓	✓	✓	✓	✓	✓
Records Review	✓	✓	✓	✓		✓
Branch Transfers	✓	✓				
Congressional Inquiries	✓	✓	✓	✓	✓	✱
Conscientious Objector Status	✓	✓	✓	✓	✓	
Exceptional Family Member Program	✓	✓				
Medical Boards (MAR2) Monitor	✓	✓	✓	✓	✓	
Reclassifications	✓	✓				
Request for Schools/Training	✓	✓				
Retirement	✓	✓	✓	✓	✓	✓

Table 4-1. Essential personnel services (EPS) responsibilities

Function/Task	Responsible Agencies					
	BN	BDE	DIV	CORPS	ASCC	IMCOM
Servicemembers' Group Life Insurance Election Certificate	✓	✓				*
Sponsorship	✓	✓				
Statement of Service		✓				✓
Suspensions of favorable Personnel Action	✓	✓				*
IMCOM Military Personnel Divisions have responsibilities for these functions/ tasks for non-Personal Services Delivery Redesign units on the installation.						
Legend: ASCC= Army Service Component Command; BDE= Brigade; BN- Battalion; DIV= Division; IMCOM= Installation Management Command; MAR2= Military Occupational Specialty Administrative Retention Review; MEB= Medical Evaluation Board; PEB= Physical Evaluation Board; SOP= standard operating procedure (Note: This list is not all conclusive)						

4-2. All EPS actions, less those items changed through Soldier self-service capabilities, are processed, verified, or routed by HR Soldiers at each level of command (battalion, brigade, division, corps, and ASCC). With brigade-centric operations the norm for HR support, some EPS actions do require processing by mission command elements above brigade. G-1/AGs at all levels have staff responsibility for EPS actions. While normally executed at brigade S-1 and below, G-1/AGs maintain oversight of all EPS functions. Common actions normally processed above brigade include awards and decorations, congressional inquiries, deletions, officer procurement, and developing EPS policies and priorities.

4-3. With limited HR resources in G-1/AGs and S-1s, determining the proper HR organization to provide EPS support to assigned or attached personnel is crucial to processing efficient and timely EPS actions. This determination is also affected by whether the unit is deployable, deployed, assigned to garrison, or geographically separated from the brigade.

HR CUSTOMER SERVICE

4-4. HR customer service is a critical service performed by all S-1 sections as it impacts a Soldier's status, readiness, career management, benefits, and quality of life. The S-1 section is the responsible office for ensuring that assigned and attached personnel receive assistance with EPS actions and answering their questions or concerns. S-1 sections must ensure they provide the time and resources to meet the customer service needs of the personnel they support. Unit personnel along with the leadership expect the HR system and processes to be responsive to them to meet their needs. As such, S-1s must strive to provide the best customer service possible. At a minimum, consider the following items when developing customer service support:

- Establish and publish specific times for providing customer service. Customer service times should be sufficient in length to ensure personnel do not have to wait long for service. Changes to customer service times should not routinely be made. Consider training or operational availability issues when establishing customer service hours.
- Consider the time necessary to process certain EPS actions. Some customer service functions are more time consuming than others and may require research or further explanation by S-1 personnel.

- Develop a plan of action for equipment failures (e.g., ID tag machine not operational). The plan of action should include alternate point for support. For example, another brigade may be able to issue ID tags.

- Ensure knowledgeable HR personnel are available to answer HR questions or to process EPS actions. This includes knowledge of specific documents that may be required to be submitted by Soldiers.

- Adjust the customer service plan as needed. Talking with Soldiers and leaders can determine if HR customer service is adequate.

- Provide a workstation for Soldiers to use. Not all Soldiers have access to HR web-based services at their unit.

AWARDS AND DECORATIONS

4-5. The awards and decorations program enables the Army to provide Soldiers and DOD Civilians tangible recognition for valor, meritorious service, and achievements. The awards program also provides a mechanism for recognizing veterans and the primary NOK (PNOK) of Soldiers, members of sister Services, military personnel of multi-national countries, and Civilians for their meritorious contributions. Multi-name award orders should be limited in number due to privacy issues. See AR 600-8-105, Military Orders, for detailed information regarding preparation of multi-name award orders. Award orders and memoranda are forwarded for placement in the AMHRR.

4-6. Approval authority for awards and decorations is prescribed by AR 600-8-22, Military Awards, AR 672-20, Incentive Awards, for DA Civilian personnel, and DODI 1400.25, DOD Civilian Personnel Management System, for DOD civilian personnel. Wartime awards approval authority may be delegated to the senior Army general officer in a documented joint command commensurate with the officer's rank.

4-7. Recommendations for awards and decorations must be initiated, processed, and submitted through the chain of command to the approval authority. Commanders in the chain of command process the award expeditiously with the goal of presenting the award prior to the individual's departure from the unit. For posthumous awards, the goal is to have the award approved for presentation to the family at the funeral. Posthumous valorous awards require special handling IAW Army policy.

4-8. Award boards may be established by commanders to review award recommendations and recommend award decisions. Awards boards, if established, must reflect the composition of the command as much as possible. For example, if an organization is task organized with Active Army and RC units, then the board should have representatives from each component. Awards and decorations are historical in nature and approval authorities maintain a record of each recommendation and decision.

4-9. During joint operations, HR elements (J-1, G-1/AG, and S-1) must determine Soldier eligibility for joint awards and decorations. During the deployment planning process, commanders with award approval level, need to ensure sufficient stocks of individual awards and certificates are included.

INDIVIDUAL AWARDS AND BADGES

4-10. Combat operations typically see an increase in certain individual awards. Published award criteria and processing guidance may be supplemented via military personnel messages from HQDA. Awards clerks and supervisors should frequently consult their G-1/AG or S-1 to ensure they have the most current guidance.

UNIT AWARDS

4-11. Commanders authorized to approve unit awards announce awards in permanent orders of their HQs. Permanent orders are published announcing the award of a unit decoration and contain the citation of the award, name of the unit or units, and inclusive dates. All unit awards approved at HQDA are announced in HQDA General Orders. Unit commanders and military records custodians must reference DA PAM 672-3, Unit Citation and Campaign Participation Credit Register, in conjunction with personnel records, to determine and confirm entitlement of individuals to wear the insignia pertinent to each type of unit recognition. All verified entitlements are entered into their personnel records IAW AR 600-8-104. HR elements should plan accordingly when requesting unit awards and anticipate a longer than usual processing timeline.

EVALUATION REPORTS

4-12. Evaluation reports provide a systematic approach for assessing the past performance and future potential of all personnel. For NCOs, warrant officers, and officers, these reports provide information to HQDA for use in making personnel management decisions that affect promotions, assignments, centralized selections, or qualitative management. For Civilian personnel, evaluations assist in making decisions concerning compensation, training, rewards, reassignments, promotions, reductions in grade, retention, reductions in force, and removal.

4-13. During deployments, mobilizations, or emergencies, HQDA may implement changes to the evaluation policy. These changes may affect report periods, reasons for submission, processing procedures, processing timeliness, use of counseling checklists, and appeals procedures. S-1s are responsible for maintaining visibility of evaluation report status to facilitate timely submission.

4-14. In addition to maintaining visibility on evaluation reports, HR leaders are expected to be subject matter experts on all aspects of the evaluation reporting process. One specific area that S-1s are often engaged for their assistance is in guidance on managing a profile. Although this profile is ultimately the responsibility of each rating official, S-1s should be prepared to discuss this topic and be ready to advise rating officials on how to maintain credible profiles that provide the flexibility to recognize top performing individuals.

4-15. AR 623-3, Evaluation Reporting System and DA PAM 623-3, Evaluation Reporting System, provide policy and procedural guidance for processing officer and NCO evaluation reports. Forms content management facilitates the process of forwarding completed evaluation reports to HRC for final action and placement in the AMHRR, except for ARNG NCO evaluation reports which route to the State Enlisted Personnel Manager for processing. The Total Army Performance Evaluation System evaluates and documents the performance of most DA Civilian personnel. AR 690-400, Total Army Performance Evaluation System (Chapter 4302), is the authority for DA Civilian employees. Additionally, certain Army civilian employees are covered by alternative civilian personnel management systems which follow other prescribed performance management systems (e.g., Defense Civilian Intelligence Personnel System, Civilian Acquisition Workforce Personnel Demonstration Project, and Science & Technology Reinvention Laboratory Personnel Demonstration Projects).

RATING SCHEMES

4-16. Commanders are required to establish and maintain rating schemes for all officer, NCO, and DOD civilian personnel within their respective commands. S-1s assist commanders by coordinating communication at all levels to ensure rating schemes are up-to-date and free of errors. Frequent checks and updates are required due to personnel turbulence units experience while in garrison or changes to task organization while deployed. Established rating schemes become critical tools when processing evaluation report appeals.

TIMELINESS

4-17. HQDA continues to emphasize timely and accurate submission of evaluation reports (officer, enlisted, and DA Civilian) while in garrison or deployed. The cover page of a senior rater's Evaluation Timeliness Report, which includes information on delinquent reports (except DA Civilian and ARNG noncommissioned officer evaluation reports), can be filed in that senior rater's AMHRR if authorized by AR 600-8-104.

PROMOTIONS AND REDUCTIONS

4-18. AR 600-8-19, Enlisted Promotions and Reductions, and AR 600-8-29, Officer Promotions, prescribe the enlisted promotions, reductions, and officer promotion functions of the military personnel system. Both provide principles of support, standards of service, policies, tasks, rules, and steps governing all work required in the field to support enlisted promotions and reductions and officer promotions. AR 600-8-19 and AR 600-8-29 provide the objectives of the Army's enlisted and officer promotion systems, which include filling authorized spaces with the best qualified Soldiers and officers. Further, both promotion systems provide for career progression and rank that are in line with potential and for recognition of the best qualified Soldiers and officers, which attracts and retains the highest caliber of Soldiers and officers for a career in the Army. Additionally, both systems preclude promoting Soldiers and officers who are not productive or not the best qualified, thus providing an equitable system for all.

4-19. It is important for all personnel involved in the enlisted and officer promotion system to understand that Soldiers and officers from all Army components may be assigned to their organization. Each component has its own separate promotion policies, rules, and steps governing promotions. In particular, when conducting enlisted promotions at unit-level, commanders and S-1s need to be knowledgeable of USAR and ARNG promotion policies and procedures as depicted in AR 600-8-19 and Army PPG, and should audit Promotion Point Worksheets to ensure compliance. For example, notification or approval may be required from the State before promoting ARNG Soldiers. Unless immediately advised otherwise by the unit commander, CMAOC posthumously promotes all Soldiers selected for promotion and on a HQDA promotion standing list.

TRANSFER AND DISCHARGE PROGRAM

4-20. The Transfer and Discharge Program provides a mechanism for the orderly administrative separation, transfer, or discharge (component/Service) of Soldiers for various reasons. AR 635-200, Active Duty Enlisted Administrative Separations, provides policy and procedural guidance for enlisted separations, and AR 600-8-24, Officer Transfers and Discharges, provides policy and procedural guidance for officer transfers and discharges. Title 10, United States Code, is the authority for voluntary and involuntary officer transfers. It includes the release of Other Than Regular Army officers and the discharge of Regular Army officers prior to the completion of their contractual obligation (both voluntary and involuntary). For RC officer separations, refer to the Army PPG.

4-21. The Army separation policy promotes readiness by providing an orderly means to:

- Judge suitability of personnel to serve in the Army on the basis of conduct and ability to meet required standards of duty performance and discipline.
- Achieve authorized force levels and grade distribution.
- Provide for the orderly administrative separation of Soldiers.

4-22. S-1s provide for the orderly administrative separation of Soldiers by preparing and tracking proper documentation and assisting with the execution of administrative separation boards. While deployed, unit S-1's establish sound policies and procedures with their respective rear detachments to move Soldiers from deployment areas to transition centers. This supports expeditious separation or discharge processing and facilitates efficient replacement operations. Close coordination with the installation MPD is required. Ensure a copy of the transfer document, separation packet, and/or discharge order is forwarded to the Soldier's AMHRR.

LEAVE AND PASS PROGRAM

4-23. The Leave and Pass Program promotes the maximum use of authorized absences to support health, morale, motivation, and efficiency of Soldiers. Army Regulation 600-8-10, Leaves and Passes, provides policy, procedures, and guidance for managing leave and passes. Upon declaration of a national emergency by Executive Order of the President or upon declaration of war by the Congress, the Secretary of the Army may suspend all leaves for Soldiers. Unit commanders and S-1s are responsible for managing leave and passes.

4-24. Special Leave and Pass Programs. During war or contingency operations, the Army may implement procedures for special leave and pass programs (e.g., environmental and morale leave and other R&R programs). All Army components are eligible for these programs. The Army G-1 publishes instructions for Special Leave and Pass programs in the Army PPG.

4-25. Rest and Recuperation. The R&R program gives Soldiers and units an opportunity to rest and recuperate at a secure location. Transportation is to a location outside the U. S. having social, climatic, or environmental conditions different from the duty station where the Soldier is serving; or to a location in the U. S. The combatant commander may establish an R&R chargeable leave program or request a non-chargeable leave program through the Secretary of Defense.

4-26. Special Leave Accrual. Special leave accrual is a program whereby Soldiers serving on active duty for a continuous period of at least 120 days, in an area in which they are entitled to special pay for duty subject to hostile fire or imminent danger, and Soldiers not authorized annual leave as a consequence of duty assignments in support of a contingency operation, may be authorized to carry over leave into ensuing years. The Army G-1 publishes Special Leave Accrual guidance in the Army PPG.

4-27. Army Post-Deployment/Mobilization Respite Absence Program. A program to recognize military personnel who are required to mobilize or deploy with a frequency beyond established rotation policy goals. The program applies to both Active Army and RC personnel. See the Army PPG for more information.

4-28. Individual Dwell Time Deployment Program. A commander's program to compensate or provide incentives to individuals required to mobilize or deploy early or often, or to extend beyond the established rotation policy goals. The program identifies dwell time as the time a Soldier spends at home station after returning from a combat deployment, operational deployment (non-combat), or a dependent restricted tour (e.g., Korea). Individual Soldiers who exceed the dwell time may accrue administrative absences.

MILITARY PAY

4-29. Military pay transactions are an integrated and embedded process within the HR architecture. Brigade and battalion S-1s are the central link between Soldiers and changes to military pay entitlements. They are responsible for resolving routine pay inquiries for their Soldiers. Military pay transactions are automatically triggered by personnel actions and other selected EPS. Soldiers have the ability to perform limited self-service pay transactions through the "My Pay" portal on Army Knowledge On-line. These capabilities include: start, stop, or modify discretionary allotments and savings bonds, modify thrift savings plans, change direct deposit information, and submit employee withholding requests (W-4).

4-30. S-1s at all levels are the supporting office for most Soldier generated pay change requests. These requests include resolving routine pay inquiries for their Soldiers (e.g., submitting a Basic Allowance for Housing request for a recently married Soldier, determining why a Soldier is in a no pay due status, and submitting documentation to change a Soldier's pay entitlements). S-1s must ensure key supporting documents for pay transactions are uploaded to the AMHRR per AR 600-8-104.

4-31. Some Soldiers are entitled to special pay. S-1s monitor special pay entitlements which may be authorized due to an ASI, MOS, SQI, or hazardous duty. Commanders and First Sergeants review the Unit Commander's Finance Report at the end of each pay period and routinely check for Soldiers receiving special pay. In cases where the S-1 or commander finds that the Soldier is not entitled to special pay, the pay entitlement is stopped and the Soldier is counseled. S-1s must be diligent to ensure reinstatement of special pay that has been erroneously terminated.

OTHER S-1 SUPPORT

4-32. Personnel action requests and other HR related S-1 support requirements include those EPS functions and tasks not discussed in the preceding paragraphs, but are services provided in support of Soldiers and units within the battalion or brigade.

4-33. S-1s have the following responsibilities for personnel action requests and other HR related support:
- Serve as the focal point for the unit in providing regulatory guidance and support as required for personnel action requests and other HR related actions.
- Process personnel action requests in a timely manner. Processing includes reviewing applications; verifying (if necessary) eligibility and completeness of the action; approval or disapproval of the request; forwarding the action, with or without comment, to HRC; or

returning the action for further information or action. S-1 sections must ensure personnel action requests are processed on a daily basis. Ensure that documentation is forwarded to the Soldier's AMHRR as required by AR 600-8-104.

- Be responsive and responsible in providing HR support to Soldiers and units. Providing effective and efficient HR support not only increases the morale and well-being of Soldiers, but can affect the readiness and personnel combat power of the organization.

LINE OF DUTY INVESTIGATIONS (LOD)

4-34. Line of duty determinations are required when a Soldier on active duty is diagnosed with an illness regardless of the cause of the illness, is injured (except injuries so slight as to be clearly of no lasting significance), or dies. Most LOD determinations require the completion of an informal or formal investigation. In appropriate cases, the assistance of the Staff Judge Advocate's office may be requested before or during a LOD investigation. Criteria and guidance for LOD determinations are found in AR 600-8-4, Line of Duty Policy, Procedures, and Investigations.

4-35. To ensure Soldiers receive appropriate medical care after leaving active duty, commanders must complete an LOD investigation or prepare a presumptive LOD determination memo at the time the injury or illness is aggravated or occurs. Presumptive LOD determinations can be made in some cases for Soldiers who die, incur, or aggravate injuries or illnesses while on active duty. LOD determinations are required for RC Soldiers serving on active duty, as well as any Active Army Soldier, who may separate from the Service prior to retirement eligibility or require continued medical treatment or disability compensation upon separation or retirement to ensure they receive appropriate medical care after leaving active duty. Active component commanders and their S-1s must be especially sensitive to the LOD requirements for RC Soldiers assigned or attached to their unit during deployments.

AR 15-6 INVESTIGATIONS

4-36. Army Regulation 15-6, Procedures for Investigating Officers and Boards of Officers, prescribes methods for conducting formal and informal investigations into allegations of misconduct or negligence or into the circumstances surrounding a serious incident or a fatality. Depending on the reason for and the type of investigation, only certain personnel as prescribed in AR 15-6, paragraph 2-1, may act as an appointing authority. Additionally, the appointed investigating officer or Board of Officers is required to consult with a representative from the Staff Judge Advocate's office before an investigation begins. AR 15-6 investigations are required for many categories of Soldier, DA Civilian, or contractor deaths. These categories include hostile deaths, military-related fatal accidents, and suspected suicides. The S-1's role and responsibility in any AR 15-6 investigation is to coordinate with the Staff Judge Advocate's office so legal counsel may initiate the necessary appointment memorandum for designated individuals and to flag individuals under investigation IAW AR 600-8-2, Suspension of Favorable Personnel Actions (Flag). S-1s may also be requested to provide administrative support to investigative boards.

OFFICER PROCUREMENT

4-37. The officer procurement program seeks to obtain personnel of a high military potential, in the right numbers, to meet the Army's authorized officer strength level. AR 135-100, Appointment of Commissioned and Warrant Officers of the Army, and AR 601-100, Appointment of Commissioned and Warrant Officers in the Regular Army, provide policy, procedures, and guidance for officer procurement in the USAR and Regular Army. NGR 600-100, Commissioned Officers – Federal Recognition and Related Personnel Actions, and NGR 600-101, Warrant Officers – Federal Recognition and Related Personnel Actions, guide officer procurements in the ARNG. During wartime, the Secretary of the Army may authorize field commanders to appoint officers to fill battlefield requirements. Officer procurement is managed by the Army G-1.

SUSPENSION OF FAVORABLE PERSONNEL ACTIONS AND BARS TO REENLISTMENT

4-38. Suspension of favorable personnel actions is mandatory when an investigation (formal or informal) is initiated on a Soldier by military or civilian authorities. See AR 600-8-2 for specific policy on flags.

4-39. Bars to reenlistment are initiated on Soldiers whose immediate separation under administrative procedures is not warranted, but whose reentry into or service beyond their expiration term of service with the Active Army is not in the best interest of the military service. Policies and procedures for bars to reenlistment are contained in AR 601-280. While bars to reenlistment are initiated in coordination with the brigade Retention NCO and the Soldier's commander, S-1s as HR managers monitor these actions.

CITIZENSHIP AND NATURALIZATION

4-40. Deploying non-citizen Soldiers who have applications for citizenship pending must call the U. S. Citizenship and Immigration Services Customer Service Number (1-800-375-5283) to inform them of mailing address changes when they occur. Soldiers with pending applications for citizenship are reminded of this requirement during SRP, during in or out processing, mobilization, extended TDY, deployment, redeployment, and reintegration (i.e., personnel processing upon return from a deployment). Soldiers who fail to notify the U. S. Citizenship and Immigration Services of mailing address changes could have their applications for citizenship denied due to not responding to mail notices from the U. S. Citizenship and Immigration Services.

4-41. S-1s have the following citizenship and naturalization responsibilities:

- Assist non-citizen Soldiers with their applications for citizenship to include cover sheets, fingerprint cards, and Form N-426 (Certification of Military or Naval Service). Note: DOD partners with the Immigration and Naturalization Service to assist non-citizen military members with their citizenship applications. The goal is to streamline and expedite the handling of their applications. S-1s serve as the conduit to assist Soldiers with their applications and to coordinate with HRC as necessary to facilitate the process. Naturalization forms and handbooks can be obtained by calling 1-800-870-3676 to request a "Military Packet" and to obtain a copy of the handbook, "A Guide to Naturalization." Soldiers and S-1 personnel can also obtain information at the www.uscis.gov website.
- Verify the application and service data and then complete the back side of Department of Homeland Security Form N-426, *Request for Certification of Military or Naval Service.*
- Certify that the character of the Soldier's service is "honorable." As a general rule, a Soldier is considered to be serving honorably unless a decision has been made to the contrary, either by the Soldier's commander or a conviction by court martial.
- Send an e-mail message to the appropriate overseas U. S. Citizenship and Immigration Services office after the Soldier's citizenship application packet is mailed. The email must contain the Soldier's name, alien number, social security number, date of birth, e-mail address, current or projected country of assignment or deployment, current or projected (if available) mailing address, and the projected date of arrival in country according to the Soldier's permanent change of station or deployment orders.
- Process posthumous citizenship applications for deceased Soldiers.

CONGRESSIONAL INQUIRIES

4-42. Congressional inquiries are specific requests made by members of Congress. Normally, commanders are required to respond to congressional inquiries within a designated timeline and format. While congressional inquiries are not always HR specific, the G-1/AG and S-1 are generally designated by the commander to process these actions. G-1/AGs and S-1s ensure congressional inquiries are processed within the designated timelines.

IDENTIFICATION (ID) CARDS AND TAGS

4-43. An ID card provides a means to identify personnel entitled to specific DOD benefits and identify personnel who fall under the 1949 Articles of the Geneva Convention. Policy, procedures, and the type of card to be issued is determined by AR 600-8-14, Identification Cards for Members of the Uniformed Services, Their Eligible Family Members, and Other Eligible Personnel and AR 690-11, Use and Management of Civilian Personnel in Support of Military Contingency Operations. Common access cards are the standard for Servicemember ID cards. The brigade or STB S-1 issues CACs for assigned or attached personnel by utilizing the TG PAT for transiting personnel. CACs and ID cards are used to:

- Identify Soldiers (active and retired), members of other Services, and their Family members.
- Identify DOD Civilians, CAAF, and EPWs.
- Provide a means to identify, control access, and track Civilians (protection warfighting function and security).
- Expedite access to stored, sharable personnel data.

4-44. ID tags are required to be worn while deployed overseas, in a field environment, and while traveling in an aircraft. ID tags are issued by brigade or STB S-1s for assigned or attached personnel and by the TG PAT for transiting personnel.

4-45. In preparing for deployments, brigade S-1s must ensure the early entry element of the S-1 has the capability to provide CACs. As such, brigade S-1s must ensure the deployable RAPIDS workstation and supporting communications equipment is shipped early in the deployment process. Deployed S-1s must coordinate with the Rear Detachment S-1 and S-6 a minimum of 90 days prior to deployment to process the RAPIDS accreditation packet through the servicing Network Enterprise Center. This ensures ID card capability is available immediately upon redeployment to home station.

4-46. Civilians (DOD Civilians and CAAF) are required to obtain a CAC prior to deploying to a theater of operations. In cases of lost or destroyed CACs, Civilians can obtain a CAC from the AFSB S-1, the TG PAT, or from a near-by brigade S-1. S-1s supporting a large population of CAAF (including other designated contractor personnel) need to ensure sufficient number of replacement cards are on-hand. Guidelines for issuing and verifying eligibility for CACs for Civilians remain the same as outlined in AR 600-8-14. Additionally, CAAF (including other designated contractor personnel) must be entered into the Trusted Associate Sponsorship System.

HR DIVISION OF LABOR

4-47. HR organizations, such as the MPD of the Installation Directorate of HR, are important partners in the overall HR support plan for units and organizations. The MPD provides HR support to all TDA units and to TOE units, battalion and below, that are geographically separated from their brigade. This partnership requires planning and preparation to ensure uninterrupted HR support to units and Soldiers whether they are deployed or at home station. ARNG Joint Forces Headquarters and USAR Reserve Sustainment Commands respectively perform similar functions in the MPD for the Guard and Reserve in non-deployed environments. To determine where organizational level HR support is conducted, leaders should use the following guidance:

- Tasks performed by TOE units while in garrison and deployed are performed by S-1 sections at brigade and battalion levels (e.g., awards and decorations, issuance of CACs and tags, promotions and advancements, and PA). The installation MPD may provide selected support to non-deployed TOE units that are geographically separated from their battalion or brigade S-1. This support may include issuance of CACs, promotions, evaluations, and PA.
- Tasks performed while in garrison only are performed by the installation MPD (e.g., retirement processing, mobilization and demobilization, Transfer and Discharge Program, Army Career and Alumni Program, and centralized in and out processing). ARNG Joint Forces Headquarters and USAR Reserve Sustainment Commands perform similar functions in the MPD for the Guard and Reserve in their garrison environments.
- Tasks performed while deployed only are performed by HR organizations (e.g., postal and wartime casualty operations).

SECTION II – POSTAL OPERATIONS

4-48. The Military Postal Service (MPS) operates as an extension of the USPS IAW USPS Publication 38. Postal services are provided to U. S. Military Services, DOD and DA Civilians, and some CAAF when USPS access is not available. Postal operations consist of a network of military HR organizations. Efficient and effective postal operations require dedicated postal organizations with trained postal clerks and HR leaders knowledgeable of postal operations laws, regulations, and procedures needed in the execution of providing mail and postal services to OCONUS locations and deployed units and personnel. There are two categories of postal operations: Postal operations and Unit Mailroom operations. Refer to ATP 1-0.2 for more detailed information on processing mail and providing postal services.

PROPONENCY

4-49. The Army's functional proponent for the postal operations management system is The Adjutant General Directorate, HRC. The adjutant general is also the executive director for the MPSA. MPSA is the DOD executive agent for military mail for all Services.

4-50. DOD 4525.6-M, DOD Postal Manual, and AR 600-8-3, Unit Postal Operations, provides mandatory policy and procedural guidance for postal operations management during military operations. Statutory requirements are found in United States Code and Code of Federal Regulations listed by topic in the above references.

RESPONSIBILITIES

4-51. The units and agencies listed in the following paragraphs, have critical roles during various stages of the deployment, sustainment, and redeployment process in establishing, executing, and managing MPS support for deployed forces.

JOINT MILITARY POSTAL ACTIVITY (JMPA)

4-52. The responsibilities of the JMPA are as follows:
- Acts as the single DOD point of contact (POC) with USPS at the postal gateways.
- Coordinates transportation of mail in the host-nation.
- Coordinates mail movement transportation needs with commercial carriers and the military Air Mobility Command.
- Coordinates mail routing scheme changes with postal gateways and maintains the military ZIP code database for the automated dispatch of mail.
- Coordinates postal supply equipment requests.
- Provides major commands and military department postal representatives with information on mail processing and irregularities.
- Assists the U. S. Postal Inspection Service when requested in matters relating to the processing, distribution, dispatch, and transportation of military mail.

MILITARY POSTAL SERVICE AGENCY (MPSA)

4-53. The responsibilities of the MPSA are as follows:
- Acts as the single DOD POC with the USPS and other government agencies on MPS policy and operational matters.
- Coordinates with other federal agencies on military postal services, to include the Federal Aviation Administration and Department of Homeland Security on any restrictions that may require the screening of mail.
- Coordinates with the theater/combatant command to determine if the appointment of a Single Service Manager (SSM) is warranted. The SSM is the POC to ensure synchronized postal support is provided to the theater prior to execution of postal service. The SSM is involved in all planning for military operations. Note: See ATP 1-0.2 for additional duties and responsibilities of the SSM.
- Advises USPS of any mail embargos or restrictions to the theater.
- Processes requests to obtain or terminate free mail only when requested by the combatant commander.

- Coordinates air and surface movement of military mail from the USPS to the postal gateways. The SSM determines commercial and military APODs and the required level of frequency, pouching, sacking, or labeling requirements.
- Requests personnel augmentation to support APOEs and SPOEs if required.
- Approves or disapproves all requests for exception to policy from the combatant commander.
- Activates/deactivates contingency MPOs in coordination with Service representatives, direct reporting units, combatant commands, and Service Component Commands (SCCs).
- Coordinates initial mail routing schemes with the JMPA(s).
- Coordinates an integrated network of major military mail distribution and transportation facilities in overseas areas.
- Establishes and maintains liaison with DOD transportation operating agencies.
- Provides military postal transportation planning support to DOD components in support of the plans of the Joint Chiefs of Staff and other military operations.

DEPARTMENT OF THE ARMY (DA) POSTAL

4-54. DA Postal provides oversight of all Army postal functions as part of the MPS to ensure efficient postal services are provided to all authorized personnel and activities within CONUS and OCONUS during normal and contingency operations. Responsibilities of DA Postal are as follows:

- Develops Army Postal policy.
- Acts as the functional proponent for AR 600-8-3.
- Conducts annual mandated inspections of the Army SCCs, IMCOM regions, and ACOM inspections programs.
- Acts as the subject matter expert for technical and functional postal operations (peacetime and contingency).
- Defines the principles of support and standards of service, policies, tasks, rules, and steps by which the Active Army, ARNG, USAR, and DOD Civilian and contractor personnel manage Army postal programs for both garrison and tactical environments.
- Informs DA leadership of initiatives and challenges regarding postal operations.
- Acts as a liaison with the ASCC, MPSA, JMPAs, and other Services.
- Assists Army Postal units with deployment, planning, preparation, execution, and transition.
- Reviews the Interservice Postal Training Activity's curriculum and Soldier Support Institute's postal doctrine to meet the needs of the Army.
- Investigates and responds to congressional inquiries concerning DA postal operations.
- Provides customer service for Army inquiries regarding mail, and monitors customer comments to identify systemic issues and/or areas that require regulatory guidance.
- Monitors budgetary transportation costs and contractual agreements to ensure Army mail is being transported efficiently with little inference for fraud, waste, and abuse.

ASCC G-1/AG

4-55. The ASCC G-1/AG is responsible for postal operations. While the G-1/AG does not execute postal operations, it is the agency responsible for developing postal policies, priorities, guidelines, and monitoring postal operations within the theater. The ASCC G-1/AG accomplishes this in coordination with the TSC/ESC and HRSC. All policies developed should adhere to Joint policy guidelines. Responsibilities of the ASCC G-1/AG are as follows:

- Plans, coordinates, integrates, and assesses postal operations within the theater G-1/AG AO.
- Ensures postal operations are included as part of Tab A (HR Support) to Appendix 2, personnel services support (PSS) of Annex F of the OPORD or contingency plan. If Army postal organizations are providing postal support to Joint and multi-national forces, they must be addressed in the OPORD.
- Maintains liaison with the SSM, TSC/ESC, HRSC, and host-nation for postal functions.

- Processes requests to the SSM for APO activations and deactivations.
- Assists the TSC/ESC, HRSC, and MMT in obtaining postal resources to support the theater postal mission.
- Monitors postal irregularities and postal offenses reported by the HRSC.
- Ensures the TSC/ESC, HRSC, and MMT have systems in place to identify deficiencies in the postal operating system and takes appropriate corrective actions to correct deficiencies.
- Develops, in coordination with the TSC/ESC, HRSC and MMT, procedures for addressing customer complaints, inquiries, suggestions, and for the expeditious return of casualty mail.
- Addresses or forwards to the SSM all theater postal issues not resolved by the TSC/ESC, HRSC, or MMT.
- Monitors force management issues within the theater.

CORPS AND DIVISION G-1/AG

4-56. Corps and Division G-1/AGs monitor postal operations for their assigned or attached units. If serving as the Army Forces G-1, the Corps and Division G-1/AG performs the duties and responsibilities of the theater G-1/AG. Corps and Divisions have no postal elements under their mission command. All postal issues or requirements are coordinated directly with the HROB within the supporting sustainment brigade. Specific postal operations responsibilities are as follows:
- Implements Joint and theater-level postal policies for assigned or attached units.
- Coordinates with the HROB and HRSC on changes to brigade mail delivery points (MDPs).
    - Coordinates with the G-6 Official Mail Manager (OMM) for the handling of official mail.
- Reconciles postal problems, issues, or changes in postal support requirements with the HROB, HRSC, or the ASCC G-1/AG.
- Includes postal operations support in all OPLANs and OPORDs.

BRIGADE S-1

4-57. The brigade S-1 develops and coordinates postal operation plans for assigned and attached units within the brigade by performing the following critical tasks:
- Establishes, manages, and supports all brigade mail operations in coordination with subordinate battalion S-1s. (Note: In cases where a brigade establishes a unit mailroom/consolidated mailroom (UMR/CMR), perform mail operations and procedures similar to the battalion S-1.)
- Provides the Division G-1/AG with grid coordinates or geographical location for the daily MDP and alternate MDPs for the brigade.
- Coordinates with the Division G-1/AG and G-6 OMM for the handling of official mail in coordination with the brigade S-6 OMM.
- Ensures that unit mail clerks handle all mail IAW all postal regulations by conducting inspections.
- Coordinates with the Division G-1/AG and/or supporting postal platoon to provide postal finance services for units and activities at remote locations.
- Coordinates with the supporting APO for establishment and execution of routine postal assistance visits for all subordinate UMRs/CMRs.
- Investigates and reconciles any problems and congressional inquiries within the brigade hindering the delivery of mail to Soldiers and units in a timely manner.

BATTALION S-1

4-58. The battalion S-1 develops and coordinates a postal operations plan for assigned and attached units within the battalion AO by performing the following critical tasks:
- Appoints in writing the unit postal officer by the battalion commander.
- Coordinates with the brigade S-1 for mail support within the designated AO.
- Supervises all subordinate unit mail operations.

- Coordinates with all subordinate units and individuals for establishment of mail pick up at the UMR/CMR.
- Collects and routes daily retro-grade mail received by unit mail clerks to the supporting postal platoon.
- Coordinates with the S-4 for transportation support for mail pick up at the servicing APO.
- Ensures mail clerks are appointed, trained, and certified by the supporting APO and can execute mail handling duties IAW DOD 4525.6-M and AR 600-8-3.
- Conducts mailroom inspections IAW DOD 4525.6-M and AR 600-8-3.
- Allows sufficient time for unit mail clerks to perform daily UMR/CMR functions.
- Informs the Assistant Chief of Staff, G-1/AG and supporting postal units, through the brigade S-1 of all individual and unit additions/deletions for routine update of the unit directory system.
- Collects and forwards mail for wounded, deceased, or missing Soldiers and Civilians to the supporting APO for further processing.
- Coordinates with the brigade S-6 OMM and brigade S-1 for handling of official mail.
- Investigates and reconciles problems within the battalion hindering the delivery of mail.
- Establishes and executes an internal UMR/CMR Inspection Program IAW the DOD 4525.6-M and AR 600-8-3.
- Immediately reports postal problems to the unit Postal Officer and/or commander and brigade S-1. Be familiar with suspicious (e.g., explosive, bio-terrorist) profiles, and be knowledgeable of what to do in the event suspicious mail is delivered.

HRSC Postal Operations Division (POD)

4-59. The HRSC is the TSC/ESC staff element responsible for ensuring that all postal policies, regulations, and guidance from USPS, MPSA, and ASCC are implemented and executed by all Army postal assets within theater. The POD provides postal assistance and technical guidance to HROBs and HR companies and ensures they are in compliance with postal operations policies and regulations. The POD directly supports the execution of the theater postal policy and the EPW mail mission and identifies appropriate resources to support the theater postal mission. Refer to ATP 1-0.2 for specific responsibilities of the POD and detailed duties of personnel assigned to the POD.

MILITARY MAIL TERMINAL (MMT) TEAM

4-60. The MMT Team provides specialized equipment and expertise to establish the Army element of a JMMT with the augmentation of an HR Company (Postal) in the port area which coordinates, receives, and processes incoming theater mail and dispatches retro-grade mail to CONUS. The MMT Team deploys initially with the sustainment brigade with the theater opening mission and then transitions to a theater distribution role. Refer to ATP 1-0.2 for specific responsibilities of the MMT Team and detailed duties of personnel assigned to the MMT Team.

HROB

4-61. The HROB plans, coordinates, integrates, and synchronizes the activities of subordinate HR elements in the deployed theater (attached to sustainment brigades) to ensure they are resourced, positioned, and properly allocated to provide postal support. Refer to ATP 1-0.2 for specific postal responsibilities of the HROB.

HR COMPANY

4-62. The HR Company provides mission command of its HQs and subordinate Postal Platoons or a combination Postal and HR Platoon. The HR Company and Postal Platoons provide augmentation to the MMT. The HR Company operates under the mission command of the supporting sustainment brigade and receives technical guidance from the MMT and HROB. Refer to ATP 1-0.2 for specific responsibilities of the HR Company.

POSTAL PLATOON

4-63. The mission of the postal platoon is to provide postal support to all individuals and units in an assigned AO or to serve as an element of an MMT. Postal platoons operate in conjunction with the Plans and Operations Section within the HR companies. Refer to ATP 1-0.2 for specific responsibilities of the Postal Platoon.

UNIT MAIL CLERK

4-64. Unit mail clerks are appointed in writing by unit commanders and key to ensuring all letters and parcels are properly and expeditiously delivered to supported populations. They assume a great deal of responsibility, and are faced with daily ethical and legal decisions in providing addressee mail delivery. They must be Army professionals who possess strong character, good judgment, not be flagged for disciplinary actions, and perform all duties IAW DOD 4525.6-M and AR 600-8-3. Unit mail clerks do not require ASI F5, but they are required to carry a valid DD Form 285 (Appointment of Military Postal Clerk, Unit Mail Clerk or Mail Orderly) and should be MOS 42A, when that MOS is available. Note: S-1s should refer to ATTP 1-0.1, Appendix D, S-1 Assessment Checklist, and use the checklist to assess the effectiveness of UMR/CMR operations. Specific responsibilities of the unit mail clerk are as follows:

- Receives mail from servicing APOs normally sorted to unit-level.
- Delivers mail to addressees.
- Collects mail from unit personnel; provides UMR level of sorting as prescribed in governing regulations; and transports mail to the servicing postal services platoon, APO, or terminal via the MDP.
- Redirects undeliverable as addressed mail to the supporting postal platoon/MDP separated by outgoing and intra-theater (local) military mail.
- Ensures mail is safeguarded and handled without exception IAW DOD postal regulations.
- Coordinates with S-1s to maintain an accountability roster of unit Soldiers (by location) to ensure efficient mail redirect for Soldiers who become casualties or change location.
- Establishes and maintains DA Form 3955(s) (Change of Address and Directory Card) either in hard copy or electronically, on all supported unit personnel. Routinely updates directory cards through coordination with supported units and agencies and provides this information to the servicing APO.
- Appropriately processes and labels redirect and casualty mail to the supporting Postal Platoon for forwarding.
- Delivers accountable mail to the addressee IAW DOD postal regulations.
- Immediately reports postal problems to the unit postal officer, commander, and/or S-1. Be familiar with suspicious (e.g., explosive, bio-terrorist) profiles and be knowledgeable of SOPs in the event suspicious mail is identified.

OTHER POSTAL INFORMATION

4-65. The information provided below outlines additional postal services as well as mail classifications.

POSTAL FINANCE SERVICES

4-66. Postal platoons provide customer service for postal finance support consistent with the commander's mail policies. These services include money order and postage stamp sales, special services, and package mailing. Postal Platoons may provide Servicemembers and other authorized personnel finance services within battalion and brigade support areas, when coordinated with supporting HR (postal) companies. Services are provided as often as the tactical situation and manning level allows at outlying locations, and can be increased or decreased based on command directives and METT-TC.

4-67. Units coordinate with the postal platoon leader to provide limited mobile postal finance services to units or teams not located near the main servicing Postal Platoon. The MTF commander coordinates with the Postal Platoon in their location to provide the MTF with necessary postal finance services to customers. Policy for mobile postal missions (rodeos) is directed by HRSC standard operating procedural guidance.

PERSONAL MAIL

4-68. Personal mail is mail addressed to individual Soldiers and Civilians. Postal Platoons receive, sort, and dispatch personal mail to appointed unit mail clerks. Personal mail is picked up daily by unit mail clerks or as directed by unit commanders IAW METT-TC. Unit mail clerks coordinate with the servicing Postal Platoon on unit and personnel status changes for mail delivery.

OFFICIAL MAIL

4-69. Official mail is mail addressed to or originating from military or other governmental organizations. Official mail is moved through the military postal system until it reaches the Postal Platoon of the unit addressed. Official mail is delivered from the Postal Platoon to the OMM who then delivers it to the addressee or agent through official mail distribution channels, the J-6. Official mail is addressed in AR 25-51, Official Mail and Distribution Management.

ACCOUNTABLE MAIL

4-70. Accountable mail is registered, insured, certified, delivery confirmation, return receipt for merchandise or express military mail service. Postal platoons receive, sort, and dispatch accountable personal mail to appointed unit mail clerks IAW DOD 4525.6-M. Once received, unit mail clerks maintain chain of custody with appropriate documentation through delivery to the recipient. Unit mail clerks ensure accountable mail is properly secured IAW DOD 4525.6-M. Return undeliverable accountable mail to the servicing APO the following day with the appropriate endorsements.

REDIRECT SERVICE

4-71. The postal network provides personal, official, and accountable mail redirect services starting at the unit mail clerk level. There are two forms of redirect services: Soldier redirect and unit redirect. Soldier redirect applies to individual pieces of mail requiring directory service prior to processing. This includes mail for individual Soldiers who changed units or locations or were separated from the unit. The unit redirect function involves redirecting bags, trays, or pallets of mail because of task organization changes, unit relocation, or unit redeployment.

4-72. Redirect services depend on the AO postal policy and the tactical situation. All Postal Platoons provide redirect services. A designated postal platoon(s) provides ASCC-level redirect services. The Corps-level Postal Platoon(s) provides the primary redirect services for the Corps. Postal platoons handle redirect of unit mail within their supported AO. The HRSC POD and ESC HROB provide personnel and unit assignment and location information in automated form via local theater unit locator services, DTAS, and the Postal Directory and Addressing system to all Postal platoons.

CONTAMINATED AND SUSPICIOUS MAIL

4-73. The postal network must make special provisions for handling and processing contaminated and suspicious mail IAW postal regulations. Suspicious mail items may consist of chemical, biological, radiological, or nuclear materials. The postal network screens for contaminated and suspicious mail and stops the mail flow when it is discovered. Any suspicious looking package or letter should be considered a potential bomb/hazard and should be treated accordingly. See FM 3-11.4, Appendix H, Multiservice Tactics, Techniques, and Procedures for Nuclear, Biological, and Chemical (NBC) Protection, for possible indicators and characteristics of suspect mail/packages, handling instructions, and reach-back capability.

CASUALTY MAIL

4-74. Casualty mail that is processed within the mail distribution system requires special attention to prevent premature casualty information disclosure and mail returned home before NOK notification. When processing casualty mail, unit mail clerks validate the Soldier's location, hold the mail for the Soldier's return, forward the mail to the MTF, or return to the servicing postal platoon. Undelivered casualty mail will not contain any endorsements or marks made or posted on the mail by the unit, and will be returned to the APO. The APO forwards casualty mail to the casualty mail section for processing. The Postal Platoon verifies casualty information; makes appropriate endorsements, then forwards casualty mail to the theater casualty section at the MMT for final processing. This only applies to unopened mail as any mail that has been previously opened by the Soldier is considered personal effects (PE) and is shipped with the rest of the Soldier's belongings.

EPW MAIL

4-75. The Geneva Convention, relative to the treatment of prisoners of war, identifies the need for EPW mail operations. The Army G-1 coordinates with the Provost Marshal, an appropriate international neutral agency, and an American neutral agency to assess EPW mail requirements. The ASCC G-1/AG identifies the Postal Platoon(s) to handle EPW mail.

FREE MAIL

4-76. Free mail is authorized by Executive Order 12556, Mailing Privileges of Members of the Armed Forces of the United States and of Friendly Foreign Nations, and Title 39, USC 3401(a), as determined by the Secretary of Defense. Free mail is a privilege specifically granted by this law and intended solely to expedite transmission of military members' personal letter and mail correspondence to the U. S. in times of operational contingency in arduous circumstances or armed conflict.

4-77. Free mail privileges apply to Servicemembers in a declared "Free Mail" operational area as well as those hospitalized in a facility under military jurisdiction as a result of service in the designated area. Free mail also applies to Civilians who are authorized through proper written guidance as directed by DOD 4525.6-M and Status of Forces Agreement (SOFA), and as designated by the combatant command.

4-78. Free mail is limited by Title 39, USC 3401 (a) to personal letters or sound recorded correspondence (to include video tapes) and must be addressed to a place within the delivery limits of the USPS or MPS. Free mail privileges are not normally allowed when mail is processed, handled, or delivered by a foreign postal administration. The Army/ASCC requests free mail through the combatant commander for the specific theater and is considered authorized when the combatant commander receives official approval from the Secretary of Defense. Upon completion of the Joint operation, the combatant commander requests termination of free mail via MPSA. Currently, review and revalidation for free mail areas is required every 180 days to ensure that the conditions that authorized free mail are still applicable.

INTERNATIONAL MAIL

4-79. The ASCC/G-1 and the combatant command assess the need for international mail exchange within the theater of operation, and in conjunction with the HRSC POD/HROB, identify the postal platoon to conduct that mission. All requests for pro-grade mail support for multinational forces are submitted by the ASCC to the combatant command to be submitted to DA Postal and MPSA for approval. Additional security measures should be implemented to safeguard against hazardous materials entering the MPS. International mail is discussed in the DOD Directive 4525.6-M and the individual country listing of the USPS International Mail Manual.

HOST-NATION POSTAL SUPPORT

4-80. If an agreement is made by the ASCC, combatant command, and the host-nation via Memorandum of Agreement and SOFA, this support can be a critical element of the postal support structure. It frees military and civilian postal personnel for more critical duties. Host-nation personnel can be military or Civilian, and they can handle all mail classes except registered mail (domestic or official). Postal unit commanders must indoctrinate Soldiers supervising host-nation personnel in the customs, language, religion, and political conditions of the AO.

USE OF CONTRACTORS FOR POSTAL SUPPORT

4-81. During military operations, it may become necessary to contract out selected postal services, to include operating entire APOs. Contracting postal support is usually an optimum option when there are insufficient numbers of Postal Platoons to maintain rotation policies or when the theater of operations is so vast that the military Services cannot support the area. Oversight of all contractual postal Statements of Work must be completed annually (or more often, as needed) by the ASCC G-1 and the HRSC POD.

4-82. The success of contracting postal operations when shifting from a "military operated and military supervised" postal operation to a "contractor operated" postal operations is ensuring the government maintains oversight of the service. The military accomplishes this by ensuring trained and experienced postal personnel serve as the primary and alternate contracting officer representative (COR). CORs are qualified individuals nominated by the requiring activity and appointed by the contracting officer to assist in the technical monitoring or administration of a contract. Although CORs can be employed on all types of service contracts, they are critically important in the more complex services, for example in the MMT. Not everyone can be a COR. CORs must be a government employee (either military or Civilian) and must possess the necessary qualifications (training) and experience commensurate with the responsibilities delegated to them.

4-83. When contractors are used to perform postal missions, a qualified, knowledgeable, postal technical supervisor must be onsite IAW USPS Publication 38 and DOD Contracting Policy DFARS 201.602.2. Consider the following recommendations when contracting postal operations:

- Establish postal operational contract support (OCS) teams to serve as the nexus for contracted postal efforts. The teams manage the COR training and appointment program and consolidated Performance Evaluation Board reports. The OCS team prepares monthly roll-up briefings to the contracting officer and for the Award Fee Evaluation Board.
- Capability to work with contract managers and legal support offices regarding requirements letters, administrative change letters, and other contract management tools.
- Periodically meet with the contracting officer and contractors to discuss postal issues.
- Plan contractor support carefully. It is imperative to identify how property is aligned early in the process to ensure it is operational and meets the standard prior to a transfer of authority. Ensure contract specifies what government furnished equipment (GFE) will be provided. Define the exact equipment, by location, to be turned over to the contractor during the transfer of authority process.
- Understand the differences between GFE, theater provided equipment, and installation provided equipment.
- Include the G-1/AG and G-8 as needed.
- Schedule COR training as necessary to meet rotation requirements.

BATTLEFIELD FLOW

4-84. Prior to deployment, the ASCC G-1/AG determines the initial postal support requirements in coordination with the combatant commands, other Service components, and the supporting HRSC. Figure 4-1 depicts postal operations in a theater of operations and mail flow from CONUS to the theater. In determining the requirements, the ASCC G-1/AG considers the infrastructure in the AO, deployment timing, force composition, and expected deployment duration. From operational analysis, the ASCC G-1/AG determines what postal unit structure is necessary to support the operation and where to place the AO MMT within the AO. The normal postal unit requirement for supporting a deployed force is one MMT per inter-theater APOD receiving bulk mail, a postal platoon providing postal finance services support for up to 6,000 Soldiers and Civilians, and a HR Company with a postal team for every three to seven postal platoons. Depending on the scope and expected duration of an operation, postal platoons and/or HR (postal) companies must deploy with the main body of the operational Army. A trained and fully equipped postal unit requires a minimum of 48 hours to establish postal operations. Postal units must be established prior to the movement of mail in or out of the AO. All METT-TC considerations must be addressed.

4-85. To support force deployment, the MPSA, in coordination with the USPS, operational combatant commands, and SCCs, assigns MPO numbers to contingency forces. The SCCs provide the contingency MPO numbers to deploying personnel at least 24 hours prior to deployment if no permanent contingency MPO numbers for the unit have been assigned. The establishment of contingency MPO numbers enables the USPS to sort mail to the brigade. However, mail for a contingency operation is not sorted or packaged for shipment until MPSA coordinates the activation of specified MPOs with the USPS. The MPSA also coordinates with the JMPA for mail transportation from CONUS to the JOA. During contingency operations intra/inter-theater mail may be transported by commercial, contract, or military ground, sea, rail, and air transportation segments.

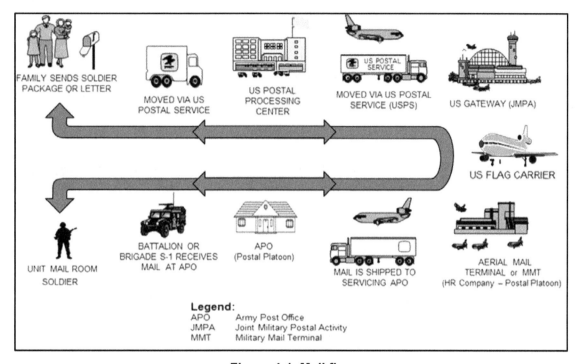

Figure 4-1. Mail flow

4-86. Upon notification from MPSA, the USPS sorts and packages mail, in time of war or emergency as determined by the Secretary of Defense. The Postal Service agrees to:

- Allow the DOD to control ZIP code assignment to all military units.
- Specify jointly with the MPSA the sorting of mail for overseas force.

4-87. The HR Company and subordinate postal platoons located at the MMT receive the mail and distribute it to HR companies supporting subordinate Corps and Division units, or postal platoons supporting subordinate brigades depending upon the size of the supported force. The postal platoon(s) receives mail dispatched from the MMT, sorts it by supported units, and prepares it for dispatch to designated MDPs. Company and battalion mail clerks pick-up mail from the MDP and coordinate delivery to addressees. Mail clerks coordinate collection of retro-grade mail from unit Soldiers and deliver it daily to the MDP at the same time as pick-up of unit mail. The same transportation used to deliver mail to MDPs transports retro-grade mail in reverse through the postal network.

4-88. The standard for JOA is unrestricted mail service, except for restrictions imposed by the host-nation. During the early stages of a contingency operation, it may be advisable for the commander to use the "X restriction" for personal mail, cassette tapes, post cards, and/or first class letters weighing more than 13 ounces. The commander may lift restrictions and permit parcels as the JOA matures, more postal personnel become available, and the theater ground transportation and airlift logistical systems mature.

4-89. It is important to note that organic transportation assets within postal units are structured to move assigned personnel and equipment, not JOA mail. The postal operations management network must coordinate all inbound and outbound mail transportation requirements with transportation managers at each level of command, from the MMT to the brigade MDP. Ultimately, effective mail movement requires assured military, contracted, and/or host-nation transportation support. The standard mail delivery time from CONUS to the JOA MMT is 14 days contingent upon a developed transportation network and METT-TC.

4-90. Postal communication requirements are voice and data connectivity. Postal elements must be capable of communicating and interfacing with USPS equipment (analog and commercial) and must be able to transmit and scan daily to AMPS. An AMPS facilitates work within the MPS and centralizes data into a single database which is universally accessed through the Internet. Determined by a user role and corresponding set of privileges, military mail transportation, finance, and MPO records and forms are immediately available to AMPS users regardless of location. Processing essential mail transportation forms and financial documents such as Postal Service Form 1412 (Daily Financial Report) are automated so the data is easily entered, edited, stored, and then transferred automatically to the USPS on a periodic basis. Ordering postal supplies, tracking postal offenses, and maintaining equipment inventories using Postal Service Form 1590 (Supplies and Equipment Receipt) are also available through AMPS.

4-91. Communication is also required with the HR Company, HROB, HRSC, MMT, and the supporting sustainment brigade. Additionally, database access to HR systems is required in order to establish and operate the postal directory, identify casualties for casualty mail operations, and to receive postal updates and alerts.

SECTION III – CASUALTY OPERATIONS

4-92. The mission of casualty operations is to record, verify, report, and process casualty information from unit level to CMAOC; notify appropriate individuals; and provide casualty assistance to the next of kin (NOK). A clear, collaborative system for casualty operations information is critical for effective management. When developing theater casualty operations policies and procedures, casualty managers must consider regulatory and doctrinal guidance. Casualty operations sections should include very clear verbiage regarding the mandate to safeguard casualty information to prevent premature and/or erroneous disclosure and to protect patient privacy.

4-93. Casualty operations include all actions relating to the production, dissemination, coordination, validation, and synchronization of casualty reporting. It includes submission of casualty reports, notification of NOK, briefing and assistance to the NOK, LOD determinations, 15-6 investigations, disposition of remains and PE (a responsibility of the MA organization of the supporting sustainment command), military burial honors, and casualty mail coordination. The role of the Casualty Assistance Center varies during contingency operations and they may be more involved in the casualty reporting functions. Casualty Assistance Centers are engaged in the notification and assistance aspect of casualty operations as prescribed in AR 600-8-1, Army Casualty Program. The following paragraphs describe critical responsibilities in a contingency operation.

4-94. Casualty Reporting: Units report casualties as they occur. A casualty is any person who is lost to the organization by reason of having been declared beleaguered, besieged, captured, dead, diseased, detained, DUSTWUN, injured, ill, interned, missing, MIA, or wounded. As depicted in Figure 4-2 on page 4-22, the DA Form 1156 (Casualty Feeder Card) , is a required template or tool Soldiers and units use to gather and report essential reporting information on all casualties as they occur. Accurate and timely casualty reporting is paramount; however, operational constraints may preclude units from meeting time requirements.

4-95. Use the DA Form 1156 template as a prompter to transmit essential elements of the casualty report by voice or electronically as soon as possible after the casualty occurs. Contingency related casualty reports are sent through command channels to the appropriate theater Casualty Assistance Center where all information is verified and forwarded to the CMAOC as soon as possible, but no later than 12 hours from the time of the incident. CMAOC is the functional proponent for Army-wide casualty operations and interfaces and synchronizes all casualty and MA operations between deployed units/commands, the installation Casualty Assistance Centers, and DOD agencies supporting Family members.

4-96. Casualty Notification: Casualty Assistance Centers are responsible for notifying the NOK residing within their area of responsibility. The method of notification varies, depending upon the type of casualty and circumstances surrounding the incident. Unit Rear Detachments must be capable of telephonically notifying the NOK of deployed injured/ill casualties when directed by CMAOC. CMAOC must approve any exception to established notification procedures outlined in AR 600-8-1.

4-97. Casualty Assistance: Provided to those receiving benefits and/or entitlements in cases of death, missing, or categorized as DUSTWUN/excused absence-whereabouts unknown. Installation Casualty Assistance Centers are responsible for providing assistance to the NOK residing within their area of responsibility. There is no time limitation for CAOs to provide assistance; however, during contingency operations, the duties of the CAO may last six months or more.

4-98. Army Fatal Incident and Family Brief: A presentation of the facts and findings of a collateral investigation of all operational and training deaths, friendly fire, and suicide incidents. The intent of the brief is to provide a thorough explanation of releasable investigative results to the PNOK and other Family members (as designated by the PNOK) in a timely, equitable, and professional manner. Additional information is available in AR 15-6 and AR 600-34, Fatal Training/Operational Accident Presentations to the Next of Kin.

4-99. Casualty Liaison Team: A CLT consists of HR personnel attached to MTFs, theater MA activities, and G-1/AG sections with the mission to obtain, verify, update, and disseminate casualty information to the appropriate personnel or organization in the casualty reporting chain. When deployed, CLTs assigned to an HR Company, report casualty information directly to the COD of the HRSC operating the theater Casualty Assistance Center and provide support to MTFs and G-1/AG and S-1 sections. CLTs begin coordination with patient administration offices to handle those casualties evacuated to military or Civilian hospitals within their AO. Mass casualty incidents or transfer of injured personnel may require treatment at hospitals outside the theater. CLTs are essential in providing updated information on all incapacitated, injured, or ill personnel through the theater Casualty Assistance Center to CMAOC. CMAOC then notifies the appropriate installation Casualty Assistance Center, who then provides updated information to the Family. CLTs also provide updated information as personnel transit through MTFs.

4-100. The Office of the Surgeon General is responsible for identifying the MTFs within the sustaining base to treat patients in the AO through MTF sourcing and outside the deployed AO for those patients evacuated from the deployed AO. Once identified, the theater Casualty Assistance Center ensures the CLT network is established, positioned, and resourced to support the deployed AO for casualty reporting.

4-101. Casualty Assistance Centers operate based upon a geographic AO and are responsible for training Soldiers from all components as CNOs and CAOs. During deployment, the theater Casualty Assistance Center is primarily involved with the casualty reporting process and, if applicable, notification of the NOK in theater.

4-102. There are five types of casualty reports: Initial (INIT), status change (STACH), Supplemental (SUPP), Progress, and Health and Welfare (peacetime only). All personnel must be sensitized to the confidentiality of casualty information. Commanders should ensure use of the DA Form 1156 as the template or tool to collect essential elements of casualty information that should be transmitted by voice or electronic means as quickly as possible. Casualty information is assigned the protective marking of "For Official Use Only" which may not be removed until verification that NOK have been notified. Information on a Soldier, DA Civilian, or CAAF (including other designated contractor personnel) in a missing status will remain "For Official Use Only" until the person is returned to military control or a change in status is made by the adjutant general. Emphasis on accuracy, completeness, confidentiality, and sensitivity of casualty information should be part of DA Form 1156 training to call in an INIT casualty report. This emphasis should be integrated into formal training programs, to include DCIPS training, at all levels. Speed is important and accuracy is essential.

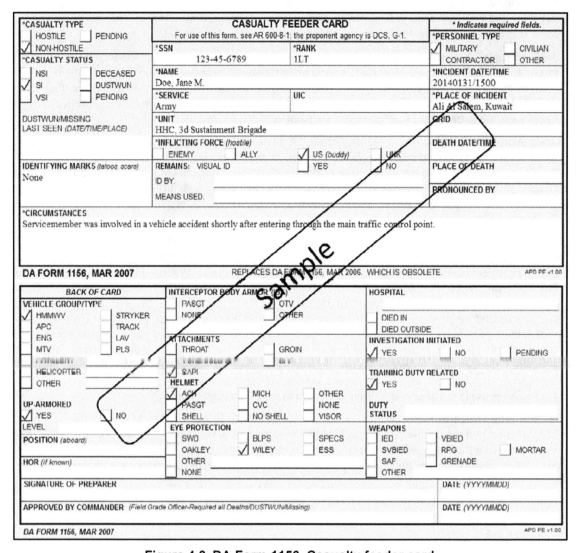

Figure 4-2. DA Form 1156, Casualty feeder card

4-103. Casualty operations management requires the production, verification, and dissemination of information from:

- DA Form 1156.
- Individual information from the supporting brigade S-1.
- Strength-related/duty status change information from CLTs and brigade S-1s.
- Admissions and disposition reports from Role 3 combat support hospitals.
- Individual diagnosis and prognosis reports from MTFs.
- Status of remains from the preparing mortuary.
- Straggler information from the Provost Marshal.

4-104. The casualty report is the source document used to provide information to the Family. Therefore, it is important that the information reported, especially the circumstances of the casualty incident, be as detailed and accurate as possible, and in terminology that can be readily understood by someone with no military background. The reportable categories of casualties and the procedures for preparing a DA Form 1156 are outlined in AR 600-8-1. Casualty information is collected on the battlefield from available sources and reported through official channels as quickly as possible. Since casualties can occur on the first day of an operation, casualty managers from the S-1 section need to deploy as part of each command's early entry element.

4-105. Each individual Soldier should carry a blank DA Form 1156 for casualty reporting purposes. The 2007 version of DA Form 1156 also serves as the witness card. Persons having firsthand knowledge of a reportable casualty should prepare the DA Form 1156. Squad leaders and platoon sergeants are encouraged to carry extra copies of DA Form 1156. Soldiers report casualties they witness or find, to include American civilians, personnel of other Services, Joint, and multi-national forces, using DA Form 1156 as a prompting tool when calling in or electronically transmitting the essential elements of the casualty report. If DA Form 1156 is not available, casualty information is written on blank paper and called in to higher command channels, where the report collector can prompt for information using the DA Form 1156 or DCIPS-CF. The written information is then forwarded to the company commander/First Sergeant as a follow-up to the initial transmission.

RESPONSIBILITES

4-106. Commanders must ensure procedures are followed IAW established timelines for AR 15-6 investigations and presentation to the NOK. G-1/AGs, C-1s, J-1s, and Staff Judge Advocates have the primary responsibility to update CMAOC on the status of investigations and provide unedited copies of approved investigations.

4-107. Multiple agencies, units, and echelons of command have critical roles in establishing and operating the casualty operations system. The levels of commands and their supporting agencies' responsibilities for casualty functions and tasks are listed in table 4-2 on pages 4-23 and continued on 4-24.

Table 4-2. Casualty operations

FUNCTION/ TASK	S-1/G-1	S-4/G-4	Mortuary Affairs	Theater Casualty Assistance Center	Installation Casualty Assistance Center	HR Platoon (CLT)	Postal Platoon	CMAOC
Report Casualty	×			×		×		
Manage Casualty File	×			×	×			×
Appoint Summary Court Officer	×				×			
Disposition of Remains		×	×		×			×
Disposition of Personal Effects		×			×			×
Line of Duty Investigation	×			×	×			
Survivor Assistance					×			×
Casualty Mail	×						×	
Burial Honors					×			×
Posthumous Awards & Decorations	×							×

Table 4-2. Casualty operations

FUNCTION/ TASK	S-1/G-1	S-4/G-4	Mortuary Affairs	Theater Casualty Assistance Center	Installation Casualty Assistance Center	HR Platoon (CLT)	Postal Platoon	CMAOC
Letter of Sympathy/Cond olence	×			×	×			
Fatal Training/Operat ional Brief	×							×
Establish Casualty Working Group					×			×
Issue Next of Kin Travel Orders					×			×
Legend: HR- Human Resources; CLT- Casualty Liaison Team; CMAOC- Casualty Mortuary Affairs Operations Center								

HRC-CMAOC

4-108. CMAOC publishes regulatory and procedural guidance governing casualty operations, assistance and insurance management, care and disposition of remains, disposition of PE, and LOD programs, and has the following responsibilities for casualty operations:

- Provides direction and assistance to Casualty Assistance Centers relating to casualty operations management, disposition of remains, LOD processing, and disposition of remains.
- Assists the HRSC in establishing connectivity for casualty reporting.
- Provides direction to mortuary liaison team(s) at the Dignified Transfer location.
- Provides coordination and transportation for Families attending the Dignified Transfer location.
- Coordinates collection of Soldier ID media.
- Synchronizes casualty operations with Casualty Assistance Centers.
- Processes travel and transportation orders for up to three Family members of very seriously injured/ill, seriously injured/ill, and at times, for not seriously injured/ill Soldiers.
- Receives AR 15-6 investigations for all deaths.
- Coordinates Army Fatal Incident and Family briefings to the PNOK.
- Acts as final determination authority for all death-related LOD determinations.
- Establishes and operates the Joint Personal Effects Depot to support the expeditious return of PE during contingency operations.
- Conducts boards required by the Missing Persons Act and Missing Service Personnel Act, IAW DODI 2310.5.
- Serves as the DOD Executive Agent for casualty operations and MA programs (to include the Central Joint Mortuary Affairs Board).
- Serves as the DOD proponent for DCIPS.
- Provides a training package to Casualty Assistance Centers for all CNOs and CAOs.

THEATER (ASCC) G-1/AG

4-109. The Army/ASCC G-1/AG has the following casualty operations responsibilities:

- Develops a casualty OPLAN and policies for theater.
- Provides oversight for theater casualty operations.

- Establishes and administers casualty reporting authorities for submission of casualty reports (based on guidance and agreements from the JTF commander, JFLCC, and CFLCC). Note: The authority to approve and release casualty reports directly to CMAOC may be granted to Corps commanders. In these cases, provide a copy of the casualty report to the theater Casualty Assistance Center.
- Establishes policy for the location of CLTs
- Coordinates with the TSC to ensure the HRSC establishes the theater Casualty Assistance Center as part of theater opening operations.
- Advises the commander on the status of casualty operations.
- Ensures casualty operations and capabilities are included as part of early entry operations.

CORPS AND DIVISION G-1/AG

4-110.   The Corps G-1/AG has the following casualty operations responsibilities:
- Develops an SOP for casualty operations.
- Submits INIT casualty reports using DCIPS to the theater Casualty Assistance Center within 8-10 hours from time of incident (dependent on routing). Note: If the Corps is granted authority by the JTF commander, JFLCC, or CFLCC, reports may be submitted directly to CMAOC with a copy provided to the theater Casualty Assistance Center.
- Administers authority levels for submission of casualty reports for assigned and attached units.
- Maintains casualty information of all assigned or attached personnel.
- Submits STACH and SUPP casualty reports in a timely manner.
- Uses DA Form 1156 as the template or tool to capture casualty information for generating the INIT casualty report.
- Ensures letters of sympathy and/or condolence are completed.
- Ensures casualty operations are included in all OPLANs and OPORDs.
- Synchronizes casualty matters between the G-1/AG and G-4.
- Ensures completion of all LOD investigations and boards as required
- Advises the commander on the status of casualties.
- Includes operations and capabilities as part of early entry operations.

4-111.   The Division G-1/AG has the following casualty operations responsibilities:
- Develops an SOP for casualty operations.
- Submits INIT casualty reports using DCIPS to the theater Casualty Assistance Center within 8-10 hours from time of incident (dependent on routing).
- Administers authority levels for submission of casualty reports for assigned and attached units.
- Maintains casualty information of all assigned or attached personnel.
- Submits STACH and SUPP casualty reports in a timely manner.
- Uses DA Form 1156 as the template or tool to capture casualty information for generating the INIT casualty report.
- Ensures casualty operations are included in all OPLANs and OPORDs.
- Includes operations and capabilities as part of early entry operations.
- Ensures letters of sympathy and/or condolence are completed.
- Synchronizes casualty matters between the S-1 and S-4.
- Ensures completion of all LOD investigations and boards as required.
- Advises the commander on the status of casualties.

4-112.   The Corps and Division G-1/AG have the following responsibilities if serving as the Army Forces G-1/AG:
- Serves as the casualty manager for the AO.
- Coordinates with the TSC to ensure the HRSC establishes the theater Casualty Assistance Center for the AO.

- Establishes connectivity with CMAOC and maintains casualty information flow.
- Ensures CLTs are located at hospitals, MA collection points, and other locations as required.
- Synchronizes casualty operations between the G-1/AGs, CLTs, public affairs, MTFs, MA, intelligence activities, and others as directed by DA.
- Includes casualty managers as part of all early entry modules and teams.

BRIGADE S-1/STB S-1 (GENERAL OFFICER-LEVEL HQS)

4-113. The brigade S-1 has the responsibility to maintain casualty reports and the status of all assigned and attached personnel at MTFs. The brigade S-1 is the point of entry for casualty data into DCIPS within six hours from time of incident, conditions permitting, and is required to submit SUPP, STACH, and Progress reports as applicable. Field grade commanders or their designated field grade representative must authenticate casualty reports for accuracy and completeness. Brigades are responsible for coordinating with the Fatal Accident section of CMAOC whenever there is a military-related accidental death or any death within the unit that is covered by AR 600-34 for the required Family briefing. Note: S-1s should refer to ATTP 1-0.1, Appendix D, S-1 Assessment Checklist, and use the checklist to assess the effectiveness of brigade casualty operations. During contingencies, the brigade S-1 has the following casualty operations responsibilities:

- Ensures the Rear Detachment maintains a roster of trained and certified CNOs and CAOs.
- Ensures the Rear Detachment makes telephonic notification for all injured and ill Soldiers as directed by CMAOC.
- Ensures the Rear Detachment identifies and trains sufficient personnel to serve as SCMOs to secure and process home station PE.
- Develops an SOP for casualty operations.
- Maintains personnel asset visibility on all assigned or attached personnel, other Service personnel, DOD and DA Civilians, and CAAF. Provides accountability information to Personnel Recovery (PR) Cells and other staff agencies to maintain 100% force accountability.
- Maintains a personnel information database as directed by the ASCC G-1/AG for the purposes of assisting PR operations; PR Cell requires information on isolated, missing, detained, or captured personnel. This is especially important if the individual in question did not complete DD Form 1833 Test (V2), (Isolated Personnel Report) or Civilian equivalent form.
- Receives casualty information from subordinate battalion S-1 sections, from tactical voice and data nets, using the DA Form 1156 as a template to collect all essential elements of the casualty report, from brigades' ad hoc CLTs.
- Verifies that Soldiers casualty information (DD Form 93/SGLV Form 8286) is current on iPERMS; forwards updates to CMAOC through the appropriate Casualty Assistance Center, as required.
- Submits casualty reports to the Corps and Division G-1/AG, or deployed theater Casualty Assistance Center, IAW ASCC G-1/AG casualty reporting guidance using DCIPS-CF/CR or directed system within six hours from time of incident, when conditions permit; PR Cell must be informed of DUSTWUN incidents and casualty reports.
- Maintains coordination with the surgeon, MTF, and medical company to monitor status of patients, both those further evacuated and those ultimately RTD from the medical company.
- Submits SUPP reports when the status of the casualty changes or whenever additional information becomes available, to include the initiation of, or completion of, any death investigation.
- Monitors and appoints SCMOs for PE, as required, and ensures compliance with provisions of AR 638-2, Care and Disposition of Remains and Disposition of Personal Effects, to include submission of the interim and final SCMO report to CMAOC. Refer to DA PAM 638-2, Procedures for the Care and Disposition of Remains and Disposition of Personal Effects, for additional guidance.
- Processes posthumous promotions, awards, and U. S. citizenship, if appropriate.

- Prepares appointment orders for investigation officers to conduct AR 15-6 collateral investigations into all hostile deaths and military-related accidental deaths and friendly fire incidents.

- Monitors and appoints LOD investigating officer for non-hostile injuries and deaths, as directed by the commander.

- Prepares and dispatches letters of sympathy/condolence as required by the commander. (Note: Battalion commanders are required to prepare letters IAW AR 600-8-1, but many brigade commanders also have the S-1 prepare a corresponding letter).

- Ensures casualty operations are included in all OPLANs and OPORDs.

- Updates status of patients to the commander, subordinate S-1s, and Rear Detachment commander as they move through the medical system using DCIPS-CF (by monitoring progress reports submitted), the brigade surgeon, and when required, verbal coordination with MTFs.

- Analyzes personnel strength data to determine current capabilities and project future requirements; tracks the status and location of recovered personnel until they complete the reintegration process. Note: PR Cells might require additional staffing to fulfill assigned responsibilities. Additional maneuver forces may also be required for PR missions.

- Ensures casualty operations and capabilities are included as part of early entry operations.

- Establishes and convenes a casualty working group to ensure all actions that are required to be completed in the aftermath of a casualty incident are coordinated and completed.

BATTALION S-1

4-114. The battalion S-1 has the responsibility to prepare casualty reports and maintain the status of assigned and attached personnel at MTFs. Battalion S-1s forward all original casualty forms (to include DD Form 93 and SGLV Form 8286) to the brigade. The battalion processes casualty reports using the DA Form 1156 as a template to capture the information needed to complete a casualty report and ensures the form is completely filled out and submitted to the brigade S-1 within three hours, conditions permitting. Field grade commanders or their designated field grade representative at battalion must approve casualty reports for accuracy and completeness. Note: S-1s should refer to ATTP 1-0.1, Appendix D, S-1 Assessment Checklist, and use the checklist to assess the effectiveness of battalion casualty operations. During contingencies, the battalion S-1 has the following casualty operations responsibilities:

- Develops an SOP for casualty operations.

- Maintains personnel asset visibility on all assigned or attached personnel. Provides accountability information to PR Cells and other staff agencies to maintain 100% force accountability.

- Ensures all S-1 personnel are trained on casualty reporting procedures, maintain required copies of DA Form 1156, and understand how to use the form as a template or prompter to relay the essential elements of the casualty report by voice or electronic means as quickly as possible after a casualty incident occurs.

- Receives casualty information from subordinate or attached units (information may be received via casualty reporting system, DA Form 1156(s), radio, or by other available methods).

- Notifies the commander and Chaplain when a casualty occurs.

- Reviews and approves casualty information (verified through CLT, MA collection points, straggler information, provost marshal channels, or individual personnel).

- Submits INIT casualty reports to the brigade S-1 using DCIPS-CF when available or via DA Form 1156 when DCIPS-CF is not available. When required, ensures a field grade officer from the battalion reviews and authenticates casualty information prior to submission of the INIT report. (If the tactical situation does not allow a review, follow-up the INIT report with a SUPP report as soon as possible).

- Coordinates with the surgeon, battalion aid station, or medical company to monitor status of patients.

- Provides SUPP reports whenever any additional casualty information is confirmed or when the circumstances as initially reported require updating.

- Processes awards and U. S. citizenship actions, if applicable.

- Appoints SCMO for PE.
- Coordinates for an investigating officer to conduct AR 15-6 investigations (required for hostile deaths, suspected suicides, deaths resulting from military-related accidents, or friendly fire incidents).
- Ensures casualty operations are included in all OPLANs and OPORDs.
- Appoints LOD investigating officer for non-hostile injuries and deaths, as directed by commander.
- Prepares, reviews, and dispatches letters of sympathy and/or condolence.
- Tracks evacuated casualties back to home station.
- Analyzes personnel strength data to determine current capabilities and project future requirements; tracks the status and location of recovered personnel until they complete the reintegration process. Note: PR Cells might require additional staffing to fulfill assigned responsibilities. Additional maneuver forces may also be required for PR missions.
- Maintains a personnel information data base; PR Cell requires information on isolated, missing, detained, or captured personnel. (Note: This is especially important if the individuals in question did not complete DD Form 1833 Test (V2), or Civilian equivalent form).
- Updates the commander on the status of casualties.
- Ensures casualty operations and capabilities are included as part of early entry operations.

HRSC, COD

4-115. The HRSC, COD establishes the theater Casualty Assistance Center and manages casualty reporting within the theater of operations IAW policies established by the ASCC G-1/AG. Refer to ATP 1-0.2 for specific responsibilities of the COD and detailed duties of personnel assigned to the COD.

HRSC, POD

4-116. The HRSC, POD develops guidance in the form of policy letters or SOPs in the area of casualty mail. The HRSC, POD is responsible for providing oversight to ensure all postal Soldiers receive and practice thorough casualty mail procedures (due to sensitive nature). Refer to ATP 1-0.2 for specific responsibilities of the POD and detailed duties of personnel assigned to the POD.

HROB

4-117. The HROB monitors casualty operations within their AO, including manning and tracking the placement of CLTs. Refer to ATP 1-0.2 for specific casualty responsibilities of the HROB.

HR COMPANY HQS

4-118. The HR Company HQs provides mission command, planning, and technical support to all assigned or attached CLTs and delivers HR area support for casualty operations in the deployed AO. The HR Company HQs ensures proper resourcing for all CLTs to perform casualty reporting tasks. Refer to ATP 1-0.2 for further information regarding the HR Company HQ's casualty operations responsibilities.

HR PLATOON

4-119. The HR Platoon receives all administrative guidance through the HR Company HQs and functions as part of the theater Casualty Assistance Center or Corps and Division G-1/AG in a deployed environment. The HR Platoon provides leadership, training assistance, and administrative support to CLTs. Refer to ATP 1-0.2 for further information regarding the HR Platoon's casualty operations responsibilities.

CLT

4-120. The mission of the CLT is to provide accurate and timely casualty reporting and tracking information at MTFs, MA collection points, and other locations. CLTs report directly to the HRSC, COD operating the theater Casualty Assistance Center and provide support to hospitals, G-1/AGs, and S-1s.

CLTs must deploy as members of all early entry elements to facilitate the casualty information flow of accurate and timely reporting. CLTs serve as a liaison for each affected commander and unit, provide updated status reports to the affected unit, and inform the unit if the affected Soldier leaves theater. Refer to ATP 1-0.2 for further information regarding the CLT. Specific CLT responsibilities include, but are not limited to the following:

- Maintains liaison with supported units, MTFs, and G-1/AGs.
- Develops an SOP for casualty operations.
- Ensures timely reporting of casualty information to the theater Casualty Assistance Center, the G-1/AG, and unit S-1.
- Verifies casualty information and forwards it to the theater Casualty Assistance Center, the G-1/AG, and unit S-1.
- Assists commanders in maintaining accurate casualty information throughout the duration of an operation.
- Ensures personnel are cross-trained to allow for rotations in duty assignments between the G-1/AG, MTF, and MA collection points to provide a break from the emotional nature of the duty.
- Assists with coordinating a Soldier's RTD with the unit and/or a PAT.
- Reviews each patient's status, documents newly arrived patients, and collects casualty related information for entry into the DCIPS database.
- Assists injured Soldiers in obtaining access to necessary services such as military pay and MWR.

CASUALTY ASSISTANCE CENTER

4-121. Casualty Assistance Centers provide casualty notification and assistance to include: assisting Families with survivor's benefits and entitlements; coordinating escorts for remains; making funeral arrangements to include Family funeral travel; and providing military burial honors and PE disposition (the Rear Detachment SCMO handles PE at home station). Casualty Assistance Centers operate based upon a geographic area of responsibility and may, depending on the situation, extend beyond their area of responsibility. They operate both in peacetime and during contingency operations. During contingency operations, the theater Casualty Assistance Center is primarily involved with the casualty reporting process, and the installation Casualty Assistance Center is mainly involved with the notification and assistance to the NOK. The Casualty Assistance Center, with direction from CMAOC, is also responsible for the following:

- Developing an SOP for casualty operations.
- Coordinating planeside honors in the AO.
- Coordinating all dignified transfer of remains travel.
- Monitoring, uploading, and updating memorial, mortuary, benefits and entitlements, and casualty assistance tracking for caseload in the AO.
- Providing training for Soldiers and personnel from all components as CNOs and CAOs.
- Coordinating fatal training accident briefs to the PNOK.

PRE-DEPLOYMENT ACTIONS

4-122. The brigade S-1 ensures the following tasks are accomplished by subordinate units prior to deployment:

- Appoints a SCMO for the AO and for the Rear Detachment to process the PE of deceased Soldiers in coordination with the S-4. Coordinates SCMO appointment with the command's servicing judge advocate.
- Ensures all deploying Soldiers and Family members view the pre-deployment casualty preparedness training videos.
- Briefs Soldiers on the importance of updating wills and gives each the opportunity to update DD Form 93 and SGLV Form 8286.

- Includes awards scrubs as part of pre-deployment operations; ensures each Soldier reviews and updates their officer or enlisted record brief, with special emphasis on awards during pre-deployment operations.
- Ensures each Soldier's current DD Form 93 and SGLV form-series are signed either digitally or personally and posted to the Soldier's iPERMS record. Maintains a copy of DD Form 93 and SGLV Form 8286 on file for each Soldier assigned or attached at Soldier's home station and with the deployed unit. Home station maintains these documents with original signatures.
- Coordinates with the S-6 to ensure capability to email casualty reports to brigade.
- Provides the Rear Detachment POC information to home station Casualty Assistance Center and ensures Rear Detachment personnel are trained on how to conduct telephonic notification to the NOK of injured and ill Soldiers.
- Ensures all DCIPS users are fully trained on casualty reporting procedures.
- Establishes a list of mature Soldiers to be trained as CNOs and CAOs and coordinates with the home station Casualty Assistance Center to ensure appointed personnel are trained and certified by the supporting center.
- Contacts Army Case Management personnel at the U. S. Air Force Mortuary Affairs Operations Center, located in Dover, Delaware, before forwarding unit patches and sets of unit crests. Contact Army Case Management personnel at (502) 613-9025, or at www.mortuary.af.mil.
- Trains Soldiers on DA Form 1156; ensures use of DA Form 1156 as a template for calling in essential information after a casualty incident.
- Develops a casualty SOP. Casualty SOPs should include DCIPS-CF/CR training (software should be loaded on several computers); procedures for processing posthumous awards and combat badges; casualty notification to Families of injured or ill Soldiers when directed by CMAOC; expediting citizenship requests; conducting unit memorial services; processing LOD investigations and determinations; and for processing of theater and home station PE, to include appointment and training of SCMOs; and define unit specifics for military funeral honors.

CASUALTY ESTIMATION

4-123. The Army G-1 is the functional proponent for Army total mission casualty estimation (KIA, captured, MIA, and WIA). The Army Surgeon General is the functional proponent for Army disease and non-battle injury (DNBI) casualty estimation. The Army G-1 is the functional proponent for overall casualty estimation, covering both total mission casualty and DNBI, in support of projected manning requirements. The Director, Military Personnel Management oversees policy and oversight of Army casualty estimation (to include methods and procedures) for the Army G-1.

4-124. Casualty estimation is conducted at division-level and above as part of the planning process for contingency operations. Casualty estimates support operations planning, future force planning, and staff training. Supported functions include:

- Commander's evaluation of a COA by assessment of force strength for missions within the concept of operations and scheme of maneuver.
- Personnel replacements flow planning, and allocation among forces (if casualty shelves are used).
- Medical support planning for both force structure and sustainment support.
- Transportation planning, including both inter and intra-theater requirements, to deliver medical force structure and to evacuate and replace personnel.
- Evacuation policy options to sustain the force by balancing minimal support force footprint, maximum in-theater RTDs, and stable personnel rotation.

4-125. The G-1/AG, as the principal staff officer for manning the force (personnel readiness requirements, projections, and recommendations), prepares the casualty estimate as part of the operations order. The G-1/AG estimates mission casualties and administrative losses and combines this with the medical staff's DNBI estimate.

4-126. The G-1/AG and surgeon (medical staff) coordinates with the commander's staff so estimated casualties reasonably reflect projected force activity in the planning scenario. The G-1/AG is to:

- Consolidate the overall casualty estimate, stratify projected losses by skill and grade, project personnel readiness requirements, and recommend and plan support for appropriate replacements from home stations and evacuation flows.
- Coordinate with other staff elements that use casualty projections to guide their planning process which includes higher command levels and Army and/or Joint lift planners.

ACHIEVING REASONABLE CASUALTY ESTIMATES

4-127. Ensuring reasonable casualty estimates requires more than a numeric estimating procedure or set of rates; a rates frame of reference is critical to show which rates relate to which variables, and how. The currently approved and mandated methodology for deriving casualty rates for operational planning is the Benchmark Rate Structure (BRS) which orients the planner by showing how rates vary as forces (size, type), time (duration of rate application), and operational settings vary. The BRS describes rate ranges and patterns seen in actual operations for both maneuver forces (battalions, brigades, divisions) and support forces across the spectrum of conventional operations, including major combat and stability operations. The operating environments described range from peer or near-peer confrontations, to overwhelming dominance by one side, to isolated asymmetric events. There is currently no approved estimation tool at this time so planners must temper their estimates with these limitations in mind.

4-128. The BRS permits bracketing optimistic-to-pessimistic rate possibilities and settling on a risk-based recommendation. An estimate may be built directly from the BRS, or the planner may use it to assess the reasonableness of rates from any source or method. Functional area planning rests, ultimately, on projected numbers of casualties. However, the reasonableness of the numbers must first be established. This requires use of casualty rates, which reference (normalize) the numbers to the population-at-risk and the time (number of days) during which the casualties are generated. Rates are expressed in numbers of casualties per 1,000 personnel (population-at-risk) per day. Standard notation is [number]/1,000/day. Figure 4-3 on page 4-32 depicts the BRS with key parameters.

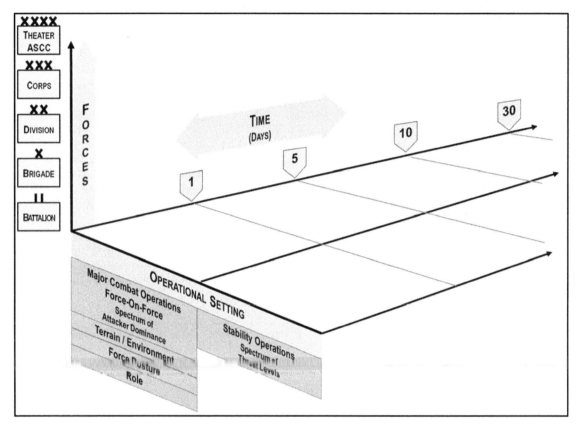

Figure 4-3. Benchmark rate structure (BRS) with key parameters

4-129. Rates vary in terms of three broad operational parameters: forces, time, and operational setting. Forces and time are straightforward. Four distinctive operational settings have been observed in modern distributed ground operations, three major combat (force-on-force) settings, and one stability operations setting. A planning projection accounts for the METT-TC to include force postures (offense/defense) and roles (shape/dominate). However, the key to rate reasonableness is the commander's intent and visualization of force results over time in the METT-TC.

4-130. Major combat (force-on-force) operational settings feature combat episodes (focused, with respect to casualty experience, in ground maneuver elements) that exhibit a spectrum of attacker dominance. The key indicator is the effect of the attack on the coherence of the main defense:

- Episodes usually involving peer opponents—where the attacker's maneuvers and fires (to penetrate, envelope, and turn) fail to undermine the coherence of the defender's main defense. Combat episodes (offensive and defensive) will recur; operations may continue indefinitely, possibly over long periods.
- Episodes involving peer or near-peer opponents—when the attacker's scheme of maneuver and fires affect one or more breaches of the main defense's coherence. Episodes may be low-order (with no, or only limited, exploitation) or high-order (deeper exploitation). However, the defender effectively resists in some sectors; the attack culminates before achieving full operational objectives.
- Episodes when the attacker overwhelmingly dominates the defender—all attacking forces (decisive and shaping) reach operational and strategic depths rapidly. Operations to secure a larger area following main defenses collapse may blend into stability operations.

4-131. Stability operations setting. Stability operations cover a spectrum of threat environments with a wide range of hostility levels. Instead of rates tied to force role and effectiveness in a scheme of maneuver, the force operates in an AO (all-aspect, 360° orientation). Casualty incidents occur across the force, centered in higher-risk regions or force elements. Force rates are defined for 30-day periods (with particular incidents then definable probabilistically and in terms of variable force risk levels across units, functions, or regions). Three broad threat environments, showing ranges of hostility levels, have been seen:

- Peacekeeping/Humanitarian Assistance—no hostilities; DNBI only (e.g., Sinai, Bosnia, and Haiti).
- Peace enforcement—a range of hostility levels seen (low, medium, high); mission casualty and DNBI (e.g., Kosovo, Afghanistan, Somalia, and Iraq).
- Foreign internal defense—a range of hostility levels seen (low, medium, medium-high, high); mission casualty and DNBI (e.g., Vietnam).

ENABLING APPLICATIONS

4-132. The BRS and its "rate patterns" approach support mission casualty estimates for field forces. There is no approved automated tool for BRS and "rate pattern" estimation.

4-133. The Medical Analysis Tool, used at senior commands, and required for Service and Joint scenarios casualty planning, is not an estimation tool. It requires that planners define their own rates.

PLANNING ESTIMATE PRODUCTS

4-134. The estimate may present three views of a casualty profile ("casualty stream"):

- Multi-day force averages as they vary over time, notably for maneuver forces.
- Peak 1-day ("hot spot") rates, especially for maneuver forces during pulses.
- Cumulative casualties – full scenario or user-defined periods (as appropriate).

4-135. The mission casualty estimate identifies:

- Killed, Captured, or MIA.
- WIA: admissions and RTD in 72 hours.

4-136. The DNBI estimate identifies both disease and nonbattle injury admissions.

BATTLEFIELD FLOW

4-137. Collect casualty information from all available sources on the battlefield and report through official channels as quickly as possible. Since casualties can occur on the first day of an operation, casualty managers from each echelon of command need to deploy as part of each echelon's early entry elements. In the absence of an HRSC, the senior element G-1/AG and S-1 must be ready to immediately assume the role of the Casualty Assistance Center. The casualty reporting mission needs to take priority and additional requirements for information from higher levels may increase the complexity of the reporting requirements. Battlefield tracking and accountability of CAAF includes providing casualty information to the theater Casualty Assistance Center and/or CMAOC. Figure 4-4 on page 4-34 depicts the theater casualty reporting flow.

4-138. The DA Form 1156 is used to submit an INIT report when a casualty incident is observed. The DA Form 1156 is used to document critical information which is forwarded to the battalion S-1 section for submission to the brigade S-1 section. The brigade S-1 section prepares the INIT casualty report in DCIPS-CF and forwards the report to the theater Casualty Assistance Center for further submission to CMAOC. (Note: Based on guidance from the JTF commander, the JFLCC, CFLCC, or Army/ASCC G-1/AG may delegate authority for Corps commanders to release casualty reports directly to CMAOC with a copy provided to the theater Casualty Assistance Center). Due to the personal nature of information within casualty reports, the theater Casualty Assistance Center reports casualty information to the CMAOC using DCIPS as the official means of casualty reporting.

4-139. Soldiers may immediately medically evacuate to an MTF where the CLT, in coordination with the Soldier's unit, may generate the DCIPS report for submission to the theater Casualty Assistance Center. Information includes date and time of the casualty, circumstances, and location. CLTs work directly for the HRSC, COD operating the theater Casualty Assistance Center and provide support to hospitals, G-1/AGs, and S-1s unless otherwise determined by the OPORD.

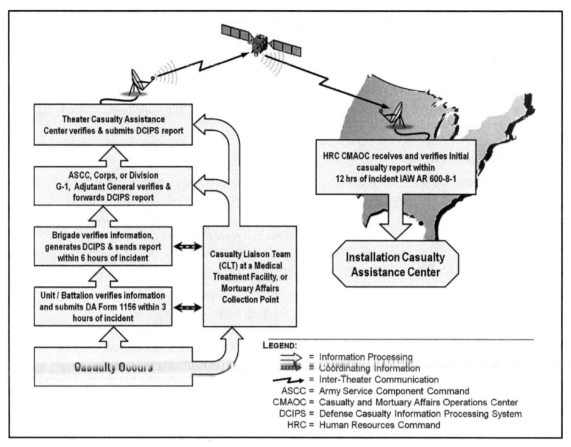

Figure 4-4. The casualty reporting flow

4-140. For injured and ill Soldiers who desire for their NOK to be notified, CMAOC contacts the supporting Casualty Assistance Center who contacts the Soldier's Rear Detachment. The Rear Detachment makes telephonic notification for injured and ill Soldiers and then reports back to the installation Casualty Assistance Center when notification is complete. Once notification is complete, and if the Soldier's doctor requests their presence, CMAOC calls the NOK and prepares Invitational Travel Orders for travel to the injured or ill Soldier's bedside. CMAOC contacts the supporting CONUS/OCONUS Casualty Assistance Center to coordinate for notification of NOK (as per the DD Form 93) for deceased Soldiers.

4-141. The DA Form 1156 data fields align with DCIPS. Data fields marked by an asterisk (*) indicate minimum requirements needed to send a casualty report forward. Validate casualty information for accuracy and completeness prior to submission. A SUPP report can follow to further document and complete the report without holding up the INIT report. Too many details included in the INIT report can lead to misinformation relayed to Families rather than accurate information provided later in SUPP reports. Figure 4-5 illustrates the casualty reporting and tracking flow (reporting process).

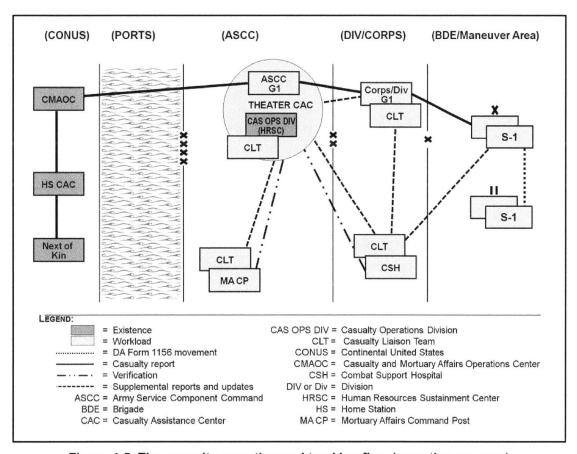

Figure 4-5. The casualty reporting and tracking flow (reporting process)

This page intentionally left blank.

Chapter 5

Coordinate Personnel Support

Personnel support activities encompass those functions and activities which contribute to unit readiness by promoting fitness, building morale and cohesion, enhancing quality of life, and by providing recreational, social, and other support services for Soldiers, DOD Civilians, and other personnel who deploy with the force. Personnel support encompasses the following functions: MWR, Command Interest Programs, and Band Operations. The G-1/AG or S-1 has staff responsibility for personnel support.

SECTION I – MORALE, WELFARE, AND RECREATION (MWR) SUPPORT

5-1. MWR programs are those activities that support and improve the morale and well-being of the deployed force. These include activities sponsored by the IMCOM G-9, other agencies, and commands at all levels. The terminology used in this publication is not synonymous with official Family and Morale, Welfare, and Recreation programs sponsored by the Army, but may include such programs.

5-2. MWR support is mission essential to combat readiness (JP 1-0). MWR programs enhance the quality of life for deployed forces and address the strategic imperatives of the Joint expeditionary Army. The deployed force includes:

- Soldiers.
- DOD Civilians.
- CAAF.

5-3. Commanders at all levels are responsible for ensuring MWR support programs are available. They are responsible for determining different levels of required support based on the mission, anticipated duration of deployment, theater environmental conditions, and higher command requirements. MWR support is METT-TC driven, and commanders must be able to quickly revise plans, programming, and support levels to adapt to changing situations and requirements. MWR support programs may include such activities as:

- Sports activities.
- Libraries.
- Clubs.
- Entertainment.
- AAFES.
- Fitness and recreation.
- ARC support.
- Internet facilities.
- Health and comfort packs (HCPs).
- Other activities that support the well-being of the deployed force.

5-4. MWR support includes a wide variety of services. During the initial deployment and early sustainment phase of military operations, only minimum MWR services are provided. Minimum services include brigade sports equipment, HCPs, ARC, and limited AAFES.

5-5. The combatant commander, through his J-1/G-1 and J-4/G-4, determines MWR needs and requirements based on operational tempo and available MWR resources. While the J-1/G-1 is the primary staff office responsible for MWR, the J-4/G-4 is responsible for the execution of MWR logistics support requirements. Depending on AO stability and actions, the commander may use alternative sources such as the Logistics Civil Augmentation Program (LOGCAP) or other contracted personnel.

5-6.   The availability of personnel and facilities provided by the MWR network depends on the combatant commander's command policies and the operational/tactical situation.   Planners at all levels ensure operational plans include requirements for fitness and recreation, AAFES support, and community support functions such as ARC.

5-7.   G-1/AG and S-1 staffs at battalion and above need to be aware of the full range of MWR services and programs and incorporate them into OPLANS and OPORDs. They must also be knowledgeable of key staff players who support the execution of MWR programs. For example, the S-4 is responsible for coordination and execution of logistics support for MWR services and programs. These services are in the form of unit recreation, library book kits, sports programs, and rest areas at brigade and higher. The MWR network also provides facilities such as recreation centers, internet cafés, and activity centers for deployed personnel that house a number of MWR functions.

5-8.   Civilian recreation staff is available to assist in the planning and execution of necessary support services. Commanders identify appropriate civilian positions on the Mobilization TDA in preparation of deployment into the theater of operations to support recreation requirements. When this method of staffing is used, civilian MWR personnel are added to the "battle-roster" of brigade and larger-sized units' staffs. These personnel normally become members of the G-1/AG and S-1 staffs, and they plan and coordinate MWR activities prior to and during mobilization. These personnel may also deploy with the unit to accomplish brigade and higher staff MWR responsibilities and assist the unit athletic and recreation (A&R) officer or NCO (military personnel) in planning and executing MWR programs.

5-9.   IMCOM HQs maintains a roster of MWR emergency essential civilian (EEC) personnel who are available to augment the G 1/AG and S-1 in coordinating and conducting MWR support activities. Upon deployment, MWR EEC specialists are paid with contingency funds. Both appropriated fund and non-appropriated fund (NAF) MWR personnel may be used, but NAF salaries of deployed personnel are reimbursed to the appropriate NAF account with contingency funds IAW DOD MWR Utilization, Support and Accountability rules.

5-10. Special duty manpower from ASCC assets and contingent hires may also be used to assist in program execution and facility operation. The Army G-3 may also provide civilian fitness and recreation staff from other installations through the Worldwide Individual Augmentation System tasking authority to IMCOM. Commanders need to establish and validate requirements on their Mobilization TDA for MWR EEC civilian positions.

5-11. Unit commanders are responsible for procurement of unit level recreation kits.   These kits are designed to be packaged and distributed to each company size unit for all components. Recreation kits are part of a unit's TOE and deploys with the unit as a portable means to fulfill recreation and leisure needs. They are part of the unit basic load and commanders must include shipment with the higher HQs lift plan and account for them as they would any other TOE equipment.

5-12. Commanders at all levels must be sensitive to conditions external to the AO that can affect morale. In emergency cases, ARC representatives inside and outside the JOA can support communications between Soldiers, DOD civilians, and their Families. Under less compelling conditions, commanders may use other means (e.g., commanders may send messages through official channels such as the Military Affiliate Radio System, facsimile transceiver, commercial telephone, or the Army mail system).

RESPONSIBILITIES

5-13. Commanders at all levels are responsible for the MWR support provided to their Soldiers and DOD civilians.   MWR programs are found at all echelons on the battlefield and in all operational scenarios. MWR requirements are based on the combat environment and availability of resources. Battalions and below self-administer their programs using their command appointed unit A&R officers or NCOs; brigades and above assist all subordinate units in planning and executing their MWR programs. Table 5-1, along with the following paragraphs, addresses the relationship between key players and other staff elements in providing MWR support.

Table 5-1. Morale, Welfare, and Recreation (MWR) support

Function/Task	Responsible Agencies				
	BN	BDE	DIV	CORPS	ASCC
Manage MWR Program/Policies	S-1	S-1	G-1/AG	G-1/AG	G-1/AG
Identify MWR Requirements	S-1	S-1	G-1/AG	G-1/AG	G-1/AG
Execute MWR Logistics Support	S-4	S-4	G-4	G-4	G-4
Issue MWR Material	S-4	S-4	G-4	G-4	G-4
Include MWR OPLAN/OPORD	S-1	S-1	G-1/AG	G-1/AG	G-1/AG
Establish Imprest Funds	S-1	S-1	G-1/AG	G-1/AG	G-1/AG
Coordinate for Family Readiness/ Support	S-1	S-1	G-1/AG	G-1/AG	G-1/AG
Establish Theater Rest Areas	S-1	S-1	G-1/AG	G-1/AG	G-1/AG
Coordinate MWR Training at CRC	S-1	S-1	G-1/AG	G-1/AG	G-1/AG
Request MWR Personnel (IMCOM G-9)	S-1	S-1	G-1/AG	G-1/AG	G-1/AG
Coordinate for Health and Comfort Packs	S-4	S-4	G-4	G-4	G-4
Plan and Coordinate Direct Operations Exchange- Tactical	S-1	S-1	G-1/AG	G-1/AG	G-1/AG
Plan and Coordinate TFE (AAFES)	S-1	S-1	G-1/AG	G-1/AG	G-1/AG
Coordinate Red Cross Support	S-1	S-1	G-1/AG	G-1/AG	G-1/AG
Allocate Soldiers Time	S-3	S-3	G-3	G-3	G-3
Legend: AAFES- Army and Air Force Exchange Service; AG- Adjutant General; ASCC- Army Service Component Command; CRC- CONUS Replacement Center; IMCOM- Installation Management Command; MWR- Morale, Welfare, and Recreation; OPLAN/OPORD- Operation Plan/Operation Order; TFE- Tactical Field Exchange					

U. S. ARMY FAMILY AND MORALE, WELFARE, AND RECREATION

5-14. IMCOM G-9 assists sustaining base commanders by maintaining MWR (includes Child, Youth, and School Services) and Family assistance and readiness support at home stations. IMCOM G-9 is the executive agent to provide necessary deployment support to the ARC; AAFES is responsible for exchange support. Activities are based on the needs of the particular community served. They are available to military personnel and their Families and usually to DOD civilians and their families.

5-15. During military operations, installation staff must be cognizant of population fluctuations and be prepared to provide expanded services. The requirement for service for the families of deployed Soldiers (Active Army and RC) and the families of those back-filling the installation may quickly stress MWR and family programs.

5-16. Prior to and during deployment, the installation Directors of HR and Family and Morale, Welfare and Recreation are responsible to:
- Assist G-1/AGs and S-1s in procurement and transportation of MWR equipment and supplies included in operations and lift plans.
- Train A&R officers or NCOs in MWR procedures and functions.
- Ensure the execution of MWR services is available during initial deployment.
- Identify MWR EEC to support deployments.
- Coordinate with the combatant command for reimbursing salaries of EEC personnel through operational funding.
- Assist MWR EEC personnel with preparations for deployment.
- Initiate temporary backfill of essential MWR personnel.
- Accomplish Army Community Service and Child, Youth, and School Services DCS tasks listed in the DCS Army Directive.
- Conduct operation resources for educating about Deployment and You training for FRG leaders, family readiness support assistants, and rear detachment commanders.
- Provide support and assistance to commanders to provide family readiness related training to Soldiers and family members throughout the deployment cycle and to establish a unit family readiness infrastructure.
- Manage the Soldier and Family Assistance Center.

ASCC G-1/AG

5-17. The ASCC G-1/AG has the following MWR responsibilities:
- Identify and input fiscal and personnel requirements for the Total Army Family Program as part of the command operating budget process.
- Coordinate, develop, and manage MWR programs and policies.
- Ensure to include MWR operations in OPLANs and OPORDs.
- Plan for deployment of MWR EEC personnel.
- Identify MWR manpower, materiel, and other assistance required to support MWR.
- Coordinate with IMCOM G-9, ASCC G-4, and Army Commands of deploying units for MWR manpower, materiel, supplies, and other assistance.
- Prepare ASCC MWR policies, procedures, and the base of operations to support units, Soldiers, DOD personnel, and other Civilians authorized access to MWR programs and services.
- Establish theater pass policies in support of MWR programs.
- Coordinate with the ASCC G-4 to establish AO rest areas.
- Coordinate with other military Services for Joint recreational operations if serving as the JTF J-1.
- Coordinate with AAFES for establishment of AAFES support.
- Coordinate with the ASCC G-4 for execution of shipping of MWR equipment and supplies.

- Coordinate and provide assistance for transporting AAFES equipment and supplies (at the equivalent security level as military convoys).
- Establish a system to allocate, distribute, and maintain MWR equipment.
- Establish a network for distribution and rotation of films and videotapes from AAFES or other services.
- Coordinate with Armed Forces Entertainment/IMCOM G-9 for live entertainment for Soldiers and authorized Civilians in the AO.
- Establish policy on volunteer or contracted live entertainment.
- Develop plans and policies for the establishment and support of unit lounge activities.
- Coordinate with IMCOM G-9 and ASCC G-4 to develop a system for procuring, transporting, accounting, training, and providing MWR technical assistance to subordinate units.
- Coordinate with IMCOM G-9 for development of a policy and operational support system for club operations.
- Coordinate necessary deployment support for the ARC.
- Coordinate with AAFES and the ASCC G-4 for manning and support for exchange sales, Name Brand Fast Food and Services, and troop-supported tactical field exchange (TFE) or Direct Operations Exchange—Tactical (DOX-T) operations.
- Coordinate and monitor MWR self-administered activities in division-size and smaller units.
- Coordinate transportation for MWR kits and the supply and distribution of HCPs in the theater.
- Monitor reading material availability in the theater and coordinate postal operations support for shipment of book kits and reading material.

Corps And Division G-1/AG

5-18. The Corps and Division G-1/AG has the following MWR responsibilities:

- Coordinate, develop, and manage MWR programs IAW ASCC guidance. (Note: If serving as the JTF or Army Forces G-1/AG, the Corps and Division G-1/AG performs those ASCC G-1/AG duties as outlined above. Policy and programs should include non-Corps/Division units in the Corps/Division area).
- Ensure to include MWR operations in OPLANs and OPORDs.
- Assist subordinate organizations in establishing MWR programs, operating unit lounges and exchange facilities, acquiring and transporting equipment and supplies, and accounting for equipment and monies.
- Plan for TFEs that are established and operated by commands using unit personnel.
- Require subordinate units to include small unit recreation kits and MWR service level kits in their load plans.
- Plan for AAFES Imprest Fund Activity (AIFA) that may be established and operated by unit personnel. See AR 215-8, Army and Air Force Exchange Service Operations for more information.
- Establish policy and schedule for rest area utilization and pass programs.
- Provide brigades with allocations for R&R.
- Plan for DOX-T operations established and operated by AAFES personnel in a secure environment (dependent on METT-TC).
- Request name brand fast food and services (concession) operations support (e.g., barber shop, alterations, gift shops, and new car sales) as the operational pace permits.
- Establish in-AO rest areas.
- Request and plan transportation for a 30-day supply of book kits from the IMCOM G-9 and the Assistant Chief of Staff for Installation Management.
- Support self-administered activities in division-size and smaller units.
- Coordinate Army band activities.

- Establish MWR policy and monitor/support Corps-level MWR programs for divisional and non-divisional units in the Corps area.
- Establish Corps and Division rest areas; assist subordinate commands in operating activity centers and lounges; and coordinate MWR services with replacement and reconstitution operations.
- Coordinate training, to include CRC processing, for MWR program personnel transiting to and from the theater.
- Request MWR personnel to assist subordinate commands in planning and assisting in MWR tasks and activities.
- Coordinate support for the ARC.
- Coordinate MWR support team activities, Family assistance, and communications with the rear detachment.

BRIGADE S-1

5-19. The brigade S-1 staff facilitates and coordinates MWR programs and has the following responsibilities:

- Ensure MWR operations are included in all OPLANs and OPORDs.
- Ensure commanders appoint A&R officers or NCOs at battalion and company as an additional duty.
- Plan for TFEs that are established and operated by commands using unit personnel.
- Plan for AIFA that may be established and operated by unit personnel.
- Plan for DOX T operations established and operated by AAFES personnel in a secure environment.
- Plan for MWR service-level kits.
- Schedule Soldiers and Civilians for R&R periods based on allocations provided by the Corps/Division G-1/AG.
- Schedule unit personnel and civilians for rest area utilization and pass programs, as applicable.
- Coordinate establishment and operation of activity centers, recreation activities, exchanges, and unit lounges for Soldiers and all other assigned personnel.
- Coordinate unit athletic and recreation programs to include acquisition, use, and maintenance of equipment and supplies.
- Ensure that commanders appoint family readiness personnel at the battalion and company as an additional duty.

BATTALION S-1

5-20. The battalion S-1 ensures the A&R officer or NCO is appointed to coordinate MWR programs and maintain equipment. The battalion S-1 has the following MWR responsibilities:

- Coordinate with the battalion S-4 to ensure Soldiers and Civilians deploy with a 30-day supply of HCP.
- Determine the type and quantity of HCP carried by individual Soldiers.
- Plan for unit MWR programs prior to deployment and upon return from deployment.
- Requisition book kits at the sustaining base or mobilization station.
- Ensure units include MWR equipment, to include unit-level recreation kit(s), and book kits in their basic load plans.
- Plan for AIFA that may be established and operated by unit personnel.
- Schedule Soldiers and civilians for R&R periods based on allocations established by the brigade.
- Coordinate establishment and operation of Soldier activity centers, recreation activities, exchanges, and unit lounges.
- Coordinate unit programs to include acquisition, use, and maintenance of equipment and supplies.

- Coordinate unit Family Readiness programs and policies.
- Ensure unit commanders appoint Family Readiness POCs as an additional duty IAW AR 600-20, Army Command Policy.
- Ensure unit commanders establish FRGs.
- Establish liaison with the ARC upon arrival in theater.

AMERICAN RED CROSS (ARC)

5-21. The ARC consistently delivers essential Red Cross services to all Army components, civilians, and their Families worldwide in order to assist them in preventing, preparing for, and coping with emergency situations. The ARC provides services such as emergency communication (e.g., deaths and births, emergency financial assistance, counseling, and comfort kits in the deployed environment).

5-22. All requests for ARC personnel to accompany U. S. Forces into the JOA are forwarded to the IMCOM G-9, the DOD executive agent for the deployment of ARC personnel during these situations. The IMCOM G-9 is responsible for coordinating and securing support for ARC personnel to support military operations, managing and monitoring military support to the ARC, funding travel to and from the AO for ARC personnel, and coordinating and preparing ARC personnel for deployment and return. The ARC National HQs is responsible for supplying the staff and managing and monitoring ARC operations in the field.

5-23. A designated ARC representative is involved with the IMCOM G-9, the appropriate military command, and the ARC National HQs in contingency planning to ensure proper coordination and clarification of requirements. In the JOA, coordination for ARC support (logistical and life support) falls under the G-1/AG. ARC representatives are available at division and higher levels to assist with Family emergencies and emergency communication between Family members and deployed personnel. Table 5-2 displays the responsible agencies for ARC support.

Table 5-2. American Red Cross (ARC) Support

Function/Task	Responsible Agencies				
	BN	*BDE*	*DIV*	*CORPS*	*ASCC*
Request ARC Support	S-1	S-1	G-1/AG	G-1/AG	G-1/AG
Coordinate Deployment with Units	S-1	S-1	G-1/AG	G-1/AG	G-1/AG
Coordinate Emergency Communications	S-1	S-1	G-1/AG	G-1/AG	G-1/AG
Red Cross Support in Theater	S-1	S-1	G-1/AG	G-1/AG	G-1/AG
Redeployment	S-1	S-1	G-1/AG	G-1/AG	G-1/AG
Legend: AG- Adjutant General; ASCC- Army Service Component Command; BDE- Brigade; BN- Battalion; DIV- Division					

ARMY AND AIR FORCE EXCHANGE SERVICE (AAFES)

5-24. An AAFES Board of Directors directs AAFES operations worldwide. The system supports major installations in CONUS, OCONUS, and units deployed to remote areas. It also supports field operations and exercises. The Army provides Afloat Pre-positioning Force support in the form of materiel, facilities, transportation, field site support, military air and logistical support of AAFES operations. Logistical support of AAFES operations and personnel is provided by direct support or through LOGCAP.

5-25. During operations, the ASCC commander, in coordination with AAFES, plans for and supports exchange operations. These plans may include a combination of DOX-T operations, TFEs, and/or AIFAs.

5-26. AAFES deploys personnel to assist the Army in establishing direct retail operations and an exchange warehousing and distribution system. The ASCC and Corps G-1/AGs coordinate with their G-4s in the process of designating, training, deploying, and employing Army and Air Force personnel to support the

AO AAFES system. AAFES may establish these activities using employees which consist of U. S. nationals, contract operators, host-nation employees, third country national employees, or vendors.

5-27. TFEs are normally military manned and DOX-Ts are manned by AAFES personnel. TFEs are designated to provide merchandise and services on a temporary basis in areas where permanent exchange activities are not present. TFE and DOX-T serves Soldiers and civilians, and may locate as far forward as the Brigade Support Area provided the tactical situation allows.

5-28. AIFA is a military-operated retail activity, usually operated in small or remote sites, when regular direct operation exchanges cannot be provided. Should commanders choose to employ AIFA, they must select and train personnel from their units to operate these activities. The unit is issued an initial fund by AAFES to purchase a beginning inventory. Money generated from sales is used to replenish the merchandise stock. A site commander can request the establishment of an AIFA from the general manager of the AAFES geographical area.

BATTLEFIELD FLOW

5-29. For planning purposes, the following guidelines establish a time-phased schedule for deploying MWR resources to support military operations. Actual timelines and operations depend on METT-TC.

5-30. C–C+30. During the first 30 days of operation, MWR may be limited to unit-level recreation kits and HCP as part of the unit's basic load. The following actions take place during this period:

- Commanders obtain book kits provided by the home installation library.
- A&R officers or NCOs procure unit-level recreation kits using mission funding. The installation Director of Family and Morale, Welfare, and Recreation may assist with procurement
- Corps and Division G-1/AGs requisition and distribute MWR service-level kits.
- The ASCC and/or Corps and Division G-1/AG establish a network for distributing and rotating AAFES-provided films and videotapes.
- AAFES begins transporting exchange items and coordinates with the theater and Corps for transportation, storage, and distribution support.
- The Defense Personnel Support Center sends additional HCPs to arrive by C+30.
- Civilian MWR EEC personnel deploy to the AO as early as the situation permits and as requested by the ASCC commander. (Note: If conditions do not permit or the commander does not request deployment of Civilians, military staffs must be prepared to establish and maintain MWR support. Coordination for supplemental civilian MWR EEC personnel is done through the IMCOM HQs.)

5-31. C+30–C+60. The following actions take place during this period:

- Coordinate with the G-4 and base camp commanders for the deployment of MWR service-level kits, electronic game kits, theater in a box kits, video messenger kit, and any other available kits. These kits contain fragile, bulky, and heavy items such as televisions, videocassette recorders, digital video disk players, basketball goals, and free weights.
- Provide appropriate personnel assets to operate MWR programs.
- Develop policies for rest area use.
- Coordinate with the G-4 for distributing HCPs with Class I supplies to units and individuals lacking access to exchange or host-nation retail facilities.
- Coordinate with the G-4 and AAFES for establishment of a base of operations and distribution centers capable of supporting DOX-T, TFE, and AIFA.
- Coordinate with their G-4 for designating, training, deploying, and employing Army personnel to support the mission.
- Coordinate with the IMCOM G-9 to implement a system for distribution of deployed unit funds, and book kits to units at C+30 and every 30 days thereafter. Coordination for supplemental MWR EEC personnel is done through the IMCOM HQs.

5-32. C+60–C+120. The following actions take place during this period:

- G-4 establishes theater-level DOD Activity Address Codes for MWR. Supply channels stock MWR items on their Common Table of Allowances. MWR supplies and equipment are ordered by and shipped to an ASCC MWR DOD Activity Address Code. Examples are weights, amusement machines, lounge and entertainment equipment, and other items for unit recreation and rest area operations.

- Corps and Division base of operations expands to provide one or more support package (Force Provider). Rest areas are developed to meet the needs of a brigade-size unit. Actual timelines and operations are based on METT-TC. This package provides recreational activities, AAFES retail outlets, vendors, and personnel services support such as postal, financial management, legal, unit ministry, and ARC services. Other services available are billeting, laundry, latrine, shower, food, and medical. The support package's primary mission is to provide rest and recuperation facilities for deployed personnel who have suffered stress associated with combat duties. The location of this support package is in the Corps and Division areas.

- The ASCC G-1/AG may establish a pass program or ASCC rest area within the AO. Assistance is requested from the Assistant Chief of Staff for Installation Management and the IMCOM G-9.

- ASCC and subordinate commands develop and implement R&R policies. Live entertainment, to include Army Entertainment productions and Armed Forces Entertainment shows (e.g., United Service Organization), are requested based on availability, ASCC policy, and the tactical situation.

- During redeployment, operations consolidate or close as the number of personnel supported decreases. Commanders ensure adequate support for residual forces. ASCC and Corps staffs establish and implement policies for equipment turn-in and redeployment. Resource accountability is critical during this phase to prevent waste, fraud, and abuse. Rest areas and R&R centers request disposition of equipment and supplies from the IMCOM G-9.

SECTION II – COMMAND INTEREST PROGRAMS

5-33. Command Interest Programs are of general interest to organizations and Soldiers. The following paragraphs briefly discuss the general responsibilities that an S-1 has with respect to any program that demands specific attention as directed by the commander. Some programs that traditionally fall within the purview are provided as examples to understand the principles of support involved but should not be considered to be all inclusive. Command interest programs generally have five key components that include the responsible agent or agency, regulatory or statutory guidance, checklist, compliance protocols, and reporting requirements.

5-34. A responsible agent or agency is someone specific or subordinate element that is appointed, in writing, by order or policy memorandum, that establishes the scope and responsibilities of the duty to be performed, the length of time the duty is performed and any applicable references authorizing the order. The commander or his designated representative must sign any order or policy memorandum that establishes a responsible agent or agency for a command interest program. The S-1 ensures the order is completed and maintained IAW the requirements for the program.

5-35. All command interest programs have regulatory guidance or statutory requirements that must be followed for successful execution of the program. S-1s ensure the responsible agent has access to the current regulation or policy that governs the program. For example, AR 600-20 establishes the Army Equal Opportunity Program. For the commander, it highlights all the essential elements of the program to ensure equal opportunity and fair treatment to all Soldiers and their Family members. Another example is The Veterans Opportunity to Work (VOW) to Hire Heroes Act of 2011 is a United States statute that requires all transitioning military Servicemembers to complete a transition assistance program such as the Army Career and Alumni Program. By law, each Soldier must complete this before separating from the Army which necessitates the S-1 to monitor and track each Soldier as part of final out-processing.

5-36. Most programs have specific requirements or procedures that must be followed. A checklist ensures each component is completed on time in the proper order. As procedures change, the S-1 ensures the checklist is updated to reflect the new method of doing business. In some cases, the S-1 may not perform some or any of the duties on the checklist beyond assuring that a responsible agent is appointed. For example, the Army Voting Assistance Program educates eligible Soldiers on the importance of voting and provides every opportunity to register and cast their votes. However, the program manager may not necessarily be in the S-1. Any Soldier that meets the requirements outlined in AR 608-20, Army Voting Assistance Program, may be appointed as the Voting Assistance Officer. That individual, once appointed in writing, would be responsible for following the checklist, maintaining compliance with the regulation, and reporting periodically to the commander the status of the program.

5-37. Compliance protocols are the methods and procedures to provide quality assurance as mandated by law for any federal agency. Simply put, these are the inspections performed by a higher headquarters, inspector general, or other agency to measure through appropriate metrics the command's compliance with the requirements established by the regulation or law. Most often these are performed when a principle responsible agent changes, the governing guidance changes, or annually if no other circumstance has prompted a review. The S-1 tracks the timeline for inspections; coordinates or schedules, where appropriate, the inspection and any follow up actions, and ensures any historical inspections are maintained as required.

5-38. Each command interest program's governing regulation or implementing guidance usually provides the time and manner by which progress reports must be presented to the commander, higher headquarters, or external agencies. Most often the S-1 acts as the staff command principle for consolidating, formatting, and presenting the required information to the commander. This is especially true for programs that require the commander's signature for certification or authentication.

5-39. In all cases it is important to understand that the S-1's role is to ensure each of the five key components outlined are executed but not necessarily perform the duty. Attempting to run each command interest program may ultimately overwhelm any S-1 staff element and threaten their ability to perform other core competencies and subordinate key functions that are required for accomplishing the unit's mission.

SECTION III – ARMY BAND OPERATIONS

5-40. Army bands provide music for ceremonial and morale support across unified land operations. They select music to inspire Warrior spirit in Soldiers and leaders and in keeping with the musical tastes of the target audience. Deployed bands are capable of creating and sustaining relationships with host-nations, multi-national forces, and Joint forces.

5-41. Army bands provide:
- Music support to military operations by tailoring music for troop support, ceremonies, and command interest programs in order to preserve customs, improve morale, inspire the Warrior spirit of troops, and promote the Nation's interests at home and abroad.
- Music support to preserve our Nation's traditions, foster the support of our citizens, support Army recruiting efforts, and enrich the morale and esprit de corps of Army professionals, organizations, and military Families.
- Music support to the commander's communications strategy as part of a comprehensive approach to support Joint, interagency, and multi-national strategic objectives.

5-42. The type of missions Army bands perform depends upon the supported command's phase of operations, the location of MPTs, or the concurrent mission capabilities of the MPTs. The modular organization of the band allows its teams to be tasked and deployed independently or collectively.

5-43. The ASCC G-1/AG, in coordination with subordinate G-1/AGs and G-3s, determines what musical support effects are required in the AO. The capabilities required to achieve those effects determine the number and type of MPTs and Band HQs that are needed in theater. In some cases, the ASCC G-1/AG may establish an Army Band Liaison Officer (42C) to synchronize and integrate musical support for Soldiers, HQs, and diplomatic organizations for ceremonial, protocol, strategic outreach, entertainment, and multi-national events.

5-44. The Band Commander is the senior staff advisor to the G-1/AG on band operations. Scheduling of music support is conducted by the G-1 through the G-3 in coordination with the band commander. For mission command purposes, Army bands are attached to the HHBn/TSC STB at division, corps, or theater-level for administrative and life support purposes.

RESPONSIBILITIES

5-45. The paragraphs below outline the responsibilities at the various echelons of command as it pertains to Coordinate Personnel Support.

ASCC/CORPS AND DIVISION G-1/AG

5-46. The ASCC/Corps and Division G-1/AG band responsibilities include:
- Coordinate with the G-3 on music support requirements and priorities.
- Coordinate with the Public Affairs Officer for input on civil affairs, off post, or community relations requests for band support.
- Ensure band operations are included in all operational plans and orders.
- Synchronize band and MWR operations.
- Develop policy for specific procedures and guidelines for requesting band support.

ARMY BAND LIAISON OFFICER

5-47. The Army Band Liaison Officer has the following responsibilities:
- Serve as a subject matter expert for United States Army Central/Coalition Forces Land Component Command providing an ongoing assessment of Army band assets in theater, COA, and musical recommendations as necessary.
- Synchronize musical support for Soldiers, HQs, and diplomatic organizations for ceremonial, protocol, strategic outreach, entertainment, and multi-national events.
- Provide weekly situational reports to the Forces Command Staff Bands Officer and Commandant, U. S. Army School of Music.
- Maintain centralized historical and operational records of deployed band missions and submit them to the Army School of Music, Directorate of Training and Doctrine.

BAND COMMANDER

5-48. The band commander has the following responsibilities:
- Provide advice on band missions and effective use of the band.
- Coordinate band operations with the G-1/AG, G-3, Public Affairs Officer, or the HHBn/TSC STB.
- Conduct mission analysis on receipt of band missions.
- Provide mission command of band personnel.

This page intentionally left blank.

Chapter 6

Conduct HR Planning and Operations

Conduct HR Planning and Operations is the means by which an HR provider articulates HR operations to support the operational commander's mission requirements. The *military decisionmaking process* is an iterative planning methodology to understand the situation and mission, develop a course of action, and produce an operation plan or order (ADP 5-0). The risk management process aligns with each step of the MDMP in order to minimize the hazards/risk level and ensures decisions are made at the proper level of command. Successful planning of HR support identifies and communicates to subordinate HR and other providers, and unit leaders, the intent, expected requirements, and outcomes to be achieved.

HR PLANNING AND OPERATIONS

6-1. Effective HR planning and operations requires HR providers to have a firm understanding of the full capabilities of HR units and organizations. This understanding allows HR providers to better anticipate requirements and inform the commander. HR providers must understand how to employ doctrine in any operating environment and be technically competent in the current HR systems, processes, policies, and procedures required to support Soldiers and commanders engaged in unified land operations.

6-2. HR staff officers at every command level, starting with the battalion S-1, perform HR planning and operations. HR planning and operations are also conducted by the HROB within the sustainment brigade and ESC, by the HR Company, and by all divisions within the HRSC. HR planning and operations is a continual process that supports a commander's ability to exercise mission command. HR planning and operations requires an understanding of how HR support is delivered in the operational environment. The need for collaboration with other staff elements, HR planners, and HR providers is necessary in order to optimize HR support across operational lines. Figure 6-1 on page 6-2 depicts the operations process to synchronize the HR planning functions which include:

- Plan: Making plans that support the operational mission and providing commanders with options on how best to use HR assets within their organizations. The HR planner is focused on translating the commander's visualization into a specific COA.
- Prepare: Preparing and setting the conditions for success requires an understanding of the operating environment. HR providers anticipate requirements and set into motion activities that allow the force to transition to execution.
- Execute: Making execution and adjustment decisions to exploit opportunities or unforecasted requirements providing commanders with the flexibility required to be proactive.
- Assess: Continual assessment allows the HR provider to learn and adapt as new information becomes available that provides a clearer picture of the operating environment.

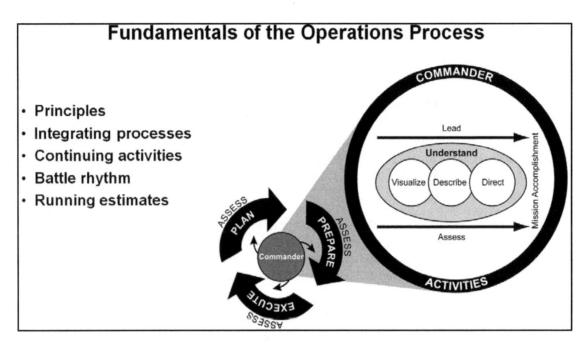

Figure 6-1. The operations process

RUNNING ESTIMATE/HR PLANNING CONSIDERATIONS

6-3. To be effective in the planning process, the most important information the HR planner should provide is the HR staff running estimate. A *running estimate* is the continuous assessment of the current situation used to determine if the current operation is proceeding according to the commander's intent and if planned future operations are supportable (ADP 5-0). Building and maintaining running estimates is a primary task of each staff section. The running estimate helps the staff provide recommendations to commanders on the best COA to accomplish their mission. Running estimates represent the analysis and expert opinion of each staff section by functional area. Running estimates are maintained throughout the operations process to assist commanders and the staff in the exercise of mission command.

6-4. Each staff section or command post functional cell is required to maintain a running estimate focused on how their specific area of expertise is postured to support future operations. For HR support, HR information is contained in the sustainment estimate and HR planning considerations. As the estimate may be needed at any time, running estimates must be developed, revised, updated, and maintained continuously. ATTP 5-0.1, Commander and Staff Officer Guide, provides detailed information on the running estimate, especially how it is used in the planning process.

6-5. An HR staff running estimate should include the following:
- Facts relating to personnel readiness, personnel accountability, casualty operations, and personnel services.
- Assumptions relating to forecasts on readiness, casualties, and personnel services.
- Friendly force status (of higher, lower, and adjacent units).
- Conclusions and recommendations for future HR operations and COAs the command and staff must be aware of.

HR PLANNING USING THE MILITARY DECISIONMAKING PROCESS (MDMP)

6-6. Each staff officer responsible for HR planning has an obligation to be thoroughly familiar with the MDMP. As depicted in Figure 6-2 on page 6-4, the MDMP consists of seven steps. Each step of the MDMP has various inputs, a method (step) to conduct, and outputs. The outputs lead to an increased understanding of the situation and to facilitating the next step of the MDMP. Commanders and staffs generally perform these steps sequentially; however, they may revisit several steps in an iterative fashion, as they learn more about the situation before producing the plan or order. The detail of each step is dependent on time, resources, experience, and the situation. The MDMP is a time consuming process that must be conducted in a detailed and deliberate process when time allows.

6-7. The MDMP is a primary tool for commanders to solve problems, make decisions, and develop plans and orders. Information collected and processed during the MDMP may be adapted by HR planners for their own organizations purpose. HR planning is a continuous process that evaluates current and future operations from the functional perspective of the HR provider.

6-8. Throughout the MDMP, the G-1/AG, S-1, and HR staff planner should consider how the information being developed impacts HR support to each phase of a military operation. While HR support is conducted across the range of military operations, HR planners must consider the frequency of occurrence for HR tasks in each element of military operations (e.g., offense, defense, stability, or defense support of civil authority). During offensive operations, units are more focused on casualty reporting and PA, while other tasks are accomplished as the situation permits.

6-9. To be effective in the planning process, it is important to locate HR officers/sections where they can not only track the current operation, but influence the operation with additional HR support. Generally, at division and higher levels of command, elements of the G-1/AG section are located in the Sustainment Cell of the Main CP. Second and third order requirements for the G-1/AG section are determined by closely tracking the COP. For example, casualties monitored on the command voice or data network should prompt the G-1/AG and S-1 of the requirement to generate casualty reports, possible EPS actions (e.g., awards and letters of condolence), and possible replacement actions necessary to replace casualty losses. By remaining engaged with the operation and maintaining situational understanding, G-1/AGs and S-1s can better support subordinate and/or supported units (HR and non-HR) in the execution of their HR mission. Similarly, HROBs must remain engaged and integrated with the sustainment brigade/ESC staff in order to influence HR support to supported organizations (G-1/AGs and S-1s) and to provide direction and guidance to the HR assets in their organization.

6-10. The following paragraphs describe each of the MDMP steps and how they relate to planning HR support. Refer to ADRP 5-0, The Operations Process, for further information on the MDMP.

Key inputs	Steps	Key outputs
• Higher headquarters' plan or order or a new mission anticipated by the commander	Step 1: Receipt of Mission	• Commander's initial guidance • Initial allocation of time
	Warning order	
• Higher headquarters' plan or order • Higher headquarters' knowledge and intelligence products • Knowledge products from other organizations • Army design methodology products	Step 2: Mission Analysis	• Problem statement • Mission statement • Initial commander's intent • Initial planning guidance • Initial CCIRs and EEFIs • Updated IPB and running estimates • Assumptions
	Warning order	

• Mission statement
• Initial commander's intent, planning guidance, CCIRs, and EEFIs
• Updated IPB and running estimates
• Assumptions
	Step 3: Course of Action (COA) Development	• COA statements and sketches
		  - Tentative task organization
		  - Broad concept of operations
		• Revised planning guidance
		• Updated assumptions

• Updated running estimates • Revised planning guidance • COA statements and sketches • Updated assumptions	Step 4: COA Analysis (War Game)	• Refined COAs • Potential decision points • War-game results • Initial assessment measures • Updated assumptions
• Updated running estimates • Refined COAs • Evaluation criteria • War-game results • Updated assumptions	Step 5: COA Comparison	• Evaluated COAs • Recommended COAs • Updated running estimates • Updated assumptions
• Updated running estimates • Evaluated COAs • Recommended COA • Updated assumptions	Step 6: COA Approval	• Commander-selected COA and any modifications • Refined commander's intent, CCIRs, and EEFIs • Updated assumptions
	Warning order	
• Commander-selected COA with any modifications • Refined commander's intent, CCIRs, and EEFIs • Updated assumptions	Step 7: Orders Production, Dissemination, and Transition	• Approved operation plan or order • Subordinates understand the plan or order

CCIR	commander's critical information requirement	EEFI	essential element of friendly information
COA	course of action	IPB	intelligence preparation of the battlefield

Figure 6-2. Military decisionmaking process (MDMP)

STEP 1. RECEIPT OF MISSION

6-11. Step 1 of the MDMP is the receipt of plans, orders, and guidance from higher HQs or a new mission anticipated by the commander. This step includes the commander's initial guidance and a decision to conduct initial planning, to include timelines. This step concludes with a warning order to the staff or subordinate units.

STEP 2. MISSION ANALYSIS

6-12. During this step HR planners conduct mission analysis. As part of the mission analysis, the mission is clearly stated and the commander provides his or her intent and planning guidance, and identifies initial commander's critical information requirements (CCIRs) and essential elements of friendly information. HR planners consider the following:

- How does the commander's intent focus HR support efforts? Should not be tied to a specific COA.
- Unit and system capabilities, limitations, and employment. This includes the ability to access voice and data systems for HR and mission command.
- Organization of the unit for HR operations; how manpower allocations are made to subordinate units.
- Analyze personnel strength data to determine current capabilities and to project future requirements.
- Analyze unit strength maintenance, including monitoring, collecting, and analyzing all data affecting Soldier readiness.
- Determine HR support and HR services available to the force (current and projected).
- Prepare estimates for personnel replacements requirements, based on estimated casualties, nonbattle losses, and foreseeable administrative losses to include critical MOS requirements.
- Prepare casualty estimates (when time permits, casualty estimation should be done on each phase of the COA).
- Command and support relationships, to include HR units and supported organizations (G-1/AGs and S-1s), and how these relationships affect the delivery of HR support.
- Resource allocation and employment synchronization of organic and supporting units.
- Locations and movement of HR units and supporting HROB.
- Current and near-term (future) execution of the planned HR support.
- Actions impacting on PA, casualty, and postal operations must flow to the supporting HROB and the HRSC (Note: This enables the HROB to assist supported units and to track the location, resourcing, and capabilities of supporting HR companies, platoons, and teams.)
- Updating the running estimate/HR planning considerations.
- Knowledge of unit mission and the mission of supported and supporting units.
- Is the MMT resourced to handle mail operations IAW theater plans/policies?
- If the MMT is serving as the JMMT, is coordination being conducted for appropriate support from Joint assets?
- Are postal facilities adequate to process, store, and distribute mail?
- Do postal organizations have adequate and operational equipment to support mail operations (e.g., forklifts and transportation)?
- What is the planned location of postal facilities?
- Can mail operations be integrated into replenishment operations?
- Are PAT elements adequately staffed to process all categories of personnel flow into and out of the APOD or SPOD?
- Have recurring transportation requirements been established and are they adequate to support transiting personnel?
- Do teams have access and resources to update personnel databases from their location?
- Where is the CLT located?

- Is planned connectivity adequate for communications between CLTs, SPO HROB, the supported unit, and DCIPS?
- Identify key specified and implied tasks.
- Identify constraints and how the end state affects HR shortfalls.
- Identify HR key facts and assumptions.
- Prepare, authenticate, and distribute the HR plan in the form of approved annexes, estimates, appendices, and OPLANS.
- Identify recommended CCIRs and status of essential elements of friendly information. Examples of CCIRs are: amount of mail not moved within 24 hours of receipt; number of transit personnel awaiting transportation beyond 24 hours; or location and status of CLTs.
- Issue/receive warning order update.

STEP 3. COURSE OF ACTION (COA) DEVELOPMENT

6-13. The COA development phase involves.
- Developing an understanding of the concept of operation and the concept of support.
- Providing HR planning guidance as necessary.
- Determining HR resources required to support each COA.
- Ensuring HR capabilities, strength impacts, and HR asset vulnerabilities are considered.
- Ensuring deployment, intra-theater transit or movements, and redeployment are considered.
- Ensuring current and future HR operations are included in COA.

STEP 4. COA ANALYSIS (WAR GAME)

6-14. The COA (war game) step is where COAs are refined, the running estimate is updated, and changes are made to the planning guidance. Specific actions include:
- Refining the status and location of all HR friendly forces.
- Listing critical HR events in war gaming.
- Determining how to evaluate HR events.
- Assessing the results of the war gaming (from an HR perspective).

STEP 5. COA COMPARISON

6-15. This step compares the COAs evaluated in Step 4 with the results of the war game to determine the recommended COA. Specific actions include:
- Refining COAs based on war game results.
- Comparing relative success of achieving HR success by each COA.
- Identifying the advantages and disadvantages of each COA.
- Identifying any critical areas of HR support which may impact on each COA, if any.
- Identifying major deficiencies in manpower or in number of HR units, teams, or squads.
- Recommending the best COA from an HR perspective.

STEP 6. COA APPROVAL

6-16. During this step the commander selects and modifies the COA. Specific actions include:
- Selecting best COA; modifies as necessary.
- Refining commander's intent, CCIRs, and essential elements of friendly information.
- Issuing the warning order.

STEP 7. ORDERS PRODUCTION, DISSEMINATION, AND TRANSITION

6-17. Prepare, authenticate, and distribute the OPLAN/OPORD.

HR INPUT TO OPERATION ORDERS

6-18. ATTP 5-0.1 provides the format and instructions for preparing an OPLAN/OPORD. The OPLAN/OPORD format has been modified to integrate the warfighting functions. HR staff officers are normally responsible for providing input to the base plan/order, input to Annex A (Task Organization), and writing portions of Annex F (Sustainment), specifically Appendix 2 (Personnel Services Support).

6-19. HR planners, when developing their portion of the OPLAN/OPORD, need to ensure the following capabilities, units, and functions are addressed in the plan or order. HR planners must also recommend appropriate command relationships and support relationships for the HR specific units supporting the command and subordinates. Units, locations, and functional area support provided by a supporting unit should be addressed by HR support to Annex A, Task Organization. This includes, but is not limited to:

- HRSC.
- TG PAT.
- MMT Team.
- HR Company HQs.
- Postal Platoon.
- HR Platoon (include PATs and CLTs).
- HROB, SPO, ESC, or sustainment brigade.
- ASCC G-1/AG.
- Corps G-1/AG.
- Division G-1/AG.

6-20. Man the Force:

- Personnel readiness management (personnel augmentation and manning requirements-stop-move); priority of fill; individual Soldier readiness; replacement operations; cross-leveling guidance; and key leader/crew replacements).
- Personnel accountability (system of record; initial manifesting/processing; support provided by PATs; guideline for reporting; accountability of DOD Civilians and CAAF (including other designated contractor personnel); location of PAT processing sites; processing tasks and roles; and data integration).
- Strength reporting (timeline; reporting format; and PERSTAT or JPERSTAT instructions) .
- Personnel information management (data integration; database hierarchy; and software requirement).

6-21. Provide HR Services:

- Essential personnel services (CACs/ID tags, awards authority and processing; promotion processing; military pay/entitlements; personnel action requests; leaves and passes; R&R guidance and allocation by subordinate unit; close-out evaluation reports; LODs; and other EPS functions as necessary).
- Postal operations (initial restrictions; addresses; supporting postal organization; scheduled delivery/retro-grade; APO location/supporting units; retro-grade mail; redirect mail; casualty mail; and OCS).
- Casualty operations (casualty reporting; location of CLTs; reporting system/format; reporting timelines; and release authority for reports).

6-22. Coordinate Personnel Support:

- Morale, Welfare, and Recreation Operations (initial deployment instructions; ARC support/procedures and processing; in-country MWR support; and AAFES support).
- Command interest programs.
- Army band operations.

6-23. Conduct HR Planning and Operations:

- Conduct HR planning and mission preparation (HR planning considerations; casualty estimates; track current and future HR operations; redeployment planning; and preparation of OPLANs/OPORDs).
- Establish HR Mission Command Nodes (communication access, equipment, NIPRNET and SIPRNET access).

6-24. Coordinating Instructions:
- Commander's Critical Information Requirements (loss of battalion or higher commander, CSM, or primary staff; casualty rates greater than 15% of any battalion's available strength; capture of friendly personnel; unauthorized release of casualty information; loss of any mail flight or convoy; delay of mail flow of 24 hours or more; loss of a replacement flight or convoy; and delay in replacement flow of more than 24 hours).
- Rear detachment operations (e.g., replacement push; records custodian; support to stay-behind Soldiers and units; and IMCOM/MPD CAC coordination) .
- Personnel policies and procedures (Red Cross messages; rotation policy).
- EPWs, civilian internees, and other detained personnel.
- Formerly captured, missing, or detained U. S. personnel.
- Travel procedures.
- Medical RTDs.
- Unit commanders identify deployable and non-deployable Soldiers (based on the Army PPG).
- Non-standard reporting requirements.
- Congressional inquiries.
- Civilian personnel.
- Religious support.
- Legal.

POSTAL INPUT TO OPERATION ORDERS

6-25. List unit, location, and functional area support provided by supporting unit. All may not apply.
- HRSC.
- TG PAT.
- MMT Team.
- HR Company HQs.
- Postal Platoon.
- HROB.
- ASCC G-1/AG.
- Corps G-1/AG.
- Division G-1/AG.

6-26. Assumptions:
- Restrictions on inbound mail will be guided by SOFA, Memorandum of Agreement, USPS International Mail Manual, DOD 4525.6-M, and agreement between the combatant command and host-nation.
- Special services will be restricted IAW DOD 4525.6-M, USPS International Mail Manual, SOFA, and other regulatory guidance agreed upon by the host-nation and combatant command.
- During early operations there is no military airlift to support intra-theater mail transport requirements.
- Postal personnel to man and operate the Aerial Mail Terminals, Mail Control Activities, Fleet Mail Centers, MMTs, and MPOs will arrive in theater prior to supported forces to prevent mail restrictions.

6-27. Planning Factor: The planning factor of 2.0 pounds per Servicemember per day is used to determine mail volume. One 20 foot container equals 8,000 pounds and one 40 foot container equals 16,000 pounds.

6-28. Coordinating Instructions:

- Consolidate official and personal mail processing and distribution operations.
- Consolidate official mail centers to one per geographic location.
- No restrictions will be placed on in-coming or out-going official mail.
- "Any Servicemember" mail is not authorized.
- All MMTs and MPOs will scan accountable bar-coded mail including customs tags.
- Mail transit times are reported weekly to MPSA.
- SCCs designate a minimum of one Postal Finance Officer per theater. Personal mail policies are IAW DOD Instruction 4525.7, Military Postal Service and Related Services.
- Personal mail procedures are executed IAW DOD 4525.6-M.
- Official mail policies are IAW DOD Instruction 4525.08, DOD Official Mail Management.
- Official mail procedures are executed IAW DOD 4525.8-M, DOD Official Mail Manual.
- Identify administration and logistics requirements to support postal operations.
- Identify space criteria required for military postal facility to support population served.
- Establish and maintain postal operations to the extent required.
- Process mail originating in or destined for overseas theaters.
- Implement instructions for international agreements affecting postal operations.
- Identify restrictions for retro-grade mail.
- Identify unit sorting requirements (if applicable).
- Identify expected source of transportation for secure mail movement.
- Outline procedures for obtaining postal unique supplies and equipment.

RULES OF ALLOCATION (ROA) FOR HR UNITS

6-29. HR organization ROAs allow HR planners to determine the number of HR units required to provide intended support. These ROAs are also used in the Total Army Analysis system to model operational requirements of units and may change based on a number of environmental factors including geography. The following are the ROAs for modular HR organizations:

- HRSC — One per TSC.
- TG PAT — One per inter-theater APOD.
- MMT Team — One per inter-theater APOD that dispatches mail via aircraft (Existence Based).
- HR Company — One per three to seven platoons (HR, Postal, or any combination); One per MMT Team; One per TG PAT.
- HR Platoon (3 x HR Squads) — Two per TG PAT (1st 3,600 daily pax flow); One per 1,800 daily pax flow (additional).
- HR Squad (CLT) – One per Role 3 MTF; One per MA Company; One per HRSC, COD; and one per General Officer-level command (w/exception to ASCC/TSC).
- HR Squad (PAT) – One per 600 personnel transiting through an intra-theater APOD (when daily transit numbers exceed 600). For example, the senior mission commander is required to maintain accountability of the first 600 personnel transiting through an intra-theater APOD. At 601 personnel, two HR Squads (PAT) are required to process personnel transiting through an intra-theater.
- Postal Platoon — One per 6,000 personnel (i.e., cumulative population); Four per MMT Team.

OPERATE HR MISSION COMMAND NODES

6-30. Operation of HR mission command nodes includes establishment, operation, and maintaining connectivity to HR data and voice communications nodes needed for HR operations. HR mission command nodes are required to enable HR personnel access to HR databases and must provide access across all commands and echelons, and to higher and lower elements.

This page intentionally left blank.

Chapter 7

Theater Opening and Redeployment Operations

Theater HR support operations are complex and involve the integrated actions of various G-1/AG staff sections, HR units and staff elements found in sustainment organizations, and the S-1 sections operating within battalion and brigade units.

GENERAL

7-1. This chapter describes key HR support functions required for successful HR operations during theater opening and those actions that need consideration after military operations are terminated. The primary focus of this chapter is on the tasks of PA, casualty, and postal operations; all of which are critical functions and the primary responsibility of HR elements. While G-1/AGs and S-1s are involved in these functions from their unit-level perspective, it is also necessary to ensure maximum participation from qualified G-1/AG postal subject matter experts. Their involvement in planning all operational, logistical and transportation priorities help to ensure postal mission readiness.

7-2. Lessons learned from current and previous operations validated the importance of including HR support as part of the early entry mission as some HR functions must be immediately available after arrival into an AO. As with all military operations, success is dependent on the careful planning, coordination, and synchronization required prior to, during, and after military action.

SECTION I – THEATER OPENING

7-3. Effective, accurate, and timely HR support during theater opening requires the same detailed preparation and planning required in all military operations. They must be initiated as early as possible within operational timelines. As previously discussed, Chapter 6 provided detailed information on planning and discusses the specific and critical HR functions and capabilities required during the initial phase (theater opening) of operations that must be considered during the MDMP.

7-4. HR capabilities required by HR support elements and personnel in theater opening are listed below. These capabilities include tasks that are performed as part of the RSOI process:

- Establish initial theater PA.
- Establish initial theater Casualty Assistance Center operations.
- Establish initial theater postal operations.

7-5. To accomplish the above capabilities requires the designation of selected personnel as members of the early entry element from the following organizations:

- ASCC G-1/AG.
- HRSC—personnel from the PA Division and COD.
- TG PAT.
- MMT Team.
- HROB of the ESC and designated sustainment brigade dedicated to theater opening.
- HR Company.
- HR platoons to support PA and casualty missions.
- Postal platoons to support the MMT.

PERSONNEL ACCOUNTABILITY

7-6. PA is the most critical of all HR theater opening tasks. It is also the primary task conducted during the HR portion of the RSOI process. The most crucial task in the PA process is establishing a deployed personnel database and infrastructure that has the ability to capture accountability data on personnel entering the theater. This includes accounting for all personnel participating as members of the early entry element. Careful and detailed planning for accountability of these personnel is crucial as they include personnel and units involved in the RSOI process, personnel opening APOEs or SPOEs and coordinating with the AFSB to account for CAAF, when directed, participating in theater opening operations. Prior to deployment to the theater, all personnel involved as database administrators should be identified, designated, and trained on theater PA systems.

7-7. To establish initial PA operations, personnel from each of the following organizations are required
- ASCC G-1/AG.
- HRSC—personnel from the PA Division.
- TG PAT.
- HROB of the ESC and designated sustainment brigade dedicated to theater opening.
- HR Company.
- HR Platoon to support TG PAT.

7-8. The ASCC G-1/AG is responsible for planning, establishing policy, setting priorities, and managing PA for the theater. The ASCC G-1/AG also identifies internal and external HR support requirements for the theater and coordinates with the combatant commander to ensure Army PA policies are in sync with Joint policies.

7-9. Actual establishment of the initial theater database is the responsibility of the HRSC, PA/PRM/PIM Division. The HRSC establishes HR database nodes, initiates theater database hierarchy, and continues the coordination to maintain projected personnel flow rates with CONUS APOD, CRCs, and Air Force planners. They also provide technical guidance to the TG PAT and the HROB in the ESC or sustainment brigade. During initial HR operations, the HRSC element may co-locate with the HROB.

7-10. The function of the TG PAT is to establish communications nodes with the HRSC element for PA and establishment of a PPC at the primary APOE. Establish the PPC at the most favorable location based on projected flow rates in the area of the APOE. Once the PPC is established, PA and database integration of all personnel entering the theater becomes the responsibility of the TG PAT and supporting HR Company. More than one TG PAT is required if multiple inter-theater APOEs become active.

7-11. HROB personnel also play an important role in theater HR opening operations. The HROB is the integrating link between the HRSC, TG PAT, and assigned or attached HR units (HR Company/HR Platoon).   The HROB, as part of the ESC or sustainment brigade SPO, not only provides technical guidance to HR units, but coordinates and synchronizes the execution of logistical and other non-HR support required to ensure HR units can accomplish the PA mission (e.g., incoming flights are met and transported to the PPC for accountability; transit personnel are fed, billeted, and transported after processing). These non-HR specific tasks are not part of the PA process, nor do HR units have the responsibility or capabilities to accomplish or coordinate these non-HR tasks. These types of non-HR tasks must be coordinated with the theater opening sustainment brigade for execution of specific tasks.

CASUALTY OPERATIONS

7-12. Initial entry operations often sustain casualties and generate the requirement for casualty reporting and tracking. As such, it is crucial that casualty operations and casualty reporting capabilities be in place on "Day one" of military operations. While Chapter 4 discussed casualty operations, the focus of this section is on the roles and responsibilities for establishing initial theater casualty operations.

7-13. To establish initial casualty operations personnel from each of the following organizations are required:
- ASCC G-1/AG.

- HRSC—COD.
- HROB of the ESC and designated sustainment brigade dedicated to theater opening.
- HR Company.
- HR Platoon.

7-14. The HRSC must be prepared to handle initial casualty operations. Casualty protocol must be established to maintain proper procedures and expedite information back to CMAOC for NOK notification. The initial establishment of the Casualty Assistance Center does not require the entire division of the HRSC and is METT-TC dependent.

7-15. The ASCC G-1/AG is responsible for planning, coordinating, and managing casualty operations for the theater. When establishing casualty operations policy, the ASCC G-1/AG will:

- Designate or delegate authority to approve and release casualty reports (e.g., the ASCC G-1/AG may delegate the authority to approve and release casualty reports to Corps commanders).
- Identify any additional locations requiring placement of CLTs. These locations are in addition to the normal General Officer-level HQs, G-1/AGs, hospitals, and MA collection points.
- Ensure casualty operations are included as part of all OPLANs and OPORDs.

7-16. The ASCC G-1/AG coordinates with the TSC to ensure the HRSC has established the theater Casualty Assistance Center. The HRSC is the theater-level element with the responsibility to execute the casualty operations mission. The HRSC, COD has the responsibility to ensure connectivity is established with the CMAOC, HRC, and that INIT casualty reports flow from the theater to CMAOC within 12 hours of the incident. The HRSC, COD maintains communication with the ESC and sustainment brigade HROB as they are the element responsible for planning and resourcing CLTs to perform casualty operations area support.

7-17. The HRSC, COD is responsible for ensuring casualty operations for the theater are executed. This includes:

- Establishing the theater Casualty Assistance Center.
- Coordinating with the HROB of the ESC and/or sustainment brigade to ensure the HR Company establishes the required CLTs at designated locations.

7-18. The HROB is responsible for planning and coordinating casualty operations support within the HROB AO. This includes planning and resourcing CLTs to General Officer-level HQs, G-1/AG, Role 2 and Role 3 MTFs, mortuary collection points, and other areas as designated by the ASCC G-1/AG. The HROB provides technical guidance to the HR Company and coordinates CLT staffing, locations, and other non-HR support for CLTs.

7-19. The HR Company is a primary player for the conduct of casualty operations. The HR Company, through its HR Platoons, forms CLTs in the HROB AO. CLTs are provided to the following:

- HRSC COD.
- Corps and Division G-1/AGs.
- Role 3 MTFs.
- MA Company.
- Other locations (CONUS and OCONUS) as determined by the ASCC G-1/AG.

POSTAL OPERATIONS

7-20. Postal operations are not part of the initial RSOI process. Postal services may not be available within the first 30 days after forces begin arriving in theater. However, to ensure postal services are available on D+31, it is necessary to ensure a minimum number of postal personnel are included as part of the theater opening force. Postal operations require a significant amount of planning to ensure there are an adequate number of postal units with operational equipment. Military operations, theater constraints, and transportation priorities also impact the ability to establish postal operations.

7-21. To establish initial postal operations requires personnel from each of the following organizations:

- ASCC G-1/AG.

- HRSC POD.
- HROB of the ESC and designated sustainment brigade dedicated to theater opening.
- HR Company.
- Postal Platoon.

7-22. The ASCC G-1/AG is responsible for planning, coordinating, establishing, and managing postal operations for the theater. When establishing initial postal operations, the ASCC G-1/AG will:
- Develop theater postal policies and procedures.
- Coordinate with other Service components to ensure postal operations are in synchronization and capable of providing postal support to all personnel who deploy with the force.
- Identify and coordinate with the TSC and HRSC to ensure adequate postal operations resources are available throughout the theater AO.
- Ensure postal operations are included as part of OPLANs and OPORDs.

7-23. During theater opening, the HRSC, POD is responsible to assist the MMT Team in establishing and executing initial postal operations. They accomplish this by coordinating with the ASCC G-1/AG and TSC to ensure adequate resources are available to conduct postal operations. Resources include identifying the number of postal elements needed to support theater operations and ensuring appropriate transportation assets, facilities, and equipment is available. The POD also appoints the AO Postal Finance Officer and coordinates with each Custodian of Postal Effects to enforce postal finance policies, procedures, and support. The POD provides technical guidance to the MMT and the HROB in the ESC and sustainment brigade.

7-24. The MMT Team deploys to the theater as an element of an sustainment brigade that has a theater opening mission. The primary function of the MMT is to establish a theater gateway mail terminal at the inter-theater APOD. This requires direct coordination with the HRSC POD, MPSA, and the HROB at the ESC and sustainment brigade. The MMT relies on the sustainment brigade SPO for execution of non-HR support (e.g., transportation and airfield facilities). The MMT is augmented by an HR Company and postal platoons for receiving, processing, and dispatching mail.

7-25. The HROB of the theater opening sustainment brigade is responsible for planning, coordinating, and integrating postal operations within the HROB AO. The HROB works closely with the HRSC POD, MMT, and the HR Company providing augmentation support to the MMT, and postal platoons operating APOs. Responsibilities include:
- Coordinate and assist HR elements in receiving non-HR sustainment support (e.g., recurring transportation and facilities).
- Ensure postal operations requirements are included in OPLANs and OPORDs.
- Coordinate with the HRSC, POD on locations for postal operations elements.
- Synchronize and monitor postal operations support provided by HR elements.
- Establish and manage the sustainment brigade CCIRs for postal operations.
- Provide technical guidance and assistance to HR postal elements.

7-26. The HR Company, with assigned postal platoons, is responsible for establishing postal services at designated locations and providing augmentation support to the MMT. The HR Company provides short and long-term postal planning, manages postal platoons, and establishes and manages postal directory service for all postal platoons. The HR Company receives technical guidance from the sustainment brigade HROB and the MMT when providing augmentation support. Mission command of the HR Company remains within the sustainment brigade. This includes the company supporting the MMT.

SECTION II – THEATER REDEPLOYMENT

7-27. The redeployment of forces from a theater of operations requires the same level of preparation and planning as it does for theater opening. For the HR community, there are four major redeployment concerns:
- Ensure an adequate number of HR units/elements remain in theater to conduct the redeployment process while reducing the HR support structure.

- Maintain PA of redeploying forces.
- Assist in the reconstitution or reorganization effort, if applicable.
- Manage the flow of personnel to home stations.

7-28. Throughout the redeployment process, the HRSC maintains the capability and ability to maintain PA, casualty operations, and limited postal support during all phases of redeployment. This is crucial, as all forces do not redeploy simultaneously. As forces redeploy incrementally, so should the drawdown of HR units.

7-29. Like theater opening, planning for the redeployment of forces from a theater is critical to successful execution of the redeployment process. HR planners from the ASCC G-1/AG, HRSC, and ESC HROB are involved in all phases of redeployment planning to:

- Ensure the theater-wide plan for redeploying includes incremental drawdown of the HR support structure.
- Determine if HR units or support elements should redeploy by unit or element.
- Determine the need, if any, to sustain a residual force to support post conflict activities.
- Develop redeployment procedures for individuals and deploying units.
- Identify specific HR requirements or functions that must transfer and to what agency.
- Decide how to conduct unit reconstitution or reorganization prior to redeployment (if necessary or required).
- Identify any additional theater departure points. (Note: As forces redeploy, additional departure points may be used. As such, planning should include the need to provide or add PAT capabilities at these locations).
- Consider if additional liaison personnel are needed, and if so, the proposed location. This includes liaison with aero medical evacuation to maintain accountability.
- Determine if a need exists to add additional CAC issuance capability at departure points. May be necessary to replace a large number of lost or expired CACs.
- Maintain connectivity during the redeployment process for PA and casualty operations.
- Identify other specific requirements (e.g., when redeployment and deployment and sustaining operations occur simultaneously, the TSC/ESC and HRSC may find it necessary to rebalance or surge HR support personnel to effectively support on-going operations and redeployment).

7-30. The "first in, last out" concept applies to redeployment of HR operations. The same HR elements that conducted PA, casualty operations, and postal operations during theater opening or HR sustainment perform similar roles during redeployment.

7-31. HR support requirements vary depending on the nature and scale of redeployment operations. For example, redeployment operations could range from limited personnel to entire units. Depending upon the military strategy, unit rotations may still occur while other units redeploy. Key considerations include, but are not limited to: size of the force redeploying and deploying; infrastructure requirements and limitations; staging area capacities; and transportation decisions. The challenge for planning HR support operations is the effective coordination and synchronization, vertically and horizontally, to ensure responsive and simultaneous support to on-going HR support operations and redeployment operations. The HROB in the ESC and sustainment brigade is critical to the coordination and synchronization effort.

PERSONNEL ACCOUNTABILITY

7-32. Throughout the redeployment process, the most critical of all HR functions is PA. Accountability includes all personnel listed in the theater database and includes Soldiers, Joint and multi-national personnel, DOD Civilians, and CAAF.

7-33. The following organizations have responsibilities for the redeployment of personnel:

- ASCC G-1/AG. Develops the theater-level plan in coordination with the HRSC and the ESC HROB. The redeployment plan includes unit and command responsibilities; processing procedures for Joint, DOD civilians, and CAAF; and specific procedures for processing for demobilizing RC Soldiers.

- HRSC. Establishes and maintains the theater database; coordinates with the ESC HROB to identify points of departures; determines how HR support is provided during the drawdown; identifies HR units and planned redeployment schedules; and if necessary, develops a plan to sustain any residual force for post conflict activities.
- ESC/sustainment brigade HROB. Develops a redeployment schedule for redeploying HR units while simultaneously ensuring PA is maintained, and ensures HR units redeploying late in the plan have the necessary communications and logistics support.
- HR Company. Provides HR unit redeploying recommendations to the HROB; PAT coverage at designated points of departure; CAC support at departure points; and considers use of CLTs from departing units as augmentation to PAT or the Plans and Operations section.

7-34. Generally, most unit personnel redeploy with their unit. However, there are some unit personnel who redeploy prior to the unit. These personnel are unit advance parties, IAs, or other personnel who deploy separately from their units. Unit S-1s have a responsibility to maintain accountability of personnel redeploying with the unit. They also have the responsibility to manifest their personnel and to provide the PAT at the theater exit point a list of their manifested personnel. The PAT then has the responsibility to ensure personnel are deleted from the database. PATs perform the same responsibilities for redeploying personnel as they do for theater opening and sustainment operations.

CASUALTY OPERATIONS

7-35. Depending on the operational environment, casualties may continue to occur. Individuals may also be killed or injured as a result of nonbattle injuries. As such, the capability to conduct casualty operations during the redeployment of personnel and units must be maintained. This includes the operation of the theater Casualty Assistance Center. As forces drawdown, the size of the Casualty Assistance Center can be reduced. Similar to theater opening, casualty operations are one of the last theater HR functions to close.

7-36. Once the decision is made to close the Casualty Assistance Center, the synchronization and coordination to transfer the casualty function is made with CMAOC to ensure files are transferred, disposed of, or retired as appropriate, and that other casualty reporting responsibilities are appropriately handed off to another designated Casualty Assistance Center or casualty element.

POSTAL OPERATIONS

7-37. The redeployment of postal units in theater requires more detailed planning than PA and casualty operations. Redeployment planning involves not only theater-wide postal units, but supporting HROBs, ESC, HRSC, and the ASCC G-1/AG. It also involves coordination and synchronization with external agencies (e.g., JMPA/MPSA). Redeployment of postal elements and closing of APOs is synchronized with the redeployment schedule for units supported by the APO or postal element.

7-38. It is critical that HR planners at all levels be involved early in the redeployment planning process. At a minimum, closing or relocating an APO requires 90 days advance notification. If possible, notifications should be at least 120 days prior to closing the APO. This notification is needed to:

- Ensure appropriate notifications are submitted to JMPA and MPSA and approved.
- Provide time to coordinate and synchronize turning-in excess postal supplies and equipment.
- Conduct necessary audits for accountable items (e.g., stamps and money orders).
- Notify supported organizations when mail services will be terminated.
- Notify the MMT at the APOD for redirecting mail.

7-39. The ASCC G-1/AG responsibilities for managing the redeployment of postal operations and closing of APOs are:

- Participate with HRSC and ESC HROB in preparation of a redeployment postal support plan.
- Provide ASCC level guidance and establish redeployment priorities.

7-40. The HRSC POD and Plans and Operations Division are responsible to notify MPSA and the servicing JMPA, by message or alternate means, as far in advance of the actual closure date as possible. Notification to MPSA includes:

- Affected ZIP codes.
- Closing dates by ZIP codes.
- Listing of all organizations and activities that use the APO as their mailing address.
- Disposition instructions for mail.
- Designating an APO to which active postal offense cases are forwarded, and all postal files and records are maintained due to closure of postal facilities.
- Requesting disposition instructions from the appropriate JMPA for USPS equipment and supplies.
- Coordinating and synchronizing with the ESC or sustainment brigade HROB on redeployment schedules and closing of APOs and the MMT.

7-41. The ESC, HRSC POD, and the HROB, in a coordinated effort, are responsible for developing a redeployment plan and schedule for redeploying theater postal units. The plan includes redeployment schedules of postal units and ensures postal units have the connectivity needed to conduct postal operations as units redeploy. The HRSC POD and the HROB ensure all issues that arise during the redeployment are resolved. It also ensures (in coordination with HRSC) the MMT initiates redirect surface mail for affected units prior to closing the APO.

7-42. The HRSC POD provides assistance and oversight to the HR Company for ensuring the HROB is aware of proper procedures for closing APOs. The HR Company Plans and Operations section ensures the following requirements are considered:

- Provides supporting units/customers with at least a 90 day termination of support notice.
- Transfers active postal offense case files to the designated APO.
- Complies with the DOD Postal Manual for disposition instructions for money orders, stamp stock, and meters.
- Refers to DOD 4525.6-C and USPS Publication 247 for supplies and equipment.
- Ensures an audit of accountable postal affects, including equipment, is performed at the close of business on the last day of operation or as soon thereafter as practical. (Note: Two postal officials appointed for this purpose must conduct the audit. The Custodian of Postal Effects shall not be an auditor, but must be present during the audit.)
- Disposes of records, and complies with appropriate Military Department, USPS, and MPSA disposition instructions.
- Coordinates new address and mail routing instructions for all units redeploying.
- Coordinates and publicizes APO closures to coincide with the drawdown of personnel.
- Reduces postal services 30 days prior to closure.
- Includes instructions for disposing mail and equipment in evacuation and destruction plans of all units operating a mail facility. When sufficient advance warning is received APOs will:
  - Deliver to addressee or dispatch mail on hand to the nearest postal facility by the safest and most expeditious means available.
  - Suspend operations and transport postal affects and supplies to a safe and secure location.
- When there is insufficient advance warning, emergency destruction of mail and postal affects take place in the following order:
  - Official registered mail.
  - Directory service information.
  - Blank postal money order forms.
  - Postal stamps and stamped paper.
  - Paid money orders and checks on hand.
  - Money order printer.
  - Other accountable mail.
  - All remaining mail.
- All-purpose date and canceling stamps.

- All other records, equipment, mail sacks, and furniture.

7-43. If possible, personnel conducting emergency destruction ensure there is a witness and that a list of destroyed items is submitted to the ASCC G-1/AG.

BRIGADE AND BATTALION S-1

7-44. Brigade and battalion S-1s plan for unit redeployment with the same attention to detail that they apply to pre-deployment planning and execution. In many respects, this is another deployment; albeit back to home station. Key areas of emphasis for S-1s during redeployment include:

- Maintaining accountability of Soldiers and civilians; this is even more challenging given the phased redeployment of units.
- Coordinating transfer of support provided other units.
- Identifying personnel for early redeployment and providing information to the supporting HR Company.
- Finalizing all awards and evaluation reports.
- Ensuring all LOD investigations are completed.
- Completing change of address cards.
- Planning and preparing for possibility of unit block leave.
- Coordinating with the supporting HROB for guidance on reception activities.
- Coordinating briefings to unit personnel.

Chapter 8

Civilian Support

Civilian personnel have always accompanied deployed Armed Forces. The increasingly hi-tech nature of equipment and rapid deployment requirements significantly increased the need to properly integrate civilian personnel support into all military operations. Recent reductions in military structure, coupled with high mission requirements and the unlikely prospect of full mobilization, mean that to reach a minimum of required levels of support, deployed military forces often have to be significantly augmented with civilian personnel. As these trends continue, the future battlefield requires ever-increasing numbers of often critically important contractor employees.

GENERAL

8-1. The primary focus of this chapter is to:
- Identify the role and responsibilities of HR organizations in providing selected HR support to Civilians who deploy with the force. This includes DOD civilians and CAAF.
- Provide OCS information to HR leaders. In some operational scenarios, contracted support is required to support PA, casualty operations, or postal functions within a theater.

8-2. Numerous examples exist throughout our Nation's history, from settlers supporting the Continental Army, nurses supporting the Civil War and other wars, Army and DOD civilians, to contractors supporting complex weapons and equipment systems. Without the support and services the civilian force provides, the military would be unable to accomplish many of its missions.

8-3. Army mobilization planners of each functional component, at all organizational levels, plan for DA Civilians and contractors who provide weapons systems, equipment maintenance, and other support services. Deliberate planning is accomplished to effectively integrate DA Civilians and CAAF. The planning process includes logistical, administrative, medical, and other support to ensure sufficient theater resources are available in the AO to support them. Planning for civilian and CAAF support is a key factor and is included in the early operational planning stage.

8-4. The following are functional proponents for various categories of civilians who may deploy in support of an operation:
- The functional proponent for Army personnel support to DA Civilians (appropriated and NAF employees) is the Army G-1.
- The functional proponent for CAAF is the Army G-4. (Contracting activities and contracting officers provide contractual oversight for contractors. AAFES performs NAF civilian personnel management for AAFES personnel.)
- The functional proponent for deployed ARC, Army Continuing Education System, and MWR personnel is the Assistant Chief of Staff for Installation Management. (MWR support is executed by the IMCOM G-9. Deployed ARC personnel are considered special staff under the G-1/AG of the unit they are deployed or collocated with. Army Continuing Education System support is executed through a Functional Support Team member assigned by the IMCOM Army Continuing Education System. The unit G-1/AG is responsible for coordinating and providing his or her personnel support while deployed.)

8-5. Emergency-essential (E-E) personnel. DOD civilians who deploy with the force are usually coded E-E on authorization documents and deploy with the unit. Typically, DOD civilians deploy in a TDY status for a period of 179 days. Army commands or units with deployed DOD civilians remain responsible for replacing them after 179 days. If Army commands are unable to provide a replacement, fill requirements are developed and requested by the ASCC via the Worldwide Individual Augmentation System. All DOD civilians are required to process through a CRC prior to deployment. The following guidelines apply:

- An E-E position is a position overseas or expected to transfer overseas during a crisis situation, and requires the incumbent to deploy or perform a TDY assignment overseas in support of a military operation.
- E-E civilians must be U. S. citizens and not subject to military recall. Family members of forward deployed E-E civilians are evacuated from a crisis location with the same priority and afforded the same services and assistance as Family members of military personnel.
- A signed E-E statement of understanding is required to ensure that civilian members are fully aware of the Army's expectations. However, a commander can direct DOD civilians, not designated E-E, to deploy in a TDY status or to remain in an area already on TDY or permanent assignment in order to perform duties essential to the military mission.

8-6. DOD civilians generally receive the same level of support as Soldiers, and like Soldiers, the military leadership provides mission command over them. Again, like Soldiers, the HR support mission is to provide HR support to them. While the official database of record for DOD civilians is currently separate from the military, they receive the same level of accountability, are included in PERSTATs, provided postal and MWR support, eligible for certain awards and decorations, and receive evaluation reports.

8-7. Non-governmental personnel. Non-governmental personnel include those employed by private organizations, such as ARC personnel, civilian media representatives, visiting dignitaries, representatives of DOD-sponsored organizations such as the United Service Organization, banking facilities, and citizens for whom local State Department officials have requested support. In certain situations, their presence may be command-directed or sponsored, and require the Army to provide limited support.

8-8. Types of contractor employees and their legal status. Contingency contractor employees fall into two primary categories:

- CAAF are contractor employees specifically authorized through their contract to accompany the force and have protected legal status IAW international conventions. IAW these international conventions, CAAF are non-combatants, but are entitled to prisoner of war status if detained. CAAF employees receive a Geneva Convention ID card or common access card and are accounted for in SPOT or its successor.
- Non-CAAF personnel are employees of commercial entities not authorized CAAF status, but who are under contract with the DOD to provide a supply or service in the operational area. Non-CAAF includes day laborers, delivery personnel, and supply contract workers. Non-CAAF employees have no special legal status IAW international conventions or agreements and are legally considered civilians. They may not received a Geneva Conventions ID card, thus are not entitled to prisoner of war treatment if captured by forces observing applicable international law. Non-CAAF employees are normally not included in PA reports.

RESPONSIBILITIES

8-9. The following paragraphs outline the civilian support unit responsibilities.

ASCC G-1/AG

8-10. The ASCC G-1/AG has the following responsibilities:

- Establish theater policy for support of civilian personnel (DOD civilians and CAAF). Policy should include specific entitlements (e.g., protection warfighting function and sustainment).
- Include CAAF and other theater designated contractor personnel in PERSTAT submissions.
- Ensure CAAF support is included in all OPLANs and OPORDs.
- Establish requirements for E-E employees (e.g., numbers and skills in the theater of operations).
- Establish procedures and coordinate (with the G-3) for DOD civilian replacements and augmentees.

- Coordinate with the TSC and HRSC to identify and resolve CAAF and other theater designated contractor personnel accountability and reporting issues. CAAF and other theater designated contractor personnel are integrated into the theater database.
- Account for and report the status of all Civilians, to include contractors, assigned or attached in support of contingency operations.
- Ensure DOD civilians, CAAF, and other theater designated contractor personnel receive appropriate HR support (e.g., postal, casualty, and MWR).
- Establish and announce the administrative workweek to ensure E-E employees receive proper payment for all hours worked.
- Determine AO specific operation deployability requirements such as medical and physical, clothing and equipment, weapons issue policy for E-E employees and CAAF, deployed personnel tracking and reporting procedures, and theater unique cultural and environmental training. Provide this information to Army G-1 prior to deployment of civilians.

HRSC

8-11. The HRSC has the following responsibilities:
- Ensure all DOD civilians, CAAF, and other theater designated contractor personnel are entered into the deployed database (i.e., DTAS for DOD civilians and SPOT for contractors).
- Coordinate with the ESC/TSC HROB to resolve any PA, casualty, or postal issues.
- Receive and process casualty reports for DOD civilians and contractors.

Army Field Support Brigade (AFSB)

8-12. The AFSB has the following contractor personnel responsibilities:
- Receive the CAAF Coordination Cell as part of theater opening operations in order to assist in establishing initial contractor accountability in theater (representatives are normally located at each APOD).
- Conduct CAAF reception activities at the APOD to assist in accounting for, receiving, and processing CAAF arriving in and departing from the operational area.
- Assist in maintaining visibility, accountability, and tracking of all Army CAAF and other contractors as directed by the ASCC. The AFSB accomplishes this through the attached CAAF Coordination Cell using SPOT. SPOT maintains contract employee data and reflects the location and status of all contractors based on information entered by the contract company and JAMMS scans.
- Maintain the JAMMS hardware and software.
- Coordinate with the TG PAT or the sustainment brigade HROB supporting the APOD or SPOD to resolve contractor accountability issues.
- Provide SPOT contractor accountability data through the TSC/ESC to the ASCC G-1/AG IAW established timelines.

HROB

8-13. HROBs have the following responsibilities:
- Ensure CAAF support is included in all OPLANs and OPORDs.
- Ensure subordinate units maintain visibility and accountability of unit contractors.
- Coordinate or provide life support (e.g., protection, billeting, feeding, and transporting) at the APOD/SPOD IAW contract entitlements.
- Coordinate with the HRSC, HR Company, and COR to resolve contractor accountability, postal, or casualty issues.

HR Company

8-14. The HR Company has the following responsibilities:

- Synchronize PA with the AFSB CAAF Coordination Cell (if established) at the APOD/SPOD.
- Coordinate with the HRSC POD and the HROB to identify and resolve postal or PA issues.
- Provide full or limited postal service to DOD Civilians and CAAF IAW theater policy.

PERSONNEL ACCOUNTABILITY

8-15. It is the overall responsibility of the ASCC G-1/AG to collect strength related information on all personnel who deploy with the force. This includes Soldiers, DOD civilians, CAAF (including other theater designated contractor personnel), and non-governmental civilians (i.e., ARC and AAFES) who provide support to the deployed force. Without accurate strength and accountability information, it becomes difficult for the combatant commander to synchronize support with the operational Army being supported into the overall operation. PA for Soldiers, Joint Service- members, and DOD civilians is outlined in Chapter 3, Section II.

8-16. For CAAF (including other theater designated contractor personnel), visibility and PA are of crucial concern by the HR community. As the ASCC G-1/AG has responsibility for reporting strength data to the combatant commander, accurate reporting of contractor strength is necessary in determining and resourcing government support requirements such as facilities, life support, and protection warfighting function in hostile or austere operational environments.

8-17. As stated in AR 715-9, HR is responsible to report CAAF and other designated contractor personnel as found in the SPOT database. Accuracy of this data is the responsibility of the prime contractor, the supporting contracting office, and associate requiring activities. The U. S. Army Materiel Command, normally through the supporting AFSB, assists in establishing and maintaining accountability of Army CAAF in the AO. During major operations, the AFSB may establish a CAAF Coordination Cell to assist with PA of CAAF. They ensure the CAAF are aware of the requirement to maintain their specific theater location by using the SPOT database to accurately reflect their location within the theater. SPOT is capable of providing by-name accountability data for all contractors deployed in theater, including pre-deployment certification, contract and POC information, and area of performance. The ARFOR G-1 is responsible to ensure subordinate sustainment command HR staffs are prepared to pull applicable SPOT contractor PA data to be included in standard Army personnel reports. It is anticipated that SPOT will eventually provide a bridge link to DTAS. Refer questions on SPOT functionality and reliability to the G-4 OCS personnel for resolution. Contract companies are responsible for the accuracy of the SPOT data for their employees to include employee's status and location.

CASUALTY OPERATIONS

8-18. Casualty reporting for deployed DOD civilians is conducted in the same manner as for Soldiers. This includes proper notification of Civilians' NOK. Casualty reports are submitted through casualty channels back to the CMAOC. The CMAOC then contacts emergency POCs at their organizations. Categories of civilians for which a casualty report is required are listed in AR 600-8-1. Upon notification of an Army Civilian casualty, a representative from the Army's Benefits Center makes contact with the NOK to discuss benefits and entitlements.

8-19. Casualty reporting of CAAF, to include other theater designated contractor personnel, is conducted in the same manner as for Soldiers and DOD Civilians (i.e., casualty reports are submitted through casualty channels back to the CMAOC). Upon receipt of reports, CMAOC notifies the contracting company or firm who conducts the NOK notification. Units with embedded civilians are responsible for ensuring that all embedded/assigned civilians meet individual readiness processing requirements prior to deployment. Personnel managers at battalion, brigade, division, corps, and ASCC account for and coordinate HR support to all civilians, which include CAAF and other theater designated contractor personnel.

POSTAL SUPPORT

8-20. When authorized via Memorandum of Instruction, SOFA, or contractual agreement in written orders, postal services are provided to qualified, deployed DOD civilians and CAAF personnel in the same manner as for Soldiers, or as spelled out in the above mentioned guidance. CAAF authorized postal support may use the ZIP code of the primary unit they support (e.g., the ZIP code of the HHC of the division or TSC) unless the MPSA designates a separate ZIP code for them. The Postal Platoon and the S-1 provide the same support to DOD civilians and CAAF who move from unit to unit as they would for a Soldier who changes units. Just as with Soldiers, Civilian addresses must be kept current, primarily with change of address and directory cards (DA Form 3955).

8-21. The nationality of the contractor employee usually determines postal support. U. S. citizen CAAF in support of U. S. Armed Forces, may be authorized to use the MPS if there is no USPS available and if MPS use is not precluded by the terms of any international or host-nation agreement. Local nationals hired in-country by DOD, or subcontracted by a DOD contractor, normally are provided with postal support through the existing host-nation system or through arrangements made by the employing contractor.

MWR SUPPORT

8-22. Maintaining acceptable quality of life is important to the overall morale of any organization, including contractors. Deployed DOD civilians have access to recreational activities, goods, services, and community support programs such as the ARC, Family support, and the exchange system.

8-23. Generally, contractors are not entitled to MWR support. However, the military may provide MWR support to contractor employees when contractor sources are not available, subject to the combatant commander's discretion and the terms of the contract. Local nationals are not provided MWR support.

8-24. The availability of MWR programs in an AO vary with the deployment location. MWR activities available may include self-directed recreation (e.g., issue of sports equipment), entertainment in coordination with the United Service Organization and the Armed Forces Professional Entertainment Office, military clubs, unit lounges, and some types of rest centers.

8-25. U. S. citizen CAAF may be eligible to use AAFES, Navy Exchange, or Marine Corps Exchange facilities for health and comfort items. Use of these facilities is based on the combatant commander's discretion, the terms and conditions of the contract, and any applicable status of forces agreement.

OTHER HR SUPPORT

8-26. For DOD Civilians, the home station and the deployed supervisor ensure deployed DOD Civilians receive HR services and treatment comparable to that received by Civilians not deployed. These services may include such areas as DA Civilian awards (e.g., performance or monetary awards for special acts, suggestions, or inventions), DA Civilian performance appraisals, supervisory documentation, appointments, career programs, promotions and reductions, identification documents, health insurance, and leave. Normally, the deployed supervisor provides input to deployed Civilians' awards and performance appraisals. That input is used by the home station supervisor in the completion of the official performance appraisals and awards.

DEPLOYMENT AND REDEPLOYMENT OF CIVILIANS

8-27. The Army created several sites within CONUS for expeditiously preparing DOD civilians and contractors for deployment. These sites, like the CRC, receive, certify theater entrance eligibility, and process individuals for deployment. Redeploying individual's process through the same CRC as they initially processed to ensure recovery of issued government equipment. When it is not practical or affordable, contractors or DOD civilians deploying from Hawaii, Alaska, or Europe may not be required to process through a CRC, but may process from locations with similar processing capabilities as a CRC.

8-28. Each deploying civilian should have a deployment packet prepared and provided by the individual's home station/installation civilian personnel office or employer. A copy of the deployment packet should be hand carried to the CRC. The CRC validates the completion of deployment requirements and provides the individual with a copy to take to the personnel support activity in the AO. The deployment packet serves as a field file. It consists of a personnel data sheet from the civilian personnel office, DA Form 7425, medical documents, copy of the DD Form 93, clothing and organizational equipment record, AO clearance, and other requirements listed on the DA Form 7425.

8-29. For contractor personnel, the company name and its emergency POC and phone number is obtained by the CRC, mobilization station, or the AO point of entry. This information is entered into the civilian personnel data system, currently the Civilian Tracking System, and also placed in the deployment packet. Contractor personnel also ensure appropriate information is updated in SPOT.

8-30. For various reasons, some system and external support contractors may inadvertently deploy without processing either through a force-projection-platform processing center, an authorized contractor run deployment site, or a CRC. When this occurs, the contract employee is normally returned to their point of origin at company expense. Pre-deployment processing is conducted in the AO by the CAAF Coordination Cell as soon as possible during the reception processing.

8-31. Upon completion of an operation, contractors redeploy out of the AO as quickly as METT-TC allows. The timing of the departure of contractor support operations is as critical as that for military forces. Orderly withdrawal or termination of contractor operations ensures that essential contractor support remains until no longer needed and that movement of contractor equipment and employees does not inadvertently hinder the overall redeployment process. Essentially, contractor personnel should undergo the same redeployment process as military personnel. However, planners must determine the specific steps desired and be aware of the cost associated with doing so.

8-32. Redeployment processes are essentially the same functions as those involved in deployment. The procedures are similar, whether contractors are redeploying to their point of origin (home station) or to another AO. Contractors normally redeploy in the same manner in which they deployed (either under government control or self-deploy).

8-33. Prior to arriving at the APOE/SPOE, contractors accomplish the same preparations as military forces. Similar to deployment, contractor accountability requirements continue, enabling the military to maintain accountability of and manage contractors as they proceed through the redeployment process.

8-34. Contractor employees who deployed through the CRC or individual deployment site should be required to return through the same processing center for final out processing. The CRC or individual deployment site is responsible for assisting the return of individual DOD Civilian and contractor employees to their organization or to their home. Contractor employees who deploy with their habitually supported unit normally redeploy with that unit.

CONTRACTING HR SUPPORT FUNCTIONS

8-35. During contingency military operations, HR leaders continually assess the capability of HR units to provide or maintain adequate support within their AO. During these assessments, HR leaders may in some cases, determine that the same level of support cannot be sustained without additional resources. Additional resources include manpower, equipment, and supplies. This shortfall may be caused by an insufficient number of HR units to support theater rotation policies or when the theater of operations is so vast that current HR organizations cannot provide adequate area support.

8-36. One method to overcome a shortfall in manning, equipment, or supplies is for HR leaders to consider OCS to provide needed supplies, equipment, and in limited cases, HR related services. This is not a new idea, but one that has been successful in various operational scenarios (e.g., mail is moved by contractors to and from the MMT). Contractors are also used to perform selected functions within APOs. While contracting-out HR functions may not be the preferred method, it is an option that may be considered by HR leaders. In all cases, OCS requires detailed planning and proper government oversight. As such, all HR leaders should consider attending the COR Course as a priority prior to deployment.

8-37. HR leaders need to understand that all military operations are not defined as "contingency operations." *Contingency operations* are military operations, designated by the Secretary of Defense, where members of the Armed Forces are or may become involved in military actions, operations, or hostilities against an enemy of the U. S. (JP 1, Doctrine for the Armed Forces of the United States). Contingency operations may also be an operation requiring the use of the military during a national emergency declared by the President or Congress. Examples may be major theater war, small scale contingencies, and stability and support operations. Routine exercises are not categorized as a contingency operation.

8-38. Risk assessment. To properly evaluate the value and feasibility of contracted support to any given military operation, the requiring unit or activity and the supported commander and staff make an assessment of risk. This assessment evaluates the impact of contractor support on mission accomplishment, including the impact on military forces, if they are required to provide protection warfighting function, lodging, mess, or any other support to contractors. This assessment determines if the value the contractor brings to operations is worth the risk and resources required to ensure its performance.

8-39. While a detailed analysis and availability of funds determines if contracting is feasible or desirable, HR leaders must understand the contracting process and the roles they may have in this process. The HR community is more involved in contracting as the Army continues its transformation. HR personnel may act as requiring activity planners or as CORs. As such, it is crucial for HR personnel to become familiar with operational contract support terms, procedures, roles and responsibilities they have in the process. HR leaders must ensure contracts include requirements for the protection of personally identifiable information IAW all applicable policies and regulations.

8-40. OCS is a key capability for deployed Armed Forces. Due to the importance and unique challenges of OCS, HR leaders need to fully understand their role in planning for and managing contracted support. Current doctrine describes three broad types of contracted support: Theater support, external support, and systems support.

- Theater support contracts: Supports deployed operational forces under prearranged contracts, or contracts awarded from the mission area, by contracting officers under the mission command of the supporting Contracting Support Brigade or designated Joint Theater Support Contracting Command. Theater support contractors are used to acquire goods, services, and minor construction support, usually from local commercial sources, to meet the immediate needs of operational commanders. Theater support contracts are contracts typically associated with contingency contracting. HR personnel may serve as requiring activity planners for theater support OCS actions. Theater support contracts in support of HR missions are normally executed through a general support manner through a Contracting Support Brigade contingency contract team or the Joint Theater Support Contracting Command regional contracting office.

- External support contracts: Provides a variety of support to deployed forces. External support contracts may be prearranged contracts or contracts awarded during the contingency itself to support the mission and may include a mix of U.S. citizens, third-country nationals, and local national subcontractor employees. The largest and most commonly used external support contract is the Army's LOGCAP contract. This Army program is commonly used to provide many sustainment related services to include HR support such as mail and MWR.

- System support contracts: These are pre-arranged contracts used by the acquisition program office and are generally not related to HR operations.

8-41. For HR leaders and staff officers, the major challenge is ensuring that any HR related theater support and LOGCAP support actions are properly planned for and incorporated into the overall HR effort in the AO. It is imperative that HR personnel work closely with the supporting Contracting Support Brigade and/or supporting team LOGCAP-Forward personnel during both the planning process and the post-award process. It is also imperative that HR staff be trained on their role in the operational contract support planning and execution process as described in the next two paragraphs.

8-42. OCS Requirements Development: HR staff must be prepared to develop an "acquisition ready" requirement packet to submit to the supporting contracting activity. The packet must include a detailed performance work statement (sometimes referred to as a statement of work) for service requirements or a detailed item description/capability for a commodity requirement. In addition to the performance work statement, the packet must include an independent cost estimate of the item or service required along with a required command and staff (including resource management) approved DA Form 3953 (Purchase Request and Commitment). Additionally, certain items or specific dollar amount requests may require a formal acquisition review board packet as directed by local command policies.

8-43. Post-award Contract Management: HR staff also plays a key role in the post-award contract management for all theater support contracts and LOGCAP task orders that directly support the HR mission. One of the most important sustainment brigade tasks in this process is to nominate and track CORs for service contracts and receiving officials for all commodity contracts. Quality CORs and receiving official support are key to ensuring contractors provide the service or item IAW the contract. HR leaders must also manage funding for each HR related contract and request funds in advance of depletion of current funds or all contract work is ceased until adequate funds are available. HR receiving officials and CORs are responsible for completing receiving reports, which certifies the goods or services contracted for were received by the Army.

8-44. In addition to the basic OCS requirements development and post contract award actions described above, there are many specific OCS planning and management tasks that HR leaders and staff officers should be familiar with when contemplating requesting contract support. The following recommendations should be considered when planning to contract out HR or postal operations:

- Establish specific OCS coordination personnel or teams to serve as the nexus for the planning and integration effort. (For example, an OCS postal support team is established for planning and integrating contracted postal functions and a PAT is established for PA. These teams manage the COR program and consolidate Performance Evaluation Board reports. The OCS postal support team may also be required to prepare monthly roll-up briefings to the supporting Contracting Support Brigade contracting officer and for the Award Fee Evaluation Board).
- HR OCS teams should have the capability and ability to work with supporting contracting officers, contract managers, and logistics support officers regarding requirements letters, administrative change letters, and other contract management tools.
- Routinely meet with the supporting Contracting Support Brigade contracting officer to discuss contractor tasks issues. Meetings should be conducted at least bi-weekly.
- Plan OCS carefully. It is imperative to identify how property or equipment is aligned early in the process to ensure it is operational and meets the standard prior to a transfer of authority. Ensure contracts specify what GFE is provided. Define the exact equipment, by locations, to be turned over to the contractor during the transfer of authority process.
- Understand the differences between GFE, theater provided equipment, and installation provided equipment.
- Include the G-1/AG and G-8 throughout the contracting process.
- Schedule COR training as necessary.
- Specify the exact period of the contract need, what the deliverable items are, if needed, and the desired degree of performance flexibility.
- Describe the desired output rather than "how" the work is accomplished or the "number" of hours provided.
- Determine the availability of government support (includes protection warfighting function/security support) provided to contractors, and any conditions or limitations upon the availability or use of such services. This must be clearly set forth in the terms of the contract.
- Identify potential degradation of contractor effectiveness during situations of tension or increased hostility.

8-45. It is also crucial to understand that the terms and conditions of the contract establish the relationship between the military (U. S. Government) and the contractor; this relationship does not extend through the contractor supervisor to his or her employees. Only the contractor can directly supervise its employees. The military chain of command exercises management control through the contract.

Glossary

A&R	athletic and recreation
AAFES	Army and Air Force Exchange Service
ABCS	Army battle command system
ADP	Army doctrine publication
ADRP	Army doctrine reference publication
AFSB	Army field support brigade
AG	adjutant general (Army)
AIFA	AAFES Imprest Fund Activity
AMHRR	Army Military Human Resource Record
AMPS	Automated Military Postal System
AO	area of operations
APO	Army post office
APOD	aerial port of debarkation
APOE	aerial port of embarkation
ARC	American Red Cross
ARFORGEN	Army force generation
ARNG	Army National Guard
ASCC	Army Service component command
ASI	additional skill identifier
ATP	Army techniques publication
ATTP	Army tactics, techniques, and procedures
BCS3	Battle Command Sustainment Support System
BRS	Benchmark Rate Structure
CAAF	contractors authorized to accompany the force
CAC	common access card
CAISI	Combat-Service-Support Automated Information Systems Interface
CAO	Casualty Assistance Officer
CCIR	commander's critical information requirement
CFLCC	coalition forces land component commander
CLT	Casualty Liaison Team
CMAOC	Casualty and Mortuary Affairs Operations Center
CNO	Casualty Notification Officer
COA	course of action
COD	Casualty Operations Division
COIC	current operations integration cell
CONUS	continental United States
COP	common operational picture
COPS	Common Operational Picture Synchronizer

COR	contracting officer representative
CP	command post
CRC	CONUS Replacement Center
CSM	Command Sergeant Major
CSSB	combat sustainment support battalion
DA	Department of the Army
DA PAM	Department of the Army pamphlet
DCIPS	Defense Casualty Information Processing System
DCIPS-CF	Defense Casualty information Processing System - Casualty Forward
DCS	deployment cycle support
DEERS	Defense Enrollment Eligibility Reporting System
DMSL	distribution management sub-level
DNBI	disease and nonbattle injury
DOD	Department of Defense
DOX-T	direct operations exchange - tactical
DTAS	Deployed Theater Accountability Software
DUIC	derivative unit identification code
DUSTWUN	duty status whereabouts unknown
E-E	emergency essential
EEC	emergency essential civilian
eMILPO	electronic Military Personnel Office
EPS	Essential Personnel Services
EPW	enemy prisoner of war
ESC	expeditionary sustainment command
FBCB2	Force XXI Battle Command, Brigade and Below
FM	Field Manual
FRG	Family Readiness Group
G-1	assistant chief of staff, personnel
G-3	assistant chief of staff, operations
G-4	assistant chief of staff, logistics
G-6	assistant chief of staff, signal
G-8	assistant chief of staff, financial management
GFE	government furnished equipment
HCP	health and comfort pack
HHBn	Headquarters and Headquarters Battalion
HQ	headquarters
HQDA	Headquarters, Department of the Army
HR	human resources
HRC	Human Resources Command
HROB	Human Resources Operations Branch
HRSC	Human Resources Sustainment Center

IA	individual augmentee
IAW	in accordance with
ID	Identification
IMCOM	installation management command
INIT	Initial
iPERMS	interactive Personnel Electronic Records Management System
JAMMS	Joint Asset Movement Management System
JFLCC	joint force land component commander
JMMT	joint military mail terminal
JMPA	joint military postal activity
JOA	joint operations area
JP	Joint Publication
JPERSTAT	joint personnel status
JTF	joint task force
KIA	killed-in-action
LAD	latest arrival date
LOD	line of duty
LOGCAP	Logistical Civilian Augmentation Program
MA	mortuary affairs
MAR2	MOS Administrative Retention Review
MDMP	military decisionmaking process
MDP	mail delivery point
MEB	Medical Evaluation Board
METT-TC	mission, enemy, terrain and weather, troops and support available, time available, civil considerations
MIA	missing-in-action
MMT	Military Mail Terminal
MOS	military occupational specialty
MPD	Military Personnel Division
MPO	military post office
MPS	Military Postal Service
MPSA	Military Postal Service Agency
MPT	Music Performance Team
MRE	mission readiness exercise
MRX	mission rehearsal exercise
MTF	medical treatment facility
MWR	Morale, Welfare, and Recreation
NAF	non-appropriated fund
NCO	noncommissioned officer
NIPRNET	Non-Secure Internet Protocol Router Network
NOK	next of kin
OCONUS	outside the continental United States

OCS	operational contract support
OMM	Official Mail Manager
OPCON	operational control
OPLAN	operation plan
OPORD	operation order
PA	Personnel Accountability
PAT	Personnel Accountability Team
PDY	present for duty
PE	personal effects
PEB	Physical Evaluation Board
PERSUM	personnel summary
PERSTAT	personnel status
PIM	Personnel Information Management
PNOK	primary next of kin
POC	point of contact
POD	Postal Operations Division
PPC	Personnel Processing Center
PPG	personnel policy guidance
PRM	Personnel Readiness Management
PRR	personnel requirement report
PR TM	Personnel Readiness Team
PSS	personnel services support
R&R	rest and recuperation
RAPIDS	Real-Time Automated Personnel Identification System
RC	Reserve Component
RLAS	Regional Level Application Software
ROA	rules of allocation
RSOI	reception, staging, onward movement, and integration
RTD	return to duty
S-1	battalion or brigade manpower and personnel staff officer
S-3	battalion or brigade operations staff officer
S-4	battalion or brigade logistics staff officer
S-6	battalion or brigade signal staff officer
SCC	Service Component Command
SCMO	Summary Court Martial Officer
SGLV	Servicemembers' Group-Life Insurance Election and Certificate
SGM	Sergeant Major
SIDPERS-ARNG	Standard Installation/Division Personnel System – Army National Guard
SIPRNET	SECRET Internet Protocol Router Network
SOFA	Status of Forces Agreement
SOP	standard operating procedures

SPO	support operations
SPOD	sea port of debarkation
SPOE	sea port of embarkation
SPOT	Synchronized Pre-deployment and Operational Tracker
SQI	special qualification identifier
SR	Strength Reporting
SRC	standard requirements code
SRP	Soldier readiness processing
SSM	Single Service Manager
STACH	status change
STAMIS	standard Army management information system
STB	special troops battalion
SUPP	supplemental
TAPDB	Total Army Personnel Database
TDA	Table of Distribution and Allowances
TDY	temporary duty
TFE	tactical field exchange
TG PAT	Theater Gateway Personnel Accountability Team
TOE	Table of Organization and Equipment
TSC	theater sustainment command
UIC	unit identification code
UMR/CMR	unit mailroom/consolidated mailroom
U. S.	United States
USAR	United States Army Reserve
USPS	United States Postal Service
USR	unit status report
VSAT	very small aperture terminal
WIA	wounded-in-action

This page intentionally left blank.

References

REQUIRED PUBLICATIONS

These documents must be available to intended users of this publication.

ADRP 1-02, *Terms and Military Symbols*, 24 September 2013.

JP 1-02, *Department of Defense Dictionary of Military and Associated Terms*, 8 November 2010.

RELATED PUBLICATIONS

These documents contain relevant supplemental information.

JOINT PUBLICATIONS

Most CJCS Directives are available online: http://www.dtic.mil/doctrine/doctrine/cjcs.htm

Most DOD Issuances are available online: http://www.dtic.mil/whs/directives/corres/ins1.html

Most Joint publications are available online:
http://www.dtic.mil/doctrine/new_pubs/jointpub_logistics.htm

CJCSM 3150.13C, *Joint Reporting Structure – Personnel Manual*, 10 March 2010.

Defense Federal Acquisition Regulation Supplement (DFARS) and Procedures, Guidance, and Information (PGI) 201.602.2, *Contracting Officer Responsibility*, 12 February 2014.

DOD 4525.6-C, *DOD Postal Supply Catalog*, 01 April 1990.

DOD 4525.6-M, *Department of Defense Postal Manual*, 15 August 2002.

DOD 4525.8-M, *DOD Official Mail Manual*, 26 December 2001.

DOD Instruction 1215.07, *Service Credit for Non-Regular Retirement*, 24 January 2013.

DOD Instruction 1400.25, Volume 100, *DOD Civilian Personnel Management System*, 13 April 2009.

DOD Instruction 2310.5, *Accounting for Missing Persons – Boards of Inquiry*, 31 January 2000.

DOD Instruction 3001.02, *Personnel Accountability in Conjunction with Natural or Manmade Disasters*, 03 May 2010.

DOD Instruction 4525.08, *DOD Official Mail Management*, 11 August 2006.

DOD Instruction 4525.7, *Military Postal Service and Related Services*, 02 April 1981.

DOD Instruction 8320.02, *Sharing Data, Information, and Technology (IT) Services in the Department of Defense*, 05 August 2013.

JP 1, *Doctrine for the Armed Forces of the United States*, 25 March 2013.

JP 1-0, *Joint Personnel Support*, 24 October 2011.

JP 3-35, *Deployment and Redeployment Operations*, 31 January 2013.

JP 4-10, Operational Contract Support, 17 October 2008.

ARMY PUBLICATIONS

Most Army doctrinal publications are available online: http://www.apd.army.mil

ADP 3-0, *Unified Land Operations*, 10 October 2011.

ADP 4-0, *Sustainment*, 31 July 2012.

ADP 5-0, *The Operations Process*, 17 May 2012.

ADRP 3-0, *Unified Land Operations*, 16 May 2012.

ADRP 4-0, *Sustainment*, 31 July 2012.

ADRP 5-0, *The Operations Process*, 17 May 2012.

AR 15-6, *Procedures for Investigating Officers and Boards of Officers*, 02 October 2006.

AR 25-51, *Official Mail and Distribution Management*, 30 November 1992.

AR 135-100, *Appointment of Commissioned and Warrant Officers of the Army*, 01 September 1994.

AR 215-8, *Army and Air Force Exchange Service Operations*, 05 October 2012.

AR 220-1, *Army Unit Status Reporting and Force Registration – Consolidated Policies*, 15 April 2010.

AR 340-21, *The Army Privacy Program*, 5 July 1985.

AR 600-3, *The Army Personnel Development System*, 26 February 2009.

AR 600-8-1, *Army Casualty Program*, 30 April 2007.

AR 600-8-2, *Suspension of Favorable Personnel Actions (Flag)*, 23 October 2012.

AR 600-8-3, *Unit Postal Operations*, 07 January 2013.

AR 600-8-4, *Line of Duty Policy, Procedures, and Investigations*, 04 September 2008.

AR 600-8-11, RAR 001, *Reassignment*, 1 May 2007.

AR 600-8-14, *Identification Cards for Members of the Uniformed Services, Their Eligible Family Members, and Other Eligible Personnel*, 17 June 2009.

AR 600-8-19, RAR 001, *Enlisted Promotions and Reductions*, 30 April 2010.

AR 600-8-22, RAR 002, *Military Awards*, 11 December 2011.

AR 600-8-24, RAR 003, *Officer Transfers and Discharges*, 12 April 2006.

AR 600-8-29, *Officer Promotions*, 25 February 2005.

AR 600-8-101, *Personnel Processing (In-Out, Soldier Readiness, Mobilization and Deployment Processing)*, 18 July 2003.

AR 600-8-104, *Army Military Human Resource Records Management*, 02 August 2012.

AR 600-8-105, *Military Orders*, 28 October 1994.

AR 600-20 RAR 005, *Army Command Policy*, 18 March 2008.

AR 600-34, *Fatal Training/Operational Accident Presentations to the Next of Kin*, 02 January 2003.

AR 601-100, *Appointment of Commissioned and Warrant Officers in the Regular Army*, 21 November 2006.

AR 601-280, RAR 001, *Army Retention Program*, 15 September 2011.

AR 608-20, *Army Voting Assistance Program*, 28 October 2004.

AR 623-3, *Evaluation Reporting System*, 05 June 2012.

AR 635-200, RAR 003, *Active Duty Enlisted Administrative Separations*, 6 June 2005.

AR 638-2, *Care and Disposition of Remains and Disposition of Personal Effects*, 22 December 2000.

AR 672-20, *Incentive Awards*, 17 December 2013.

AR 690-11, *Use and Management of Civilian Personnel in Support of Military Contingency Operations*, 26 May 2004.

AR 690-400, *Total Army Performance Evaluation System (Chapter 4302)*, 16 October 1998.

AR 715-9, *Operational Contract Support Planning and Management*, 20 June 2011.

ATP 1-0.2, *Theater-Level Human Resources Support*, 04 January 2013.

ATP 4-91, CHG 1, *Army Field Support Brigade*, 15 December 2011.

ATP 4-93, *Sustainment Brigade*, 09 August 2013.

ATP 4-94, *Theater Sustainment Command*, 28 June 2013.

ATTP 1-0.1, *S-1 Operations*, 16 May 2011.

ATTP 1-19, *U. S. Army Bands*, 07 July 2010.

ATTP 4-10, *Operational Contract Support Tactics, Techniques, and Procedures*, 20 June 2011.

ATTP 5-0.1, *Commander and Staff Officer Guide*, 14 September 2011.

DA PAM 220-1, *Defense Readiness Reporting System-Army Procedures*, 16 November 2011.

DA PAM 623-3, *Evaluation Reporting System*, 05 June 2012.

DA PAM 638-2, *Procedures for the Care and Disposition of Remains and Disposition of Personal Effects*, 22 December 2000.

DA PAM 672-3, *Unit Citation and Campaign Participation Credit Register*, 29 January 1988.

Department of the Army Personnel Policy Guidance (PPG) for Overseas Contingency Operations, 1 July 2011.

FM 3-11.4, CHG 1, *Multiservice Tactics, Techniques, and Procedures for Nuclear, Biological, and Chemical (NBC) Protection*, 2 June 2003.

FM 7-15, CHG 10, *The Army Universal Task List*, 27 Feb 2009.

FM 27-10, CHG 1, *The Law of Land Warfare*, 18 July 1956.

NGR 600-100, *Commissioned Officers – Federal Recognition and Related Personnel Actions*, 15 April 1994.

NGR 600-101, *Warrant Officers – Federal Recognition and Related Personnel Actions*, 01 October 1996.

OTHER PUBLICATIONS

Title 39 U.S. Code 3401, *Mailing Privileges of Members of Armed Forces of the United States and of Friendly Foreign Nations*, 1 February 2010.

Convention (IV) Relative to the Protection of Civilian Persons in Time of War. Geneva, August 1949.

Executive Order 12556, *Mailing Privileges of Members of Armed Forces of the United States of America and of Friendly Foreign Nations*, 16 April 1986.

USPS Publication 38, *Postal Agreement with the Department of Defense*, February 1980.

USPS Publication 247, *Supply and Equipment Catalog*, July 2002.

RECOMMENDED READINGS

ADP 6-0, CHG 1, *Mission Command*, 17 May 2012.

AR 215-1, *Military Morale, Welfare, and Recreation Programs and Nonappropriated Fund Instrumentalities*, 24 September 2010.

AR 600-8, *Military Personnel Management*, 01 October 1989.

AR 600-8-6, *Personnel Accounting and Strength Reporting*, 24 September 1998.

AR 600-8-10, RAR 001, *Leaves and Passes*, 15 February 2006.

AR 600-85, *The Army Substance Abuse Program*, 28 December 2012.

AR 608-1, *Army Community Service*, 13 March 2013.

AR 608-18, RAR 001, *The Army Family Advocacy Program*, 30 October 2007.

AR 614-30, *Overseas Service*, 30 March 2010.

AR 614-100, *Officer Assignment Policies, Details, and Transfers*, 10 January 2006.

AR 614-200, RAR 002, *Enlisted Assignments and Utilization Management*, 26 February 2009.

AR 690-12, *Equal Employment Opportunity and Affirmative Action*, 04 March 1988.

AR 930-4, *Army Emergency Relief*, 22 February 2008.

AR 930-5, *American National Red Cross Service Program and Army Utilization*, 01 February 2005.

ATTP 4-0.1, *Army Theater Distribution*, 20 May 2011.

DOD 1348.33, Vol. 1, CH2, *Manual of Military Decorations and Awards: General Information, Medal of Honor, and Defense/Joint Decorations and Awards*, 07 March 2013.

DOD Instruction 1000.01, *Identification (ID) Cards Required by the Geneva Conventions*, 16 April 2012.

DOD Instruction 1300.18, CH 1, *Department of Defense (DOD) Personnel Casualty Matters, Policies, and Procedures*, 8 January 2008.

FM 5-19, *Composite Risk Management*, 21 August 2006.

PRESCRIBED FORMS

None.

REFERENCED FORMS

Most Army forms are available online: www.apd.army.mil

DA Form 1156, *Casualty Feeder Card.*

DA Form 2028, *Recommended Changes to Publications and Blank Forms.*

DA Form 2173, *Statement of Medical Examination and Duty Status.*

DA Form 3953, *Purchase Request and Commitment.*

DA Form 3955, *Change of Address and Directory Card.*

DA Form 4187, *Personnel Action.*

DA Form 4591, *Retention Data Worksheet.*

DA Form 7425, *Readiness and Deployment Checklist.*

DA Form 7631, *Deployment Cycle Support (DCS) Checklist.*

Department of Homeland Security Form N-426, *Request for Certification of Military or Naval Service.*

DD Form 93, *Record of Emergency Data.*

DD Form 261, *Report of Investigation Line of Duty and Misconduct Status.*

DD Form 285, *Appointment of Military Postal Clerk, Unit Mail Clerk or Mail Orderly.*

DD Form 1833 Test (V2), *Isolated Personnel Report.*

Postal Service Form 1412, *Daily Financial Report.*

Postal Service Form 1590, *Supplies and Equipment Receipt.*

Postal Service Form 2942A, *Military Mail AV7.*

SGLV Form 8286, *Servicemembers' Group Life Insurance Election and Certificate.*

Index

A

AAFES, 1-6, 3-13, 5-1, 5-2, 5-5, 5-7, 5-8, 5-9, 8-1, 8-4

AMHRR, 2-11, 3-2, 3-26, 3-32, 4-1, 4-4, 4-5, 4-7

AR 15-6, 4-8, 4-22, 4-24, 4-28, 4-29

Army band operations, 1-6, 5-10, 6-7

Army Body Composition Program, 1-6

Army field support brigade, 3-13, 8-3

ASCC G-1/AG, 1-9, 2-2, 2-4, 2-12, 2-13, 2-16, 3-2, 3-3, 3-4, 3-13, 3-14, 3-16, 3-21, 3-22, 3-27, 3-37, 4-13, 4-19, 4-26, 4-29, 5-4, 5-9, 5-11, 7-2, 7-3, 7-4, 7-6, 7-8, 8-2, 8-4

awards and decorations, 1-5, 4-3, 4-4, 4-10, 8-2

B

Battalion S-1, 1-7, 2-10, 2-11, 2-12, 2-26, 3-5, 3-15, 3-22, 3-28, 3-29, 4-7, 4-13, 4-14, 4-27, 4-28, 5-6, 6-1, 7-8

Brigade S-1, 1-5, 2-8, 2-9, 2-10, 2-11, 2-12, 3-2, 3-4, 3-12, 3-14, 3-15, 3-20, 3-30, 4-3, 4-10, 4-13, 4-14, 4-27, 4-29, 4-34, 5-6

Brigade S-1/STB S-1, 3-21, 3-27

C

CAAF, 2-9, 3-3, 3-10, 3-13, 3-15, 3-18, 3-19, 3-22, 3-30, 3-36, 3-37, 4-10, 4-11, 4-22, 4-34, 6-7, 7-2, 7-6, 8-1, 8-2, 8-3, 8-4, 8-5

CAISI, 2-10, 2-11, 2-12, 3-34, 3-38

Casualty Assistance Center, 2-14, 2-21, 2-26, 3-29, 4-21, 4-22, 4-25, 4-26, 4-28, 4-29, 4-30, 4-34, 4-35, 7-3, 7-6

casualty estimation, 2-6, 4-32, 6-5

casualty feeder card, 4-21, 4-23

casualty mail, 4-13, 4-17, 4-21, 4-29

casualty operations, 1-5, 2-7, 2-10, 2-15, 2-21, 4-1, 4-21, 4-25, 4-26, 4-28, 4-30, 7-3, 7-5, 7-6, 8-4

Casualty Operations, 2-13

casualty reporting flow, 4-34

citizenship/naturalization, 4-9

civilian support, 8-1

CLT, 1-5, 2-7, 2-18, 2-19, 2-21, 3-14, 3-29, 4-22, 4-26, 4-27, 4-30, 4-35, 6-6, 7-3

CMAOC, 2-21, 3-29, 3-32, 4-6, 4-21, 4-25, 4-26, 4-27, 4-28, 4-31, 4-34, 4-35, 7-3, 8-4

command interest programs, 1-6, 2-10, 5-9

common access card, 2-9, 2-17, 3-29, 3-33, 3-38, 4-10, 6-8, 8-2

conduct HR planning and operations, 1-6, 2-9, 6-1, 6-8

congressional inquiries, 2-6, 4-1, 4-3, 4-9, 4-12, 4-14

contractors, 1-1, 2-9, 2-18, 3-13, 3-19, 3-29, 4-18, 8-1, 8-3, 8-4, 8-6, 8-7, 8-8

coordinate personnel support, 1-6, 2-9, 2-11, 5-1, 6-7

COPS, 2-9, 2-15, 3-30

Corps/Division, 3-24, 5-5, 5-6

customer service, 2-9, 4-1, 4-3, 4-12, 4-16

D

DCIPS, 2-9, 2-21, 3-10, 3-28, 3-29, 4-28, 4-29, 4-30, 4-31, 4-34, 6-6

DEERS, 2-22, 3-10, 3-28, 3-29

Deployment and Redeployment of civilians, 8-5

DTAS, 2-9, 2-11, 2-13, 3-2, 3-3, 3-5, 3-11, 3-13, 3-15, 3-16, 3-21, 3-22, 3-28, 4-17, 8-3, 8-4

E

EDAS, 3-31

eMILPO, 2-9, 2-11, 3-2, 3-5, 3-11, 3-13, 3-21, 3-28, 3-29, 3-31, 3-33, 3-35, 4-1

enduring principles, 1-1

Equal Opportunity Program, 1-6, 5-9

essential personnel services, 1-5, 2-6, 4-1, 4-3, 6-7

evaluation reports, 1-5, 2-11, 3-10, 3-32, 4-1, 4-5, 7-8, 8-2

F

family readiness, 1-6, 1-7, 5-4

FBCB2, 2-10, 2-11, 2-15, 3-35

functions of HR support, 1-3

H

HR and sustainment relationships, 1-7, 2-27

HR company, 1-5, 1-8, 1-11, 2-2, 2-14, 2-16, 2-18, 2-19, 2-20, 2-21, 3-17, 4-15, 4-19, 4-20, 4-21, 4-22, 4-30, 7-4, 7-7, 8-4

HR platoon, 2-17, 2-19, 2-21, 4-15, 4-30, 7-2, 7-3

HR sustainment roles, 1-9

HRC, 1-3, 2-1, 2-13, 3-1, 3-2, 3-3, 3-4, 3-7, 3-8, 3-10, 3-12, 3-17, 3-28, 3-29, 3-31, 3-32, 3-33, 4-1, 4-8, 4-25

HROB, 4-30, 6-1, 6-3, 6-5, 6-8, 7-1, 7-2, 7-3, 7-4, 7-5, 7-7, 8-3, 8-4

HRSC, 1-5, 1-8, 1-10, 2-2, 2-5, 2-12, 2-13, 2-15, 2-17, 3-13, 3-16, 3-28, 3-37, 4-13, 4-14, 4-19, 4-25, 4-26, 4-27, 4-34, 6-1, 6-5, 6-9, 7-2, 7-3, 7-4, 7-5, 7-6, 7-7, 8-3, 8-4

HRSC COD, 4-29

HRSC POD, 4-29

I

IMCOM, 1-3, 2-2, 4-12, 5-1, 5-2, 5-4, 5-6, 5-7, 5-8, 5-9, 8-1

information systems, 2-1, 2-2, 2-5, 2-10, 2-17, 3-29, 3-34

iPERMS, 3-10, 3-26, 3-28, 3-32, 4-28, 4-31

J

JMMT, 2-16, 4-15, 6-5

JMPA, 4-11, 4-12, 4-19, 7-6, 7-7

JPERSTAT, 3-16, 3-17, 3-18, 3-19, 3-21, 3-22, 6-7

L

Leave and Pass Program, 2-6, 4-6, 4-7

LOD investigations, 2-7, 4-26, 4-31

M

mail clerks, 2-21, 4-14, 4-15, 4-16, 4-17, 4-20

Man the Force, 1-1, 1-3, 1-4, 2-9, 2-11, 3-1, 6-7

MDMP, 2-14, 3-36, 6-1, 6-3, 6-5, 7-1

military pay, 1-5, 2-12, 2-13, 2-17, 4-7, 4-30, 6-7

MMT Team, 1-8, 2-12, 2-16, 2-17, 2-20, 4-15, 7-4

MPS, 4-11, 4-12, 4-18, 4-21, 8-5

MPSA, 1-3, 2-16, 3-29, 4-11, 4-12, 4-14, 4-18, 4-19, 4-20, 7-4, 7-6, 7-7, 8-5

MWR, 1-3, 1-6, 2-9, 5-1, 5-2, 5-4, 5-6, 5-8, 5-9, 6-7, 8-1, 8-2, 8-3, 8-5

N

NIPRNET, 2-5, 2-10, 2-11, 2-15, 3-15, 3-22, 3-26, 3-29, 3-35, 3-36, 3-38, 6-8

O

officer procurement, 4-3, 4-8, 4-9

official mail, 4-13, 4-16

P

personal effects, 4-26, 4-28

personnel accountability, 1-5, 1-8, 2-17, 2-21, 3-12, 3-13, 3-30, 3-36, 6-2, 6-7, 7-2, 7-6, 8-3

personnel action requests, 4-7, 6-7

personnel policy guidance, 1-1, 4-17

PERSTAT, 2-9, 3-13, 3-16, 3-17, 3-18, 3-19, 8-2

PIM, 1-4, 2-4, 2-12, 2-13, 3-1, 3-13, 3-26, 3-27, 3-28, 3-30

postal operations, 1-5, 1-11, 2-13, 2-16, 2-18, 2-19, 2-20, 4-11, 4-12, 4-13, 4-14, 4-18, 4-19, 4-20, 6-5, 7-1, 7-4, 7-5, 7-6, 7-7, 8-8

Postal Operations Division, 2-13, 4-14

postal platoon, 2-16, 2-18, 2-20, 2-21, 4-15, 4-16, 4-17, 4-19, 4-20, 7-4, 8-5

PRM, 1-4, 2-4, 2-9, 2-10, 2-11, 2-12, 2-13, 3-1, 3-2, 3-3, 3-4, 3-5, 3-6, 3-12, 7-2

promotions, 1-2, 1-5, 2-11, 4-1, 4-5, 4-10, 8-5

promotions and reductions, 4-6

provide HR services, 1-5, 2-9, 2-11, 4-1, 6-7

R

RAPIDS, 3-10, 3-29, 4-10

retention operations, 1-4, 1-5, 3-23

RLAS, 2-9, 2-11, 3-2, 3-5, 3-11, 3-32, 4-1

running estimate, 6-2

S

SCMO, 2-26, 4-27, 4-30

SIDPERS-ARNG, 2-11, 3-2, 3-5, 3-10, 3-11, 3-32, 3-33, 4-1

SIPRNET, 2-5, 2-10, 2-11, 2-15, 3-15, 3-22, 3-26, 3-29, 3-30, 3-36

special troops battalion, 1-8

SPOT, 3-13, 3-37, 8-2, 8-3, 8-4, 8-6

SRP, 2-22, 3-5, 3-9, 3-11, 3-29, 4-9

STB, 1-10

STB S-1, 2-9, 2-10, 2-16, 3-4, 3-14, 4-10

strategic HR support, 1-2

strength reporting, 1-5, 3-12, 3-17, 3-18

suspension of favorable personnel actions and bars to reenlistment, 4-9

T

TAPDB, 2-9, 2-11, 3-4, 3-14, 3-29, 3-30, 3-31, 3-32, 3-33

TG PAT, 1-8, 2-2, 2-12, 2-14, 2-17, 2-18, 2-19, 3-16, 3-17, 4-10, 7-2, 8-3

theater opening and redeployment operations, 7-1

Transfer and Discharge Program, 4-6, 4-10

U

unit mailroom/consolidated, 4-13

unit reset, 3-7, 3-8, 3-9

USPS, 4-11, 4-12, 4-14, 4-17, 4-18, 4-19, 4-20, 6-8, 7-7, 8-5

V

Voting Assistance Program, 1-6, 5-10

VSAT, 2-10, 2-11, 2-12, 3-34, 3-38